HANDBOOK

THE DUKE OF EDINBURGH'S AWARD

The Duke of Edinburgh's Award
Gulliver House, Madeira Walk,
Windsor, Berkshire SL4 1EU

Revised first edition: June 1988
Second edition: June 1990

© The Duke of Edinburgh's Award.

Typeset, printed and bound in Great Britain by
Jolly & Barber Ltd., Rugby, Warwickshire

Designed by Richard Brown FCSD

ISBN 0 905425 02 2 (Paperback)

BUCKINGHAM PALACE.

Young people growing up in this modern complicated world have many difficulties to face, and opportunities for personal achievement are often limited. At the same time, parents, teachers, voluntary organisation leaders and employers, who recognize their responsibilities towards young people, also have their problems.

This scheme is intended to help both the young as well as those who are concerned for their welfare. The object is to provide an introduction to worthwhile leisure activities and voluntary service; as a challenge to the individual to discover the satisfaction of achievement and as a guide for those people and organisations who would like to encourage the development of their younger fellow citizens.

I hope that all those who take part in this scheme will find an added purpose and pleasure in their lives. I am quite sure that all those who help to run it will gain that special sense of satisfaction which comes from helping others to discover hidden abilities and to overcome a challenge.

Preface

This Handbook replaces all former editions of *Award Handbook*.

Additional guidance on the requirements and conditions contained in *Award Handbook* is given in several companion publications published by the Award. These include: *Operating Authorities Guide; Guide for Briefing Adult Helpers; A Challenge to the Individual; Expedition Guide.* Details on these publications are available from the Headquarters of the Award Scheme or the Literature Department at the Scottish Office, the addresses of which are given at the back of this book.

Contents

7

Chapter 1   What The Scheme Is

Opportunity and Challenge

Young people are eager to grasp opportunities for enjoyment, excitement and new experiences. They wish to make their mark in a world where the individual often appears insignificant, and are willing to take on substantial challenges if they perceive them to be worthwhile and relevant to the needs of society. They want to prove themselves, to discover new talents and develop their relationship with friends and the wider community.

The Duke of Edinburgh introduced his Award Scheme to encourage and stimulate their enthusiasms and energies by presenting a challenging programme of activities open to young people between the ages of 14 and 25. The Scheme is intended to develop those qualities of maturity and responsibility which will help them throughout their lives, in their homes, their jobs and in their relationships, whatever their personal abilities or circumstances. The Award now operates in over 50 countries. In some it is known by a different title although the underlying philosophy and basic principles of operation are the same.

To quote HRH The Prince Philip: "The Philosophy of the Scheme is neither very profound nor very complicated. It is simply this: a civilised society depends upon the freedom, responsibility, intelligence and standard of behaviour of its individual members and if the society is to continue to be civilised each succeeding generation must learn to value these qualities and standards. . . . Above all, it depends on a willingness among younger generations to find out for themselves the factors which contribute to freedom, responsibility, intelligence and standards of behaviour. These are all rather abstract concepts. The Scheme . . . has attempted to bring them down to earth; to give individual young people the opportunity to discover these ideas for themselves through a graduated programme of experience."

Challenge is the essence of the concept. The Award presents to young people a balanced non-competitive programme of voluntary activities which encourages responsibility, self-reliance, personal discovery and perseverance.

The value to the Scheme of adult helpers is paramount and fundamental. Adults have a wealth of experiences, abilities and attitudes which can have a profound influence on the development of young people. In Prince Philip's own words: "If there is one thing which the experience of the Scheme re-affirms and re-emphasises time and again, it is the involvement and dedication of adults that is absolutely critical to its success."

The Scheme

The Scheme itself is not a youth organisation. It is a programme of practical, cultural and adventurous activities designed for use by all agencies having a concern for the development of young people; a programme flexible enough to meet their enthusiasms and aptitudes whatever their background or culture, however plentiful or limited their resources may be.

Participants follow their chosen activities, largely in their own time, with guidance from someone knowledgeable in each subject. Minimum standards of achievement are laid down and when these are met they qualify for an Award. These minimum standards may be exceeded, where appropriate, in order to create a truly personal challenge. A badge and certificate are presented on behalf of The Duke of Edinburgh to mark an attainment which represents the successful completion of a co-operative venture between the young and not-so-young, so that in this way, barriers between generations are eroded.

In gaining Awards, young people learn by experience the importance of commitment, enterprise and effort. They discover a great deal about themselves and come to know the enjoyment of working with and for other people.

The Scheme is voluntary and entry must be a participant's free choice. It is not competitive since each individual is assessed on their progress, perseverance and achievement and Awards are within the reach of all. The Scheme is available to all young people whether members of a youth organisation or not. They may take part individually or together with others of their own age group.

This, then, is the essence of the Award Scheme. Through a commitment to its programmes, young people will be acquiring self-reliance and a sense of responsibility to others, both essential qualities of citizenship. The Award programme is a vehicle for spiritual, personal and social development and the overall benefits of the Award are, therefore, greater than the sum of its component parts. It is hoped that adults who help young people towards an Award will bear these aspects in mind.

The Awards

There are three separate Awards—**Bronze**, **Silver** and **Gold**.

For each Award the participant has to fulfil the requirements of each of the four Sections of the Scheme in accordance with the Conditions set out in Chapter 4 and the Sections.

The four Sections and their aims are:

Service—to encourage service to others.

Expeditions—to encourage a spirit of adventure and discovery.

Skills—to encourage the discovery and development of personal interests and social and practical skills.

Physical Recreation—to encourage participation in physical recreation and improvement of performance.

Activities in the four Sections are intended to complement each other and so provide a balanced programme reflecting different aspects of young people's development.

The detailed conditions for each Section of the Scheme are given in the following Chapters. It is emphasised that these are the minimum requirements to qualify for an Award; **many young people will be able to undertake, and will gain greater value from undertaking, more than the stipulated minimum.**

There is no time limit within which the programme for each Award must be completed, other than a young person's 25th birthday. There are minimum starting ages for each Award and minimum periods of time for which the chosen activities have to be sustained, details of which are given in Chapter 4 and the four Sections.

Subject to these requirements, young people may enter for whichever Award is best suited to them; those completing Bronze or Silver can go on to attempt the next higher Award, in which case they will be exempted from some aspects of training which they have already completed.

The starting point for entry into the Award Scheme, whichever Award is chosen, is marked by the acquisition of an *Entrance Pack* containing a *Record Book*, in which is recorded details of activities undertaken. It forms a record of progress through the Scheme, verified by the adults who have carried out the assessment in each Section.

The Philosophy

The nature and philosophy of the Award can be encapsulated in the following ten points.

Non-competitive

The Award is a personal challenge and not a competition against other individuals. The only set standards are those necessary to ensure the safety of those taking part. The Award programme is based on personal choice, initiative and perseverance and should reflect an individual participant's unique combination of abilities, resources and interests. No two programmes should be identical.

Available to all

Because the criteria for gaining an Award are individual improvement and achievement, disadvantaged young people and those with special needs are able to participate fully. There is one Award which is available to all with no discrimination against participation on grounds of sex, cultural background, religion or political affiliation.

Voluntary

The Award is run by volunteers for volunteers. Every young person makes a free choice to take on the challenge and they are supported through the Award by a huge network of adult volunteers. Participants must commit their own leisure time to complete Award activities.

Flexibility

The Award programmes can be geared to local facilities, and designed for the individuals taking part. If the basic age requirements are met there are no maximum time limits for completion of any Award and young people may enter for whichever level of Award is best suited to them.

Balanced programme

Whatever the level of Award, there are four Sections which must be completed—Service, Expeditions, Skills and Physical Recreation. The challenge is there to extend and develop existing abilities and also to try something new. The Sections will make varying levels of demand on each participant depending on their experience, interests and abilities.

Progression

Through its three levels the Award Programme demands more time and an increasing degree of commitment and improvement. Young people should also take an increasing role in organising the activities for their Award. At Bronze level, participants will need strong support from adult helpers but at Gold they should be responsible for organising their own Award programme with the guidance of adults.

Record of Achievement

The *Record Book* notes positive achievement and improvement only. If a participant does not complete the conditions on one occasion, the opportunity exists to try again.

Marathon not a Sprint

The Award demands persistence and commitment. It cannot be completed in a short burst of enthusiasm. The time limits are minimum requirements for completion of each Award and therefore individuals can work at their own pace, depending on the time available, up to their 25th birthday.

Value

The Award is a process of personal and social development. It should introduce participants to a range of new opportunities, allow them to learn from their experiences and enable them to discover unknown capabilities. The value and significance of an Award to participants is directly proportional to the quality of the experiences and the degree of personal commitment they have invested.

Enjoyment

Above all, it is important that both young people and adult helpers find participation in the Award enjoyable, exciting and satisfying. The intention is that participants should pursue Award activities in their future lives and not be discouraged from ever trying them again.

Chapter 2   How The Scheme Works

Administration

HRH The Duke of Edinburgh is Chairman of the Board of Trustees, which controls The Duke of Edinburgh's Award programme.

The Scheme in the UK is administered on behalf of the Trustees by the Head Office in London which deals with matters of overall policy and central administration. There are also Territorial Offices in Scotland, Wales and Northern Ireland, and seven Regional Offices covering the North-East, North-West, Midlands, East, London, South-East and South-West of England.

Outside the UK, the Award programme is administered by autonomous National Award Authorities which are serviced by the International Secretariat. All National Award Authorities whose Award programme conforms to the following four internationally agreed principles are members of the International Award Forum which meets every few years in different parts of the world.

The four principles, which represent the only formal link between National Award Authorities throughout the world, are:

■ The voluntary nature of participation by young people.

■ The age range of participants i.e. 14 to 25 years.

■ The basic structure of the Award Programme, i.e. its four mandatory Sections and its three levels of Award.

■ The minimum time requirement laid down for the completion of each Award, i.e. for direct entrants, 6, 12 and 18 months.

Operation

Responsibility for the operation of the Scheme is delegated under licence to **Operating Authorities** who are authorised to grant Awards on behalf of HRH Prince Philip or the Head of State as the case may be. In order to obtain this licence, Operating Authorities have to satisfy the National Award Authority that they understand the full implications of the Scheme, are in a position to safeguard its aims and standards and can establish the necessary administrative framework to enable the Scheme to function and to ensure it continuity. 15

Any organisation or body concerned with the education, welfare or training of young people may be licensed as an Operating Authority, and any young person wishing to participate in the Scheme must do so through one of these Authorities, though they do not necessarily have to belong to a particular group or organisation.

Examples of Operating Authorities are:

- National Voluntary Youth Organisations.
- Local Government Authorities.
- Public Services i.e. Armed Forces, Police, Fire Service etc.
- Government Departments
- Industrial and Commercial Concerns.
- Independent Schools.

Operating Authorities may sponsor the Scheme in any number of **user units** under their control, as shown in the following table, through links at County, Borough or local level as appropriate.

Operating Authorities	User Units
National Voluntary Youth Organisations	Clubs/Groups, Units, etc.
Local Government Authorities (County or equivalent level)	Secondary Schools. Youth Service. Further Education. Other Groups
The Armed Forces, Police, Fire Service	Training Establishments. Service Schools, Cadet Units
The Home Office	Detention Centres
Industrial and Commercial Concerns	Firms. Factories. Shops
Independent Schools	Schools

As will be seen, the Scheme may be operated in many different environments and because of this, it offers the means of linking together a great number of organisations and individuals concerned with young people.

Responsibilities

Operating Authorities must carry out the following responsibilities.

■ Monitor the general conduct of the Scheme by User Units operating under their control.

■ Advise User Units on the operation of the Scheme and on the availability and suitability of Instructors.

■ Approve Instructors and Assessors where so required by the conditions.

■ Supply *Entrance Packs* and other literature to User Units.

■ Check *Record Books* and grant Awards.

■ Supply badges and certificates.

■ Arrange suitable public liability insurance to cover possible injury to or damage caused by, young people and adults engaged in the Scheme.

■ Arrange initial and regular training for leaders and helpers (see Chapter 3 "Learning about the Scheme").

In the case of large Operating Authorities, some of the above responsibilities may be delegated, but overall supervision of all aspects of the Scheme remains with the Operating Authority itself.

Some Operating Authorities may also be able to:

■ Support young people who wish to enter the Scheme but who do not belong to any particular organisation.

■ Hold stocks of equipment for use in training and on expeditions.

Further information relating to the functions of Operating Authorities and advice concerning many operational and administrative matters is contained in the Award Scheme publication *Operating Authorities Guide*.

Local Award Committees

Local Award Committees which are usually composed of representatives from different Operating Authorities, User Units and Assisting Organisations, as well as individual helpers, may be formed to provide a forum for consultation and discussion.

The functions of local Award Committees include:

■ Promoting the Scheme in the locality, including publicity and recruitment of adults.

■ Pooling resources of staffing, equipment and facilities. This may include the sharing of Instructors and Assessors and the joining up of groups for various activities to ensure the most efficient use of the services of Assisting Organisations.

■ Helping participants who have started the Scheme under one Operating Authority (say a school) to link up with another agency to complete an Award.

■ Helping individual participants not belonging to any organisation.

■ Arranging presentation ceremonies.

■ Maintaining contact with Gold Award Holders.

■ Comparing standards to ensure an acceptable degree of uniformity.

It should be stressed that Award Committees are normally consultative although, in areas of little Award activity, they may, with the approval of an Operating Authority, assume the role of a User Unit. The operational nature of such a Unit may be appropriately combined with some of the consultative functions listed above.

Instruction and Assessment

In all Sections of the Scheme it is necessary for young people to be guided by adults who are knowledgeable about the activities being followed and are acceptable to the Operating Authority. For some activities, qualified Instructors are required.

On completion of each individual programme it is necessary for a participant's achievement to be assessed. The Assessor's signature in the *Record Book* certifies that the Award requirements for that Section have been satisfactorily completed.

The basis of assessment is laid down in the detailed conditions for each section of the Scheme.

Assisting Organisations

A large number of National and International Organisations have pledged their support to the Award Scheme and are able to offer assistance in many different specialist fields. This help is often needed to meet the requirements for instruction and assessment outlined above. Further reference to appropriate bodies is made in the detailed conditions for each Section of the Award.

Gold Award Holders

Gold Award Holders wishing to continue their involvement in the Award Scheme are encouraged to do so by acting as Instructors and Assessors, helping at Award Centres, assisting with publicity and fund raising and sponsoring individual participants.

Gold Award Holders' Associations have been formed in many places, the main aim of which is to assist with the further promotion of the Scheme in their respective areas.

Further details are available from Territorial and Regional Offices or through the London Award Office.

Publicity

The successful operation of the Award Scheme depends on the active involvement and support of all sections of the community, and this in turn depends on keeping the Scheme, its purpose and achievements, continually in the public eye.

Full advantage should be taken of every opportunity to bring the activities of young people taking part to the notice of the local press and radio and, where appropriate, television stations.

Chapter 3 Guidance on Operation

General

As with all activities for young people, success in the Award Scheme depends on good preparation and organisation. The Programme must be simply explained and sensibly interpreted both to the young people themselves and to the adults who will help them through the Scheme.

Although at first sight, acceptance of responsibility for running the Award Scheme may present a somewhat daunting prospect, closer study will reveal the flexibility of its programme and the way in which it can be used to complement current activities and adapted to suit local conditions.

The purpose of this chapter is to offer guidance to users of the Award Scheme, especially those preparing to adopt it for the first time.

Responsibilities

In every unit there should be one adult with the responsibility for co-ordinating the work of participants and their adult helpers; to ensure continuity it is desirable that a deputy should also be appointed.

The leader need not necessarily be involved with the detailed running of any particular part of the Scheme, but should aim to build up a team of helpers, each having responsibility for one of the Sections.

The role of the leader is partly promotional and partly operational. Responsibilities will include:

- Learning about the Scheme.
- Contacting the appropriate Operating Authority.
- Contacting any local Award Committee.
- Obtaining both promotional and operational literature.
- Launching the Scheme.
- Discussing choice of activities with potential participants.
- Obtaining parental consent and support.
- Ordering *Record Books* from the Operating Authority and issuing them to participants.
- Finding Instructors and Assessors in co-operation with the Operating Authority and, where appropriate, the local Award Committee.

- Ensuring that Award Scheme activities are dovetailed into other unit programmes.
- Reviewing financial arrangements.
- Keeping appropriate records.
- Arranging Award Presentations.
- Helping young people to continue in the Scheme on relocation.
- Publicity.

Learning about the Scheme

The importance of training cannot be over-emphasised. A training course should be attended by potential users as soon as possible after becoming involved as it can prevent hours of abortive work by adults and ensure that the young people they support derive maximum benefit from participation in the Award. Courses are run at National, Regional or Local level, and are designed to explain the philosophy of the Scheme and the conditions of the three Awards. They also explain the local administration of the Scheme, and provide useful local contacts. Refresher courses are also useful for keeping helpers up to date.

Contacting the Operating Authority

The Operating Authority will often be responsible for running these training courses, and it is from them that all items of Award literature, including *Entrance Packs* and *Record Books*, badges and certificates, have to be obtained. Contact must therefore be established and maintained with the appropriate person exercising this responsibility.

The full responsibilities of Operating Authorities are set out in Chapter 2. Their advice should be sought in all cases of difficulty or doubt.

Local Award Committees

Local Award Committees, where they exist, can be of great assistance to users and close contact should be maintained with them. Their work can save duplication of effort and ensure more efficient use of adult help. Time spent in these committees will be repaid many times over.

The principal responsibilities of local Award Committees are listed in Chapter 2. Even though such committees may not exist it will nevertheless be found helpful to maintain close liaison with all other Award users in the area.

Award Literature

Promotional material is supplied free of charge to Operating Authorities, from whom the necessary supplies can be obtained. Items available include a leaflet for potential participants, a more detailed outline of the Scheme, and a leaflet for those involved with young people with Special Needs.

This *Award Handbook* is the principal item of operational literature. There are also *Operating Authorities Guide; Expedition Guide;* and *A Challenge to the Individual. Notes for Instructors and Assessors* are also available in leaflet form.

Details of all these publications may be found in the colour *Catalogue and Order Form* which is published annually.

Information of importance in the UK is published in the *Award News* section of *Award Journal*, the Scheme's house magazine in January, April and September each year. Users should make certain of receiving copies from their Operating Authorities. *Award Journal* is distributed free of charge to those operating and using the Scheme.

Similar information is contained in the publication *Award World*, for users of the Scheme outside the UK. It is published at four-monthly intervals and distributed free of charge to National Award Authorities to whom application should be made for copies.

All involved with the Scheme in any capacity should be supplied with, or have access to, the relevant items of Award literature.

Launching the Scheme

The success of the Scheme in any unit may well depend on the way in which it is first introduced, so launching should be well prepared.

Sufficient adult help must be recruited prior to launching. For any one person to run the Scheme and to oversee each Section as well, is a near impossible task.

When adult support has been assured, an introductory session should be arranged when one of the films or videos available could be shown or a guest speaker invited. A display of Award material, with local photographs if possible, could be mounted. Particularly valuable on such occasions can be Award holders talking about their own experiences.

It may then be desirable to suggest that the young people go away to think about the Scheme and discuss it with parents and friends, before deciding to enter. Care should be taken to avoid starting with too many participants; the first year's Bronzes may become the next year's Silvers, when there will be another crop of Bronzes; in the third year there could be Golds as well. Direct Entrants at Silver and Gold also have to be considered.

Choice of Activities

It is important to remember that as far as practicable participants should themselves select the activities they wish to pursue, having regard to the local facilities available.

Whilst participants are free to choose an activity with which they are already familiar, they should be reminded that work undertaken prior to entering the Scheme cannot be allowed to count towards an Award—except as provided in paragraph 6 of the General Conditions. The detailed programme followed in each Section of the Scheme should be tailored to the needs and capabilities of each participant.

Parental Support

It may be desirable to obtain parents' consent for participants under the age of 18, not only to satisfy any legal requirement but also to arouse their interest. Parents can often help as Instructors and Assessors (or persuade others to do so) and act as providers of equipment, transport and other facilities. Their support and encouragement may inspire participants to persevere when the initial novelty has worn off.

Entrance Packs and Record Books

Entrance Packs and *Record Books* are issued on entry into the Scheme and become the personal property of the participant. One *Record Book* is used for both the Bronze and Silver Awards whilst a separate Gold *Entrance Pack* is used for the Gold Award by both progressive and direct entrants. It should be remembered that only success should be recorded. If an Assessor feels that the requirement has not been met, the participant should be encouraged to make further effort, and no entry made in the *Record Book*.

When making entries, Assessors should be asked to make appropriate comments and instructed fully on how to complete the correct page. Leaders must ensure that the following particulars are absolutely correct:

Name and address of participant, in block letters
Date of Birth
Date of Issue (which is also date of entry)
Name of Operating Authority

On completion of an Award, the *Record Book* should be sent to the appropriate official in the Operating Authority, **not** to the Award Office, so that the pages headed "Certificates and Awards" may be signed and the appropriate certificate and badge awarded.

Instructors and Assessors

Any adult who is interested in the well-being of young people and who is qualified or otherwise skilled in an Award activity may act as an Instructor or Assessor. The suitability of adults is determined by the Operating Authority who will often maintain lists of names. Award Committees can often also be helpful in finding Instructors and Assessors.

The larger the number of adults prepared to help in this way, the wider the choice of activities which can be offered to young people. The aim should be to seek a little help from many, rather than a lot of help from a few.

In seeking such assistance, the important aspect of the Award Scheme in offering to adults a practical and congenial way of interesting themselves in the upbringing of younger citizens and of influencing their lives should not be overlooked. The Scheme is directed as much to adults as to young people themselves. Experience in recruiting adult help has emphasised the value of a personal approach, as opposed to a general call for volunteers, and of specific requests for assistance in a particular capacity or area of interest. Having secured the co-operation of adults it is important to sustain their interest and enthusiasm and to ensure that they fully understand their role.

Dovetailing the Scheme

It should be remembered that the Scheme is not an organisation, but a programme available to all young people. Being flexible, the programme may be followed by units having a wide diversity of aims and should be looked upon as a means of helping to fulfil those aims. A group can be set up specially for Award Scheme purposes but, equally, established units, such as Scout Groups, Girl Guide Ranger Units, youth clubs etc, may use the Scheme as an extension of their existing programme of activities.

There may be close similarity between some of the activities undertaken by young people for their Awards and those they are required to undertake for special qualifications or badges within their own particular youth organisation. In these circumstances, the activities followed may also be allowed to count for Award purposes, provided that the appropriate Award conditions are fulfilled.

Financial arrangements

Cost to the Individual There is normally an entry fee payable on first joining the Scheme which covers the cost of the *Entrance Pack* and *Record Book* and also represents a young person's own contribution to the expenses of running the Scheme.

Other costs will depend on individual circumstances but they need not be great. They will probably consist of fares to attend activity classes, possibly membership fees of a club and perhaps evening class fees. There is no need to buy expensive equipment. Apart from personal items such as clothing and footwear, much can be borrowed, particularly in the early stages.

Costs to the Organisation This ought not to be high. It will include the cost of the operational handbooks and hire of films. It may be necessary to reimburse Instructors and Assessors for out-of-pocket travelling expenses and also, on occasion, to pay for the transport of participants for their expedition or other activities.

Financial Assistance The Local Authority or other statutory department should be contacted to ascertain what assistance by way of grant, or loan of equipment is available; it may also be necessary to initiate local fund-raising to meet incidental expenses.

Keeping Records

Where there are several participants each pursuing different activities it will not be easy to keep track of each individual's progress. It may, therefore, be helpful to keep a simple chart showing how each participant is getting on. Records should also be kept of Awards gained.

Award Presentations

Whenever possible, badges and certificates should be presented at a suitable ceremony, arranged as soon as is practicable after participants have gained their Awards. It may be possible, for example, to present the badge within the unit immediately it is achieved and the certificate at a joint ceremony arranged by the local or area Award Committee at a later date.

At the **Gold** stage, the appropriate *Gold Award Notification Form* must be accurately completed and signed by the responsible person before forwarding to the Operating Authority, who will forward details to the National Award Office.

Continuing the Scheme

When young people are leaving school or moving to a new area, it is important to encourage them to continue with the Scheme and to take steps to enable them to do so. The person best able to help in this regard is likely to be the designated Award Officer of the Operating Authority, who will be in touch with all User Units in the area. If the participant is leaving the district, it is important that the *Record Book* should be completed up-to-date, and the tear-out page provided for the purpose in each book filled in and sent to the Operating Authority into whose area the participant is moving or to an Award Office. A similar procedure should be followed when a participant moves from one country to another.

Publicity

All participating organisations can help by mentioning the Scheme and the activities of Award Entrants in their own literature and magazines. Assisting Organisations can give similar stimulus by articles in house magazines and journals.

Award groups should make full use of promotional material and films and make sure that all concerned are kept informed of plans and progress. Local bulletins or newsletters provide a useful means of keeping everyone in touch.

Notes on the Individual Sections of the Scheme
Service Section

There are many National organisations able to offer training in this Section.

The task is, therefore, mainly one of advising participants and liaising with the appropriate organisation to arrange appropriate courses, possibly in conjunction with other User Units.

In cases where practical service is chosen, local organisations may need to be consulted to identify forms of service which are relevant to the needs of the community.

Expeditions Section

It is important that the planning of Expeditions and Explorations is thorough in all respects, not only for the safety of young people, but because ventures which go wrong attract adverse publicity, for the unit as well as for the Scheme. There can be no short cut regarding the preliminary training and practice journeys. It is important that training is given only by appropriately qualified or experienced persons.

Details of the requirements are set out in the Expeditions Section and the *Expedition Guide* provides further information and advice, particularly in respect of ventures undertaken in Wild Country areas.

Skills Section

With such wide choice of activity, it is particularly important to find Instructors and Assessors from many spheres. Where a club or society concerned with the chosen activity exists this should not be too difficult, but in other cases it may be necessary to seek the help of such organisations as Rotary, Chambers of Commerce, Trades Councils, Women's Institutes, or other similar associations.

Care should be taken to ensure that Assessors are aware that it is **progress** and **effort** that is being assessed. For this reason the Instructor may sometimes be the most appropriate Assessor as well.

Physical Recreation Section

The emphasis in this Section is on **participation** and **improvement of performance.** Expert assistance appropriate to the activity being followed should be sought.

The availability, or lack of, facilities may often govern choice in this Section.

Residential Project

As an additional requirement at **Gold** stage, participants have to complete a Residential Project. Details of suitable opportunities may be published from time to time by National Award Authorities (in the UK in *Award News* section of *Award Journal*), but other ways of fulfilling this requirement may be found. These may vary from work camps to special courses in residential centres or placements in hospitals or homes for the disadvantaged.

Interpretation of Leisure Time

The Award Scheme is accurately described as an introduction to leisure time activities and it is intended that its programme should be voluntarily undertaken during those parts of the day, the week, the month or the year, when the choice of activity or occupation is at the option of the participant.

Although, either at school or at work, some of this "free time" may fall within designated activity or recreational periods, young people are additionally required to commit a substantial effort outside normal school or employment working hours.

It is recognised that the wide range of activities from which young people may choose in the Skills Section inevitably includes a number of interests and occupations associated with subjects forming part of school curricula, vocational training or study courses of some kind. The same may be said of some aspects of the training required in the Service, Expeditions and Physical Recreation Sections.

It is not the intention, as stated in the General Conditions (paragraph 10), that such interests and occupations should be excluded, but that, in addition to whatever instruction or training may be acquired during school or works time, young people must show clear evidence of additional voluntary effort in their own genuine leisure time.

Examples of the types of activities to which the above considerations might apply are:

Service Section
Instructions in First Aid, Life Saving or Occupational Safety.

Expeditions Section
Training in Purpose Work or in Expedition Skills such as Compass Work, Map Reading or Cooking.

A limited amount of "time off" may be allowed to young people to help them undertake their practice journeys or qualifying venture, but the major part of such enterprises must be completed in a young person's own spare time, when they could equally well be doing something else of their own choosing.

Skills Section
Instruction in Workshop Crafts, Graphic Arts or Music.

Physical Recreation Section
Attempting standards in activities with Governing Body awards.

Residential Project
Courses undertaken as part of educational or vocational training are not excluded and for these some young people may receive a limited amount of "time off" but a commitment of genuine leisure time, e.g., evenings and weekends, remains a positive requirement.

Young People with Special Needs

The Award Scheme is designed to be available to all young people and Awards are made on the basis of each individual's progress, perseverance and achievement.

Some young people face difficulties arising from physical, sensory or mental handicaps which inevitably limit their achievement. Experience has shown, however, that many benefit considerably from participation in the Scheme when appropriate arrangements are made for them.

There is only one Award Scheme, with one set of principles and standards. All take part on equal terms. But some variation of the conditions in some Sections of the Scheme may be needed if young people with disabilities are to participate. Such variations in no way involve any lowering of standards or provide for soft options: they serve only to accommodate the individual's disability, abilities, and no more.

The publication *A Challenge to the Individual* contains advice on helping disadvantaged young people through the Award Scheme, and details of the kind of variations which may be considered.

Chapter 4   General Conditions for all Awards

Ages and Requirements

1. The age range of the Scheme is from the **14th to the 25th birthdays.**

2. Participation in the Scheme is to be a young person's voluntary choice.

3. There are three Awards—**Bronze, Silver and Gold.**

4. For each Award, those taking part have to complete the requirements of each of the **four** Sections:

Service

Expeditions

Skills

Physical Recreation

5. For the **Gold Award**, participants also have to complete a **Residential Project.**

6. Entry into the Scheme is open to all young people and is made by obtaining an *Entrance Pack* containing a *Record Book* from a recognised Operating Authority. This marks the starting point in the Scheme and no activities undertaken before obtaining this book may count towards an Award, unless undergone during the previous three months in accordance with the conditions of the appropriate Section with a view to entry into the Scheme.

7. The minimum starting ages for each Award are:

Bronze-14 years. Some discretion is given to Operating Authorities to permit a few who would be just too young to enter but who are part of a larger group over this age, to make a start with their friends. (This concession is primarily intended for those in schools or youth groups who plan their activities on a group basis for the year ahead.)

Silver-15 years. Some discretion is given to Operating Authorities to permit those who have completed the **Bronze Award** just below this age to make a start on the **Silver Award** without imposing an artificial delay.

Gold-16 years. No activities may be counted for the **Gold Award** below this age.

Subject to these minimum ages, entry may be for the **Bronze**, **Silver** or **Gold Award**.

8. The earliest ages for qualification for each Award are:

Bronze—All Entrants—**14$\frac{1}{2}$**

Silver—Bronze Award Holders—**15$\frac{1}{2}$**

Direct Entrants—**16**

Gold—Silver Award Holders—**17**

Direct Entrants—**17$\frac{1}{2}$**

9. The latest date for entry into the Scheme is the **23rd birthday** and the upper age limit for all Awards is the **25th birthday,** by which time all activities to count for an Award must be completed. Extensions can only be considered where illness, accident or unavoidable circumstances make this impossible, in which case requests are to be referred by Operating Authorities to the National Award Office for consideration.

Leisure time

10. Although the Scheme is essentially an introduction to leisure activities, a participant's interests within school, formal training or work will often stimulate and sustain a commitment to one or other of the Scheme's many programmes or pursuits. However, training within normal working times for examination or career advancement purposes **cannot** be counted for an Award and a participant, to qualify, **must** show adequate evidence of voluntary effort and a substantial contribution of leisure time.

Arranging activities

11. Activities followed by young people within their own particular youth organisations may count for Award purposes provided that they are already in possession of a *Record Book* and that the appropriate Award conditions are fulfilled.

12. With growing maturity, it is expected that participants at **Silver** will take some share in organising and arranging their activities and at **Gold** they are expected to take the major part in planning and arranging what they want to do. At the higher levels of the Award an increasing proportion of Award activities should be conducted outside the immediate environment of schools' or works' premises.

13. Work for a Section of the next higher Award may be started before completing all other Sections of a lower Award, provided those concerned are over the minimum starting age for the higher Award.

Instruction

14. Instruction is to be given by suitably experienced persons, holding appropriate qualifications where specified in the detailed programmes, and approved:

■ for the **Bronze Award**, with the approval of Operating Authorities, by unit Award leaders.

■ for the **Silver Award**, by representatives of Operating Authorities at local level.

■ for the **Gold Award**, by representatives of Operating Authorities at County (or equivalant) level.

Assessment

15. Assessment is to be undertaken by suitably qualified persons approved:

■ for the **Bronze Award**, by representatives of Operating Authorities at local level.

■ for the **Silver Award**, by representatives of Operating Authorities at County (or equivalent) level.

■ for the **Gold Award**, by Operating Authorities at County (or equivalent), or National level.

Authorisation of Awards

16. The *Record Book* is to be used to record successful progress through the Scheme, and entries should only be made when the requirements of each section have been satisfactorily met.

17. A participant qualifies for an Award when all the requirements have been completed to the satisfaction of the Operating Authority.

18. Authorisation of Awards is to be undertaken.

■ for the **Bronze Award**, by Operating Authorities or their representatives at local level.

■ for the **Silver Award**, by Operating Authorities or their representatives at County (or equivalent) level.

■ for the **Gold Award**, at the highest level in each Operating Authority.

The Operation of the Scheme outside the UK

19. Within the Award Programme it is recognised that there are a number of additional and equally valid forms of activity available in different parts of the world; National Award Authorities are encouraged to promote those best suited to the needs of their young people within the overall structure of the Scheme. Where specific UK organisations are quoted, these may, in all cases, be interpreted to include their local equivalents in other countries.

Aim

To encourage service to others.

General

■ This Section is based on the belief that members of a community have a responsibility to each other and that voluntary help is needed.

■ It recognises that those who offer help should receive training in appropriate skills and have some knowledge of the needs of those to whom assistance is given.

Requirement

■ Participants are required to train for, and where possible give, service to others. Consideration should first be given to the proposed form of practical service to be followed and then to the training required to enable that service to be undertaken with competence and insight.

■ This training may take the form of **either** briefing and counselling sessions leading directly to practical service of a non-specialised nature, **or** of specialised training as preparation for later practical service in that field.

■ At Gold level there is a requirement for 12 months involvement, to include both training and practical service.

Forms of Service

The various Forms of Service are set out in three categories to facilitate choice, which will be governed largely by the aptitude of each participant and the availability of resources. If an activity is listed in Group 2 or Group 3, the required training and qualification **must** be completed. The activity **cannot** be followed as a Community Service programme in Group 1.

Forms of Service

Group 1	Group 2	Group 3
Community Service	**Service requiring courses of specialised training**	**Service requiring specific qualifications**
Children	Care for Animals	Canoe Lifeguard
Environment	Cave Rescue*	Child Care
Fund Raising	Civil Aid	Cycling Proficiency Instruction
Helping to meet the community and social needs of the elderly and infirm	Coastguard Service	
	Fire Service†	First Aid
	Lifeboat Service	Home Nursing
Help with the sick or those with special needs	Mountain Rescue‡	Life Saving
	Police Service	Mountainwalking Leader Training*
People in Need	Road Safety	
	Safety in the Home	Occupational Safety‡
	Service through Religious Education	Royal Observer Corps‡
	Working with People with a Mental Handicap	Surf Life Saving
	Work with the WRVS†	Teaching of Swimming*
	Youth work:	Welfare‡
	Award Scheme Leadership*	Youth Service Uniformed Organisations‡
	Voluntary Organisations‡	
	Youth Service	CCPR Community Sports Leaders Awards‡
	Youth Club Canteen Management‡	BETA*

* *Gold* only
† *Bronze* and *Silver* only
§ *Silver* only
‡ *Silver* and *Gold* only

Notes
i Group 1—The list is not exhaustive; Operating Authorities should suggest tasks appropriate to local community needs.
ii Some of the above programmes in all Groups have a minimum age requirement.

An alphabetical index of all forms of Service is on page 105.

Conditions

1. Choose **one** of the Forms of Service listed and:

EITHER

a) For those in Group 1:

i) Undergo appropriate briefing.

ii) Undertake practical service as follows:

BRONZE: at least 15 hours, spread over 3 months
SILVER: at least 30 hours, spread over 6 months
GOLD: at least 60 hours spread over 12 months.

iii) A diary is to be kept by each participant showing the times and details of the service given, to enable a verbal, written, pictorial or taped account to be compiled for assessment. The account should indicate an understanding of the need for giving this Service.

iv) At least three counselling sessions with the Assessor are to be arranged during the period of practical service.

v) In addition at **Gold level**, participants are required to offer a **twelve month study**, either a social, environmental or cultural issue in their local community, or related to the service element of the practical work undertaken.

vi) The form of practical service may be changed if circumstances render continuation of the original choice impracticable or inappropriate.

OR

b) For those in Groups 2 and 3:

BRONZE

i) Complete the appropriate course of specialised training and reach the required standard.

ii) Participants should be encouraged to give practical service related, whenever possible, to the training undertaken.

iii) The period of involvement should be at least eight weeks.

SILVER

i) Complete the appropriate course of specialised training and reach the required standard.

ii) Participants are expected to give practical service related, whenever possible, to the training undertaken.

iii) The period of involvement should be at least sixteen weeks.

GOLD

i) Complete the appropriate course of specialised training and reach the required standard.

ii) Complete at least 40 hours of practical service, related, whenever possible, to the training undertaken.

iii) The combined period of training and practical service **must** be at least 12 months.

At least three counselling sessions with the Assessor are to be arranged during the period of practical service.

Note: It is recognised that for some Forms of Service listed in Groups 2 and 3 the required training may be made available in curriculum timetable or works time, but participants are nevertheless expected to show adequate evidence of additional voluntary effort in their own leisure time.

Instruction and Assessment

2. Instruction and assessment for Group 1 activities are to be carried out by appropriately qualified or experienced persons nominated or approved either by the Operating Authority or the appropriate Governing Body.

3. For those Forms of Service included in Groups 2 and 3, it is essential that both the Instructors and Assessors are qualified persons approved by the appropriate Governing Body. At Gold level, instruction and assessment should not be undertaken by the same person.

4. The training is to be certified in the *Record Book* by the Instructor. Only when this and any further qualification required by the Conditions have been fulfilled is the Assessor to sign the *Record Book*.

5. Young people should be encouraged to continue giving service after qualifying for their Awards.

GROUP 1—COMMUNITY SERVICE

This group comprises those Forms of Service in which there is a substantial element of practical involvement. For this practical service to be most effective, it is important that participants are adequately briefed on the needs of those they are seeking to serve or the objective of the project they propose to undertake.

It is also important that a full record of the practical service is kept by each participant and that there are regular meetings between participant and Assessor during the period of service to discuss progress and resolve any problems.

Introduction

This programme is designed to provide for those who wish to:
a) Give practical service at any stage of the Scheme
b) Take part in forms of service which are not covered by other Service Programmes

Forms of Service undertaken may be either:
a) To individuals in need of help in their own homes
b) To people either living in a residential situation or attending a meeting place, such as a Day Centre.
c) To the wider community, e.g. improving the amenities, conserving the environment or assisting community groups.

It is essential that appropriate briefing and training is given at all stages and that supervision and/or monitoring is maintained.

The Community Service Programme is intended to be broadly based and there is no single nationally recognised Governing Body appropriate to the wide variety of types of Service likely to be undertaken. A list of possible local contacts is given on page 49. Leaders should be able to discover a local source of help through its use.

Projects appropriate to each level of Award
BRONZE

Projects at Bronze level should be restricted to:

1. Those which can be carried out under the immediate supervision of an adult Social Worker or an experienced volunteer approved by the Operating Authority.

2. Those of a team nature requiring three or more volunteers where the project is of a "once and for all" nature, e.g. clearing and tidying an overgrown garden. The team should be the subject of supervision.

3. Those which participants can carry out on their own but where no particular inconvenience to a person in need will occur if the work is dropped, e.g. collection of foil, stamps or cards for charities, survey work.

SILVER

At Silver level there should be less need than at Bronze for ensuring that projects are under close supervision but arrangements for periodic checking should be made. In addition to more demanding versions of suggested Bronze stage projects, the following might be considered appropriate:

1. Projects which require a continuing commitment over the period required.

2. Projects which, after vetting, are considered suitable for a participant to execute unaided in a recipient's home.

GOLD

At Gold level participants should be mature enough to engage in any project with proper briefing and adequate supervision. Those who have satisfactorily completed service at the Bronze and Silver levels of the Scheme might usefully supervise others in their service projects. In such cases the participant should be made aware of an appropriate person who may be contacted in the event of difficulty with the project.

Note: Leaders are advised that parents or guardians should be informed of the nature of the service being given by those under 18 years of age.

Community Service

	DIARY	BRIEFING	PRACTICAL SERVICE
BRONZE	This should record: **a)** the briefing and counselling sessions **b)** the duties, times, and details of practical service. It should enable a written, verbal, pictorial or taped account to be compiled for assessment.	Participants should be adequately briefed so that they can under-take effective practical service under close supervision.	A minimum of 15 hours spread over three months of regular service
SILVER	This should record: **a)** the briefing and counselling sessions **b)** the duties, times and details of practical service It should enable a written, verbal, pictorial or taped account to be compiled for assessment.	Participants should be fully briefed so that they can undertake effective practical service with periodic monitoring or supervision.	A minimum of 30 hours spread over six months of regular service
GOLD	This should record: **a)** the briefing and counselling sessions **b)** the duties, times and details of practical service. It should enable a written, verbal, pictorial or taped account to be compiled for assessment.	Participants should receive comprehensive briefing so they can engage competently in any project with adequate supervision	A minimum of 60 hours spread over 12 months of regular service.

COUNSELLING SESSIONS	STUDY (GOLD ONLY)	ASSESSMENT
The first session should be arranged after four hours practical work. They should then be held once a month.		The participant and the project supervisor should discuss and review: **a**) the practical service **b**) the diary **c**) the account of the project.
A minimum of three sessions, the first after about 4 hours of practical work and the others as appropriate during the period.		The participant and the project supervisor should discuss and review: **a**) the practical service **b**) the diary **c**) the account of the project.
A minimum of three sessions during the 12 months.	Over the 12 month period participants should undertake: **either** **a**) a general investigation into a social cultural or environmental issue in their local community **or** **b**) a detailed investigation related to the practical service undertaken	The participant, the project supervisor and a senior official of the organisation offering the service, or a person knowledgeable about the needs of the community, should discuss and review **a**) the practical service **b**) the diary **c**) the account of the project **d**) the study.

Conditions

1. DIARY

The diary should enable a written, pictorial, verbal or taped account to be compiled for assessment. The account should display an understanding of the need for giving the Service.

2. BRIEFING

The preliminary briefing should include:

a) The nature and purpose of the Service to be undertaken and the role of the participant.

b) Practical details of the project such as how, when and where the project is to be undertaken, the clothing and equipment required and the system of supervision and monitoring.

c) Appropriate basic skills and information on health, safety and legal factors.

d) General principles of voluntary service and any specific problems or issues likely to be met in carrying out the project, e.g. problems of senility in elderly people or points to be watched when working with children.

3. PRACTICAL SERVICE

The specified minimum period of practical service, appropriate to the level of Award, is normally to be spread over the period of time indicated. However, at Bronze and Silver levels Operating Authorities have the discretion to vary the minimum period. However, in no circumstances should the period of involvement be less than 8 weeks at Bronze level and 16 weeks at Silver level.

Projects should be appropriate to the maturity of the participant as outlined for each level of Award and comply with the spirit of Community Service.

For the Gold Award, practical service **must** be maintained for a 12 month period.

4. COUNSELLING SESSIONS

The purpose of these sessions is:

a) To discuss the progress of the project with the participant, to deal with any problems which may have arisen and to arrange for continuing the project work.

b) To seek clarification or guidance where the value of the young person's contribution or involvement is unclear.

c) To help participants learn from their experiences.

d) To share concerns experienced by the young person and, possibly, review the appropriateness of the Service option.

e) To discuss with the participant the diary and the type of account to be produced, i.e. whether it is to be written, verbal, pictorial or taped.

The time which elapses between the preliminary briefing and further counselling sessions will be governed by the type of project.

5. STUDY (Gold Award only)

The Study should illustrate a broad general knowledge of the topic other than the specific practical involvement. Participants may choose one or a combination of the following methods of presentation.

1. A written project.

2. A tape, slide, video, film or photographic presentation.

3. A collection of information and resource material such as leaflets, press cuttings, sketches.

Participants should be encouraged to find other inventive ways of presenting their investigations.

6. ASSESSMENT

Assessors should normally be those who have been involved in supervising or checking the practical service carried out by the participant. At Gold level the assessment should be carried out in conjunction with a senior official of the organisation providing and supervising the practical work, or failing this, by a person who is knowledgeable in the needs of the local community such as a doctor, minister, planning officer or social worker. The signature and position of this person should appear in the *Record Book*.

The Assessment Session should:

a) Consider the practical service which has been undertaken, paying attention to:
i Reliability
ii Competence
iii Relationships and attitudes

b) Discuss and review the diary and account, and at Gold level, the study topic. Ensure participants understand the significance of the service given.

Comments concerning these factors should be entered in the *Record Book* noting the type of service given.

Some suggested forms of practical service and the local contacts who might be approached to give the briefing talk and arrange the actual service are given on page 49. It is stressed, however, that this list is by no means exhaustive. For some activities the age requirements must be borne in mind.

Forms of Practical Service

CATEGORY	SERVICE	LOCAL CONTACTS
Children	Regular visiting of: children with a physical handicap or with cerebral palsy; helping in Day Nurseries; escorting children; children's outings; looking after a disadvantaged child for a holiday.	Medical Health Officer; Local Education Authority or suitable Voluntary Organisation Social Worker; Local Authority Social Worker; Director of Social Services Voluntary Organisation or Women's Royal Voluntary Service.
Environment	Conservation; practical working parties; footpath construction; forestry work; fencing; dry stone walling; litter clearance and the demolition of eyesores.	Civic Trust; Local Conservation Corps of the British Trust for Conservation Volunteers; Nature Conservancy Council; National Trust; Commons, Open Spaces and Footpaths Preservation Society; Forestry Commission; Park Ranger Service; RSPB; Scottish Conservation Projects Trust.
Fund Raising	Through local or national charities by organising events	Cancer Research Campaign; Children's Society; Local Council for Social Services; Oxfam; LEPRA; NSPCC.
The Elderly	Old People's Clubs; Delivering meals on wheels; Gardening; Shopping; Organising entertainments	Local Old People's Welfare Officer; British Red Cross Society; Women's Royal Voluntary Service; Royal British Legion; Order of Malta.

SERVICE

49

The Sick or those with Special Needs	Hospital work (trolley shops, hospital canteens etc); Care of the Sick or those with Special Needs. Participants wishing to help people with a mental handicap should follow the programme on page 83	Hospital Voluntary Help Organiser; Women's Royal Voluntary Service; Order of Malta; St John Ambulance Association or British Red Cross Society; Local Authority Welfare Officer or Voluntary Organisation; RNIB; RNID; Gateway Clubs.
People in Need	Telephones; visiting duties	The Samaritans; Ash; Gingerbread; Alcoholics Anonymous; Local Counselling Services; Royal British Legion.
Other Service	Organising collections of magazines for hospitals or salvage; Voluntary help with animals; Overseas Students.	St John and Red Cross Hospital Libraries; Women's Royal Voluntary Service; Community Service Volunteers; RSPCA; PDSA; United Kingdom for Overseas Student Affairs; British Council of Student's Unions.

GROUP 2—SERVICE REQUIRING COURSES OF SPECIALISED TRAINING

This group comprises those forms of service which require courses of specialised training, but which do not lead to specific qualifications.

Care for Animals

Aim: To appreciate the inter-relationship between animals and the community.

BRONZE
Pets and pet-ownership.

1. Reasons for pets: animals available: owner's responsibility.

Care and keep of the following:

2. Large pet mammals; dogs, cats.

3. Small pet mammals; rabbits, hamsters, mice, etc.

4. Pet non-mammals; birds, tortoises, snakes, etc.

5. Animal services: veterinary surgeons, animal societies, police, pet shops, shows, clubs.

The course should be organised by a veterinary surgeon, a senior officer of an animal welfare society, or a biology teacher. A veterinary surgeon should give at least the first and last of these sections. The organiser may call in other experts to deal with the other sections each of which could consist of two separate sessions. There should be as much practical work as possible. Assessment should be by oral examination conducted by the course organiser and the veterinary surgeon. When these are the same person, there should be a second examiner who is similarly associated with animals. Additional practical service may be given by helping in an RSPCA Shelter or fund raising for an animal charity, for example.

SILVER
The importance of animals to the community and vice versa.

1. Their role in sport, work, as providers of food, etc.

2. Horses: various roles: principles of care and keep.

3. Cattle: providers of milk, meat, leather.

4. Sheep: providers of wool, meat.

5. Pigs: providers of meat.

6. Poultry: providers of meat, eggs.

Methods of husbandry: collection and uses of end-products of the above.

7. Domestication of animals and the role of the community in safe-guarding their welfare.

The course for the Silver Award should be organised by a veterinary surgeon, a senior officer of an animal welfare society or a biology teacher. A veterinary surgeon should give at least the first and the last of these sections. The organiser may call in other experts to deal with the other sections. Each of these could consist of two sessions but not all of them need be given. There should be as many practical demonstrations as convenient. Assessment should be by oral examination conducted by the course organiser and the veterinary surgeon. When these are the same person, there should be a second examiner who is similarly associated with animals. Participants who have not taken the Bronze Award must attend at least the first and the last sections of a course for that Award. Additional practical service may be given by helping in an RSPCA Shelter or fund raising for an animal charity, for example.

GOLD
Wider inter-relationships of society and animals illustrated by such topics as

a) Native wild animals: zoos: wild-life parks: conservation.

b) Experimental and laboratory animals and the need for a social conscience.

c) Important diseases such as rabies, tuberculosis, brucellosis, etc.

d) Role of the veterinary profession and other "animal-orientated" organisations. Their deployment, integration and significance in the community.

The course should be organised by a veterinary surgeon, a senior officer of an animal welfare society or a biology teacher. A veterinary surgeon should give at least the last one of these sections. The organiser may call in suitable experts to discuss other subjects. Visits arranged to illustrate the topics should be encouraged. Assessment may be written or oral and should be conducted by the course organiser (or one of the other experts involved in the instruction) and a veterinary surgeon. Participants who have not taken the Silver Award must have attended the first section of each of the Bronze and the Silver Award courses.

Resource material can be obtained from:

**British Veterinary Association,
7 Mansfield Street, London W1M 0AT.**

**Pedigree Petfoods Education Centre,
National Office, Freeby Lane, Waltham-on-the-Wold,
Melton Mowbray, Leicestershire LE14 4RS**

Cave Rescue (Gold only)

Aim

To train participants to become full members of a recognised Cave Rescue Team.

Conditions of entry

1. Only open to Gold Award participants over 18 years.

2. All participants must know the contents of the Caving Safety Code.

3. Participants must have sufficient caving experience to be accepted as a probationary member of a recognised Cave Rescue Team and produce a log book of underground explorations to date.

GOLD

1. Surface Organisation— This to include:

a) Call-out procedure.
b) Personal responsibility to turn out with correct clothing, equipment and food.
c) What to do on arrival.
d) Responsibilities of person in charge on the surface.
e) The role of the police and other emergency services, press and non-caving volunteers.

2. Underground Organisation and Problems

a) Leader's responsibilities.

b) Rescuer's responsibilities.
c) Problems requiring use of specialists, e.g. divers.
d) Knowledge of procedures.
e) Communications with surface.

3. An appreciation of the effect of cold water immersion as applied to caving and rescue work.

4. First Aid

a) Diagnoses.
b) Artificial respiration—mouth-to-mouth or Sylvester.
c) Treatment of haemorrhage—internal and external.
d) Treatment of chest injuries.
e) Treatment of fractures and dislocations.
f) Know how to treat for shock and offset exposure in wet caves.
g) Treatment of burns (particularly battery acid/alkali and friction).

5. Knots

a) General experience in handling of rope for protection.
b) Bowline.
c) Figure of eight.

6. The Neil Robinson Stretcher—brief history, construction and modifications. Techniques for:

a) **A simple carry**—how to secure patient in stretcher, use of waterproof casualty bag, adjustable foot and helmet.
b) **Bedding planes**—short lifts in unison—use of drag sheet or stretcher.
c) **Pitches**—ladders and single rope techniques, lifting ropes, life-lines. Responsibilities of leader climbing with patient. Rope identification and communication in wet pitches. Use of rescue harness.
d) **Traverses**—use of pitons, bolts, stemples, guide ropes and wires.
e) **Syphons or sumps**—appreciation of the use of breathing apparatus.

7. Two "Mock" Rescues

a) One from a horizontal cave system.
b) One from a pot-hole with a pitch of more than 30ft.

SERVICE

54

The object of the rescues will be to recover a supposedly injured person from a cave system and carry them to the nearest road or track.

It is not intended that any advanced techniques to negotiate syphons or traverses will be used, though participants should be aware of such techniques.

The rescues will be as realistic as possible so that participants can appreciate the difficulties and strenuous nature of cave rescue. The knowledge and experience so gained will provide a basis for further rescue work.

Training
This will be largely of a practical nature given by members of the Cave Rescue Team at their headquarters or in the field. Participants must be a member of a Cave Rescue Team for the required amount of time.

Assessment
Participants must have carried out the whole course, as outlined, and satisfy the training officers of their competence as useful members of the Cave Rescue Team.

Specific tests will be carried out if necessary.

Address:
National Caving Association
The White Lion, Ynys Uchaf, Ystradgynlais,
Swansea SA9 1RW
Telephone: 0639 849519

Civil Aid

1. The unit must either be registered with National Voluntary Civil Aid Services to conduct the Scheme, and be a paid up member of NVCAS, or a unit organised by a Local Authority offering instruction and service in the Civil Aid Course.

2. Note that the Civil Aid Course is a course by itself and is not the same as Community Service. Units signing books under the wrong section and non-registered units signing books will jeopardise the candidate's Award.

3. The course must be supervised by a registered Civil Aid Instructor, or a Local Authority Appointed Instructor.

4. Candidates may enter at Silver or Gold. In this case, the Bronze section must be included for Silver, and the Bronze and Silver for Gold.

5. It is essential that emphasis is placed on practical training.

6. No questions should be asked in assessment which have not been included in the course.

7. The pass mark is 65 per cent. NVCAS units must submit a report on each course to the NVCAS Youth Officer.

BRONZE

1. What is a Disaster?—Deal with Fire, Flood, Storm, Landslide, Railway or Aircraft incident, Explosion, Earthquake.

2. People in Distress—Behaviour and needs of people in disaster situations.

3. How we are organised—Police, Fire, Ambulance, WRVS, Red Cross, St John, Oxfam, War on Want, Save the Children.

4. Rescue—Ropes, Knots, Lashings—Casualty handling, normal and improvised—Safety—Summary of First Aid.

5. How to Communicate—Telephones, public, J,L,F, field cable and laying, message transmission and reception.

6. Practical exercise.

SILVER

1. Revision—Revise all Bronze Award training. Carry out exercise with simulated injuries.

2. Crash Planes and Call-out arrangements.

3. Needs of People in Distress—Provision of food; Provision of shelter and accommodation; Sanitation.

4. Rescue—Reconnaissance and Rescue Plan—Control at Incidents, Ladders, Improvisation.

5. Communications—Testing telephones, Field cable fault finding, Message writing.

6. Hazards from Industrial Materials—Recognition and Action.

7. Exercise and/or extra instruction.

Note: Direct Entrants (Silver) Session 1 above should consist of 1, 2 and 3 of Bronze. Item 6 of Silver is then added to Gold.

GOLD

1. Revision—Bronze and Silver Training (Cover Bronze and Silver if Direct Gold Entrant). A Practical Exercise.

2. Major Disasters—Flood, Crash (train and aircraft), Earthquake, Landslide, Explosion.

3. Organisation of Civil Aid and allied Voluntary Services.

4. Principles of Fire Fighting and extinction. Use of stirrup pump.

5. Information Centres—Sources of information; Presentation of information. Appreciation and briefing.

6. Means of communication—Messenger, Telephone, Radio, Message handling, Practical work.

7. Organisation of a Civil Aid Unit—duties of Officers and Committees.

8. Membership of a Civil Aid Unit for 12 months.

Address:
Deputy President Civil Aid, Crinoids,
106 Church Road, Teddington, Middlesex.

Note: Candidates for Gold must hold a full Adult First Aid Certificate by the end of the course.

Coastguard Service

1. HM Coastguard is the UK authority for the co-ordination and conduct of Search and Rescue at sea in the waters surrounding the United Kingdom and 1,500 miles out into the Atlantic. They operate a comprehensive communications system based on 21 Maritime Rescue Centres situated around the coast. A continuous 24 hour radio watch on the VHF distress frequency is maintained at all of these centres through some 84 remote radio transmitting and receiving sites around our coast. In addition to this radio watch, 999 emergency telephone calls from coastal areas are handled and advice on safety can be provided at anytime, day or night. The centres have direct radio or landline links with the Coast Radio Stations, Rescue Helicopters, Lifeboats, Coastguard stations and patrol vehicles in their districts and the facilities necessary for co-ordinating all forms of maritime rescue whether they be at sea or on the coastline. HM Coastguard also performs a number of other duties in connection with the beaches and foreshores.

In addition to the Rescue Centres there are Coastguard stations which are manned during periods of bad weather or high casualty risk. These stations are in the charge of a regular Coastguard Officer assisted by volunteers enrolled in the Coastguard Auxiliary Service.

The Auxiliary Coastguard also supply the personnel required for the Coastal Searching and Cliff Rescue teams and many assist the regular Coastguard at the Rescue Centres or as reporting members.

There is ample scope for interesting and active work for young men and women with an interest in the sea with particular emphasis on communications and direct assistance to the general public.

2. Operating Authorities who wish to arrange training for this type of Service should contact the appropriate Regional Controller, HM Coastguard. In coastal districts the address of the nearest Maritime Rescue Co-ordination Centre or Maritime Rescue Sub Centre will be found in the telephone directory.

3. When the class is ready to be assessed, the Operating Authority should approach the nearest Regional Controller, HM Coastguard, and ask him to fix a convenient date and place for the assessment to be held. A list of the names of the participants should accompany the request.

4. The Regional Controller, HM Coastguard, will delegate to one of his senior officers the task of making the assessments and recording the results in individual *Record Books*.

BRONZE

A minimum of 10 sessions ($1\frac{1}{2}$–$2\frac{1}{2}$ hours) of theoretical and practical work, including one session for assessment.

Participants will be expected to have a brief knowledge of the primary duties of HM Coastguard as outlined in paragraph 1 in the notes.

1. Distress Signals—To be able to describe:

a) The signals made by surface vessels when they are in distress and require assistance from other vessels or from the shore.

b) The signals made from the shore in reply to distress signals made by a ship.

c) To understand how to alert the emergency authorities should these signals be seen.

2. International Code—Describe the shapes, colours and meanings of the alphabetical flags of the International Code of Signals where applicable to a Distress Situation.

3. Lights and Sound Signals

a) Know lights carried by power driven vessels when under way and the sound signals made in poor visibility.

b) Ditto for vessels at anchor.

4. Radio Telephony

a) Know simple procedure in voice communications.

b) Know the international phonetic alphabet.

5. Compass

a) Know the cardinal and half cardinal points.

b) Know the types of compass carried by vessels at sea.

6. Resuscitation—Be able to demonstrate the "mouth to mouth" method of resuscitation, and cardiac massage.

SILVER
A minimum of ten sessions ($1\frac{1}{2}$–$2\frac{1}{2}$ hours) of theoretical and practical work, including one session for assessment.

Participants must successfully have completed the Bronze syllabus or be sufficiently knowledgeable to be assessed for this concurrently with the Silver.

1. Distress signals—Describe the signals made by R/T from a vessel in distress.

2. Communications—Have a knowledge of communications used in HM Coastguard, including the following:

a) VHF, MF, DF.

b) Satellite Communications

c) EPIRB's—purpose and use.

d) Establish and maintain communications on a VHF R/T circuit.

3. Availability of Resources—Have an appreciation of the availability and capabilities of Lifeboats, Helicopters and Coastguard rescue teams.

4. Compass—Understand the three figure notation for indicating direction.

5. Charts and Maps—Be able to plot a position on a chart by latitude and longitude, by bearing and distance and by Decca co-ordinates. Plot a position on an Ordnance Survey map by grid reference.

6. Cliff Rescue/Coastal Search—Have an elementary knowledge of Cliff Rescue and/or Coastal Search techniques, to include the following:

a) What equipment is used.

b) The main safety points/planning requirements

c) Methods of Recovery/Search techniques.

Note: Although students should have an elementary knowledge of cliff rescue techniques, and should attend exercises, they cannot be allowed to **take part** in actual rescues or training exercises.

7. Ship recognition—Describe the more obvious recognition features of the following types of vessel:

a) VLCC	**d**) Passenger ferry	**g**) Various types
b) Warships	**e**) Oil rig service vessel	of sailing vessel.
c) Ro-Ro ferry	**f**) Fishing vessel	

GOLD

A minimum of eight sessions ($1\frac{1}{2}$–$2\frac{1}{2}$ hours) of theoretical and practical work including one session for assessment.

It is expected that the candidates intending to follow the Gold Award syllabus will have already completed the Bronze and Silver training. If, however, they are direct entrants at the Gold stage, they will be expected to complete, in addition to the syllabus given below, all the training in the Bronze and Silver syllabus as required by HM Coastguard.

Participants will be expected to have a good knowledge of the primary duties and organisation of HM Coastguard.

SERVICE

Participants must be able to act as an assistant at a Maritime Rescue Centre with commensurate knowledge of Coastguard communications and Search and Rescue procedures.

1. Compass—Underground magnetic variation and its application to true bearings.

2. Chartwork

a) Have a good understanding of the information shown on a chart.

b) Understand the effects of wind and tide on a vessel both underway and drifting.

c) Be able to plot intercepts and running fixes from VHF DF information.

3. Coastal rescue—Participants will be attached as supernumaries at local CG Auxiliary stations, and should attend a minimum of 6 exercises.

4. Rule of the Road—Understand the steering and sailing rules.

5. Resuscitation—Be prepared to be tested in the mouth to mouth method of resuscitation and cardiac massage, and to explain the reasons for all action taken.

6. Practical Service—Those who have completed the Gold level training will be enrolled as "extra" supplementary watchers (unpaid) at selected Rescue Centres to satisfy the practical service requirement for the Gold Award.

They should keep watch with a Regular Coastguard Officer, and as they become more proficient, be allowed to handle telephone messages themselves, and some of the other routine duties of a watch officer.

At least 20 two-hour watches should be kept spread over a minimum period of 12 months.

Fire Service (Bronze and Silver only)

Instruction and assessment at the discretion of Chief Fire Officers of Counties or Metropolitan Districts to whom application should be made.

BRONZE

1. Introduction—Talk given by Senior Officer to include welcome, explanations of how the class should conduct themselves while on the course and of the object of the course, introduction to instructor.

2. Fire Service Organisation—History and tradition of Fire Service, how it is organised and functions today.

3. How to act if a fire occurs—Explain various methods of calling Fire Service and correct procedure, e.g. use of exchange telephone; explain what happens from lifting receiver to acceptance of call at a fire station.

4. What to do whilst awaiting arrival of Fire Service—Save life; shut doors and windows; meet fire appliance on arrival; inform officer what has been observed of fire, persons reported in building, position of fire, intensity, etc.; point out nearest water supply.

5. Inspection of Fire Station and Appliances—Tour of fire station, inspect and explain appliances and equipment carried.

6. Fire—Explain the process of combustion by means of a triangle, give examples of causes of fire, how fire spreads, emphasis on the toxic effects of smoke produced, with modern furniture and fittings, the dangers of entering such smoke and how to act if caught in smoke.

7. Methods of Rescue—Explanation of methods employed; explain and demonstrate crawling with insensible person.

8. Fireman's Lift—Teach by numbers, each student to perform. Participants should not attempt to lift persons in excess of their own body weight.

9. Knots and Lines—Instruct as per *Fire Service Drill Book*.

10. Methods of extinguishing small fires—Buckets, mat for beating or smothering, soda water syphon; briefly describe chemical extinguishers, hand pump, garden hose. Demonstrate operation of hand pump.

11. Hose Drills—Running out length of hose, connecting to hydrant and shipping branch.

12. Fire Prevention—Precautions in the home, domestic heating, airing linen, cleaning materials, petrol, coal fires, electricity, electric irons, wiring fuses, meters and switches, gas, oil stoves, storage of materials, decorations, fireworks, candles, bonfires, smoking materials, doors and windows. Explain dangers and precautions relating to each.

Instruction should take approximately 12–15 hours.

Assessment may be written and/or oral and should include where possible tests of practical ability to apply the instruction given on the course.

Practical service could include further detailed investigation into areas such as potential causes of fire in the home or public places, fire precautions or fire prevention.

SILVER
Note: Direct Entrants (Silver) have to cover Bronze training which may be compressed into four sessions, **additional to the syllabus below**.

1. Introduction—Talk given by Senior Officer to include welcome, explanation of how the class should conduct themselves on the course, of the purpose of the course, and introduction to the instructor.

2. Fire Service Organisation—Peacetime structure and how the Service functions: powers under the Fire Services Act, 1947: mobilising, first attendance, make up, type of incidents dealt with, e.g. special services, communications. Visit to a control room.

3. Water Supplies—Description of town's mains, hose reels, hydrants, private hydrants, open water, brief explanation of water relay.

4. Fire Prevention and means of escape in places of public entertainment and large buildings—sprinklers, drenchers, automatic fire alarms, fire telephones, dry and wet risers, fire resisting doors.

5. Hand Appliances—Water, foam, CO_2, Halon and powder extinguishers: how each is identified and actuated and for which type of fires each is suitable.

6. Methods of Rescue—Résumé of Bronze Award; explanation and demonstration of 2, 3 and 4-handed seat and blanket removal method.

Instruction should take approximately 12–15 hours.

Assessment may be written and/or oral and should include where possible, tests of practical ability to apply the instruction given on the course.

Practical service could include further detailed investigation into areas such as potential causes of fire in the home or public places, fire precautions or fire prevention.

GOLD
No syllabus.

Lifeboat Service

The RNLI is a voluntary organisation for saving life at sea supported entirely by voluntary contributions and administered by a Committee of Management. The British Isles are divided into seven areas, each controlled by an Inspector who is responsible to the Committee of Management through the Director. There are 126 offshore lifeboats and 137 inshore lifeboats stationed around our coastline and manned as required by volunteer crews. Training for this volunteer service will be arranged at certain suitable stations where instructors are available and application should be made to the Inspector of the area concerned through the Royal National Lifeboat Institution, West Quay Road, Poole, Dorset, BH15 1HZ. Each group under training must be limited to a maximum of six. Participants must wear a secure lifejacket when afloat which will be provided.

When a group is ready for assessment, the Inspector will be informed and the necessary arrangements made. The results will be entered in the candidate's *Record Book*. *Volume II Admiralty Manual of Seamanship* will cover most of the syllabus.

It may be possible for participants to accompany the lifeboats crew on exercise, in order to do this each participant **must be covered by their own insurance**.

BRONZE

Candidates will be taken out on exercise before finally being accepted, once in an inshore lifeboat (ILB) and once in the offshore lifeboat. They must produce certificates showing that they can swim 50 yards with their clothes on.

1. The Inspector, or a deputy appointed by him, will meet the candidates and instruct them in the system of control of a lifeboat station. Instructors will then explain launching and recovery and the candidates will help to clean up the boathouse.

2. Candidates to learn distress signals, also lights and sound signals for vessels underway and at anchor. Instructors to show and explain gear in the lifeboat and boathouse—its use and purpose.

3. Instruction on the compass (both 360 degrees and points) and how to steer a boat by it, compass to be learned by points ready for next session.

4. Revision of compass work and ships lights.

5. Repeat fourth session.

6. Instruction in general First Aid and mouth-to-mouth resuscitation.

Note: Training in simple First Aid is a necessary part of the basic training in the Award Scheme Expeditions Section so it may only be necessary to revise this training with some candidates, whereas with others new to the subject it will require instruction during this session and further practice during later sessions. Test on "boxing" the compass, followed by ILB exercise with instruction in ILB launching and recovery.

7. General review, check on resuscitation. Duty work on offshore and inshore lifeboats.

8. General revision and exercise in the offshore lifeboat.

Assessment
Candidates will be assessed by the Inspector or his nominee. They will be expected to have attended the Course regularly and to have acquired a reasonable degree of skill and knowledge in all the practical training undertaken, such as First Aid, compass, etc.

SILVER
It is expected that candidates intending to follow the Silver Award syllabus will already have completed the Bronze Award Training. If, however, they are Direct Entrants at the Silver Stage, they will be expected to cover in addition to the syllabus below, the basic training in Bronze Award sessions 1, 2, 3, 5 and 6.

1. The Inspector, or a deputy appointed by him, will give a short history of the RNLI and its principles, and brief participants on this stage. Revision, as necessary, on work done for the Bronze Stage.

2. Instruction in rope work, including bends, hitches and splices.

3. Instruction on ship types and the use of the leadline, echo sounder and use of a heaving line.

4. Instruction on lifebelts, breeches buoy drill, man overboard and scrambling net.

5. Instruction in tide tables and elementary chartwork.

6. Instruction in elementary meteorology and exercise afloat in conjunction with helicopters.

7. Further instruction on tide tables, chartwork and meteorology.

Assessment

Candidates will be assessed by the Inspector. They will be expected to have attended the Course regularly and to have acquired a reasonable degree of skill and knowledge in all the practical training undertaken.

GOLD

It is expected that the candidates intending to follow the Gold Award syllabus will have already completed the Bronze and Silver training. If, however, they are Direct Entrants at the Gold Stage, they will be expected to cover, **in addition** to the syllabus given below, whatever basic training in the Bronze and Silver syllabus deemed necessary and desirable by the RNLI instructor.

1. Inspector, or a deputy appointed by him, to describe the general organisation of the RNLI. Instruction on compass course corrections and compass bearings, followed by an ILB exercise.

2. Instruction in the responsibility of the RNLI and the necessity for and various methods of raising money.

3. Instruction in the responsibilities of a station Honorary Secretary and action to be taken on receipt of a casualty report.

4. Instruction in the duties of HM Coastguard relative to lifeboats and combined searches with other boats and helicopters. Navigational instruction and planning a search.

5. Instruction in working out the requirements for a short passage from the lifeboat station to the repair yard, followed by practical instruction in ILB handling afloat.

6. Exercise afloat in the offshore lifeboat. Candidates should be instructed in and carry out emergency drills.

Assessment

Candidates will be assessed by the Inspector or his nominees. They will be expected to have attended the Course regularly and to have acquired a reasonable degree of skill and knowledge in all the practical training undertaken.

Note: GOLD

It is a requirement of the Gold Award that participants are to give voluntary service to the community over a period of twelve months. If this practical work can in any way be linked with the service training already undertaken, this is ideal, but it is recognised that this is not always practicable and in such cases other forms of help to the community may be given.

Participants, therefore, who have taken the RNLI training and who wish to help with this service, should first consult the RNLI Inspector to see if there are any useful ways in which their service can be used locally, such as help in the boat house, in connection with the duty roster, in helping to raise funds, or in other ways.

Assessment
Candidates will be assessed on the regularity of the voluntary help given, their willingness to undertake tasks requested of them and the sustained interest shown in the Lifeboat Service.

Mountain Rescue
General
Participants should have read the *Mountain and Cave Rescue Handbook* and be familiar with the rescue methods described in it. They should also be thoroughly familiar with the BMC Booklet *Safety on Mountains*.

The standards to be aimed at in training for this syllabus are:

a) Those who qualify at Silver level would be reliable assistants in a Rescue Team.

b) Those who qualify at Gold level would be eligible to serve a probationary period as a member of a Mountain Rescue Team after their 18th birthday.

SILVER
1. Participants must be reasonably conversant with a mountain or a pot-hole area and all its rescue facilities: e.g. the Craven area or the Western Lake District. Such knowledge should be gained by practical experience.

2. They should know what precautions to take on the hills (spare clothing, food, whistle, map, compass, First Aid dressings, torch, *MRC Handbook*, etc.).

3. They must be able to find their way by using 1:50000 and 1:25000 Ordnance Survey Maps and a compass to a given six-figure grid reference.

4. They should be able to recognise and give First Aid for: shock, bleeding, fracture, dislocations, sprains, exposure, frostbite and burns, and know of the great care needed and the methods used in handling a person suffering from an injury, or suspected injury to the spine.

5. They should be able to tie a bowline and a reef knot and make a Pigott stretcher, know MRC instructions on distress signals and the pyrotechnic code.

6. They should know the correct procedure in case of an accident in their own party, i.e. the duties of the person staying behind and of the person going for help. They must know how a rescue party is prepared, and how the scene of accident should be marked by the display of clothing, rope, etc., or its position determined by a compass bearing.

7. They should know the alpine distress signal and its answer.

8. They should know something of the various rescue organisations in the British Isles and the correct "call-out" procedure.

9. They should have an elementary knowledge of the search methods and the procedure, including the square search.

10. They should know standard aircraft markings, and be aware of the dangers of, ejector seats, ammunition and explosion from fuel.

11. They should have to give practical proof of their ability in the following: map work; First Aid; knotting.

12. They should take part in an exercise with a recognised organisation which includes a search and a rough carry.

GOLD

1. Young people must meet the requirements for Silver level.

2. They must be thoroughly conversant with a mountain or pot-hole area and provide at least 21 days' practical experience in the area.

3. They must be conversant with those aspects of mountaineering which are peculiar to the area in which they intend to operate.

a) If this involves rock climbing they must have followed a "difficult" climb in their own area.

b) If this involves pot-holing they must have taken part in an expedition involving ladder pitches.

c) Whatever their area, they must have elementary practical experience of moving over snow and ice, including the use of an ice axe.

4. They must either be familiar with all the common knots and methods of rope management used by climbers, or they must be able to rig and de-rig a pot-hole pitch and be familiar with standard lifeline practice.

5. They must demonstrate their ability to use a 1:50000 and 1:25000 Ordnance Survey Map and a compass by day and night to reach a six-figure grid reference and to navigate in bad visibility (cloud or mist or in featureless or unknown country).

6. First Aid:

a) They must have passed the full First Aid qualification for the Silver Award, or its equivalent.

b) They must have injected a dummy ampoule of morphia.

7. They must know how to load and carry a Thomas Stretcher and how to use a Thomas Splint and **either** lower a Thomas Stretcher, **or** use the Neil Robinson Stretcher for pot-hole rescue, also a McInnes Stretcher.

8. They must know the rescue procedure for crashed aircraft as laid down by the *Air Ministry Pamphlet*, 6th edition 1973.

9. They must give practical proof of their ability by organising a search, rescue and evacuation for a casualty from either a cliff face or a pot-hole.

Police Service

BRONZE

Period and Activity

1. Address and Lecture
Welcome by Senior Officer. Objects of course and syllabus. Primary responsibilities of the police and the problems involved in discharging them.

2. Lecture
The organisation of a Force and police rank structure.

3. Tour
Tour of a Police Station with a brief insight into the work of the various Departments.

4. Lecture/Practical
Importance of various forms of police communications and practical use of telephone, radio and teleprinter.

5. Lecture
First action at scene of incidents and accidents generally. Trapped persons, fires, suicides, sudden deaths, childbirth. The police emergency system. Where facilities are available participants to be given an opportunity to deal with mock incidents.

6. Lecture and Demonstration
Cycle proficiency and road safety. The importance of educating the public in road safety and educating and helping young and old persons as expressed by the *Highway Code*. Maintenance of pedal cycles and how to give elementary instruction on these subjects to others.

7. Lecture/Practical
The value of good observation in detecting crime. How to improve your observation and practical tests in observation. Personal descriptions.

8. Lecture
General lecture on the various specialist officers engaged in police work, i.e. women police, drugs officers, criminal records and intelligence officers, detectives, and where possible a short talk by persons engaged in one or more of these activities.

9. Assessment
May be written and/or oral and should include where possible tests of practical ability to apply the instruction given on the course.

Note: The length of the sessions may be varied according to the circumstances but is is recommended that the lecture element in any one session should not exceed 45 minutes, and the total time taken for the whole Course should not exceed 12 hours.

Practical service could include such areas as Crime Prevention, Cycle Marking, Neighbourhood Watch or Cycleway.

SILVER

Period and Activity

1. Address and Lecture
Welcome by Senior Officer. Objects of course and syllabus. Primary responsibilities of the police, police ranks and organisation.

2. Tour and Lecture
Tour of a Police Station and lecture on the various specialist Departments by officers of those Departments where available.

3. Lecture
Motor vehicle accidents. First action, assistance to police, traffic control, care and custody of children, animals and property.

4. Lecture
Crime Prevention. Security of property, buildings and motor vehicles. Movement and activities of criminals. "Modus operandi".

5. Practical
Mechanical safety of motor vehicles, brakes, lighting, etc. How to spot and correct faults and the consequences of bad vehicle maintenance.

6. Lecture and Demonstration
Practical aids to police in preventing and detecting crimes, radio alarms, alarm systems, carriage of high value property. How fingerprints are used, plaster casts, blood groups, photography, identikit.

7. Lecture and Visit
The Magistrates' Courts, Juvenile Courts and Coroners' Courts, and the purpose of each. Where possible a visit to a Magistrates' Court and a discussion on the proceedings at the Court during the visit.

8. Practical
Procedure relating to lost and found dogs and property. Practice in receiving property from persons in the street and in the Police Station and completing appropriate records.

9. Lecture
Duties of citizens relating to preventing crime and assisting police. Citizens' powers of arrest. Training of Police Cadets and Probationary Constables.

10. Assessment
May be written and/or oral and it should include where possible test of practical ability to apply the instruction given on the course.

Note: The length of the sessions may be varied according to the circumstances but it is recommended that the lecture element in any one session should not exceed 45 minutes, and the total time taken for the whole Course should not exceed 15 hours.

Practical service could include such areas as Crime Prevention; Cycle Marking; Neighbourhood Watch or Cycleway.

GOLD

Note: Direct entrants to the Gold Award should cover briefly the following subjects from the Silver Award before commencing.

1. Police organisation and rank structure.

2. Action at road accidents.

3. Magistrates' Courts, Juvenile Courts and Coroners' Courts.

Period and Activity

1. Address and Lecture
Welcome by Senior Officer. Primary responsibilities of the police. Functions of Crown Courts. Punishment of adult offenders.

2. Practical
Dealing with a mock road accident, covering particularly first action, assistance to police, traffic control, First Aid, care of property.

3. Visit
A visit to a Crown Court.

4. Lecture
Major incidents and crashed aircraft. Police action, co-ordination of services, communications, care of victims and control of public.

5. Demonstration/Practical
Demonstration of how to give evidence and practice in giving evidence in a mock court as a witness.

6. Lecture

Care and treatment of children and young persons by Probation or Welfare Officer or if not possible, by a woman Police Officer.

7. Optional Visit (**over 18 years only**)

Visit to a Community Home, Detention or Attendance Centre to see an aspect of the treatment of young offenders.

8. Lecture and film

Specialist and higher training together with film on these aspects where possible.

9. Lecture and film

Police action after major crimes, covering initial action, large scale operations, the co-ordination of general and specialist work up to the point of Court appearance. This is done by showing appropriate film wherever possible.

10. Assessment

May be written and/or oral and should include where possible test of practical ability to apply the instruction given on the course.

Note: The length of the sessions may be varied according to the circumstances but it is recommended that the lecture element in any one session should not exceed 45 minutes, and the total time taken for the whole Course must be at least 15 hours.

Practical service could include such areas as Crime Prevention; Cycle Marking; Neighbourhood Watch or Cycleway.

Note: GOLD

For the Gold Award participants are required to devote a minimum period of 12 months to the Service Section, to include training and practical service. The training selected should lead to, be related to, or give insight into the proposed practical service.

After undertaking Police Service Training some participants may be able to work directly with the Police by assisting in station duties or becoming Special Constables. In addition the Police Service Course provides useful training for other forms of community service, e.g. work within Intermediate Treatment or the Probation Service, in night shelters, community homes or probation hostels, or with "at risk" groups of young or old people.

SERVICE

Road Safety

General Notes

Instructors and assessors will benefit from close contact with road safety practitioners who will be able to act as a source of reference for local and national accident data, documents, materials and other relevant information.

The Road Safety Officer can be contacted through the Council Offices. Most police forces also have an Accident Prevention Officer.

Wherever possible the instructor should refer to the latest edition of the Highway Code for guidance and an outline of the law's demands.

Any site visits to roads, or practical road training, should be carefully planned and younger participants should be briefed on appropriate safe practices and supervised where necessary.

BRONZE

Aim of Syllabus

To develop an understanding about the nature of road accidents, particularly in the context of the participant's own local environment and age group.

Participants should:

1. Investigate the way in which accident data is collected, how it is stored, and how it may be used.

2. Assess the relative contributions to accidents of
a) human error (e.g. alcohol, speed, inexperience)
b) environment (e.g. weather, road surface condition, visibility)
c) vehicle (e.g. defective tyres, faulty brakes)
Use press cuttings, data and case studies.

3. Put together a profile of road accidents to your own age group, e.g. male/female, location, time, circumstances, blame, vehicles. Survey friends and peers as well as using data.

4. Find out travel patterns of those in your age group. Use of public transport. Journey types. High risk behaviour. Relate to the journeys to school, and suggest improvements.

5. Select a familiar section of street or road in a town or village and identify possible dangers. Bear in mind the needs of the elderly and the disabled.

6. Using a bicycle, establish the principles of vehicle safety maintenance. Draw up a priority list of features requiring special attention. Be able to identify and correct defective parts, for checking by an expert.

7. Understand the properties of reflective and fluorescent materials and their safety application to vulnerable road users in particular. Obtain samples and test for effectiveness and customer acceptability. Compile a list of appropriate items, where they can be obtained, and prices and promote their use to a group of older people and to parents at a pre-school group.

SILVER

Note: Candidates following a road safety syllabus for the first time should become familiar with the Bronze objectives 1 and 2.

Aim of Syllabus
To build on existing understanding of the causes of road accidents, and develop a detailed awareness of some of the safety programmes available.

To prepare the participants for vehicle ownership and individual responsibilities.

Participants should

1. Investigate the relative risks faced by different age groups from road traffic accidents as compared to other types of accident. Costs and consequences of road accidents.

2. Become familiar with procedures at the scene of road accidents. Learn emergency aid skills, e.g. CPR, recovery position, dealing with severe bleeding.

3. Understand effects of alcohol and drugs, and the laws relevant to road users. Field test awareness of a sample of the public on these. Assess relative contributions of law enforcement, publicity and education to an anti-drink drive strategy.

4. Understand contribution of seat restraints to casualty reduction. Become familiar with current legislation. Prepare consumer report on availability, pricing and fitting of child seat restraints. Try and publish findings in local journal, magazine or newsletter.

5. Find out about availability of local training courses for bicyclists, motor-cyclists, horse-riders and car drivers (including disabled). Seek agreement to attach yourself to one of these organizations, and familiarize yourself with training techniques.

6. Research the costs involved in vehicle ownership, the documentation necessary, and the safety advantages and disadvantages of the chosen mode of transport. Obtain insurance premium quotation. Present your findings to a group of teenagers in a school, college or youth organization.

GOLD
Note: Participants should be familiar with the theoretical content of the Silver course. They should also discuss their proposed course of training and service with a road safety practitioner before commencing. Wherever possible, participants should arrange to give service on behalf of, or in conjunction with a Road Safety Officer or other practitioners.

The project assignment should also be one negotiated in advance with a practitioner, who may be able to give guidance on a topic offering particular relevance.

Aim of Syllabus
To develop an awareness of the more complex issues relating to road safety, such as the perspectives of different pressure groups, the various lobbies, the contribution of public transport, safety as an environmental issue, the comparative level of provision for vulnerable groups.

To assess how a local street environment succeeds or fails in incorporating fair and effective safety design.

To embark upon an extended programme of road safety service.

Participants should
1. Study a site that was improved by low-cost engineering treatment. Previous accident record analysed, reasons for treatment understood, and post-treatment record analysed. Close involvement with RSO, and engineering colleagues is necessary here.

2. Select a local site to prepare in-depth recording of road-user movements, user opinions, perceived and actual danger or conflict. Using photography, video filming, tape recordings, present recommendations to Engineering Department.

3. Make contact with a user group, or lobby group, and understand the different points of view. Study special needs of physically or mentally handicapped road users. Consider and research particular needs of ethnic minorities and citizens with English as a second language. Communicate their problems to the Council officers and assist in devising a strategy to meet their needs.

4. Embark upon extended service such as
a) Assisting with regular training of road users, whether pedestrians cyclists, motorcyclists or horse-riders after first having gained competence.
b) Assist in the training of Bronze road safety scheme participants
c) Represent the interests of your age-group on a local road safety group or committee.

Safety in the Home

Notes:
1. Leaders are advised to seek expert help from Instructors and Assessors. Material and help can usually be obtained from the local Environmental Health Department.

2. Training Packs and guides to projects on Home Safety are available from the Royal Society for the Prevention of Accidents at Cannon House, The Priory, Queensway, Birmingham B4 6BS and 117 Lisburn Road, Belfast BT9 7BS, Northern Ireland.

BRONZE

Aim of Syllabus—To teach participants about the extent, cause and results of home accidents and the need for preventive action.

To give basic training in personal safety and personal responsibility for the safety of others in the home.

1. Candidates should have an appreciation of:

a) The Home Accident statistics.

b) The most frequent accidents that occur in the home and the two age groups most vulnerable.

c) The effect of home accidents on the individual and the family.

2. They should be able to identify areas in the home where most accidents occur and offer sensible and inexpensive ways of preventing them.

3. The precautions to be taken when considering Home Safety in specific areas such as:

a) Living Room, Hall and Stairs.

b) Kitchen.

c) Bedroom and Bathroom.

d) Garage and Garden area.

4. Keep notes and collect relevant Newspaper and Magazine articles.

Design a 'Home Safety Check' suitable for either the Elderly or the Under Fives. Suggest ways of making their environment safer.

Answer Questions asked by the Assessor, choosing areas from **3 a)**, **b), c), d)**.

SILVER
Aim of syllabus—The syllabus aims at furthering the knowledge and awareness of dangers in and around the home and to increasing a sense of responsibility towards the safety of the family in general.

Candidates should:

1. Be able to explain the dangers inherent in the following and describe how they would take precautions to prevent accidents.

a) A family living room.

b) A child's bedroom/playroom.

c) A garden, complete with garden shed and greenhouse used by a family with young children.

d) A garage/workshop

2. Prepare and give a talk on Home Safety to last approximately 10 minutes to a local organisation or class or schoolchildren using one teaching aid (designed by candidate).

OR

Make a model "Hazard House" and explain the dangers.

3. Submit a project on Home Safety.

4. Keep notes and collect relevant Newspaper and Magazine articles.

GOLD

Aim of syllabus—To develop a firm foundation of safety skills and knowledge as preparation for responsible adulthood and as potential parents living in their own home environment.

Candidates should:

1. Make a study of main services with special reference to normal safety procedures:

a) Gas.

b) Water.

c) Electricity.

Understand the importance and significance of safety signs, symbols, labels and warnings.

2. Know what action to take in household emergencies concerning main services, including:

a) How to turn off the main gas supply and ensure safety of personnel.

b) How to deal with an 'overflowing cistern'. Locate the main stopvalve; deal with flooding.

c) The safe use of electricity. How to mend a fuse. How to wire a plug. Recognise when professional assistance is required. How to plan for power cuts.

d) What to do if fire breaks out. How to call the Emergency services.

3. Conduct a Home Safety Survey and present findings to a wider audience.

a) Devise a questionnaire that would obtain the information required.

b) Work out how to conduct the survey.

c) Present the results, with graphs or charts where appropriate, together with a short written summary.

Service through Religious Education

Syllabuses are available direct from the following denominations:

The Baptist Union of Great Britain and Ireland *BRONZE, SILVER* and *GOLD*
Department of Mission, Baptist House, 129 Broadway, Didcot, Oxford-shire, OX11 8RT.

The Church of England *SILVER* and *GOLD*
General Synod Board of Education (Children), Church House, Dean's Yard, Westminster, SW1P 3NZ.

Church of Ireland *SILVER* and *GOLD*
Rev. H. McKelvey, 19 Upper Lisburn Road, Belfast BT10 0GW.

Church of Scotland *SILVER* and *GOLD*
Department of Education, 121 George Street, Edinburgh EH2 4MN.

The Church in Wales *SILVER* and *GOLD*
Children's Officer, Religious Education Centre, Woodlands Place, Penarth, South Glamorgan CF6 2YQ.

Judaism *BRONZE, SILVER* and *GOLD*
Reform Synagogues of Great Britain, Sternberg Centre for Religious Education, 80 East End Road, Finchley, London N3.

Methodist *SILVER* and *GOLD*
MAYC Training Officer, Youth Department, 2 Chester House, Pages Lane, London N10 1PZ.

IMAYC, Aldersgate House, University Road, Belfast BT7 1NA.

Roman Catholic *SILVER* and *GOLD*
Our Lady Catechists, Chairman, 67 Alexander Drive, Cirencester, Glos. GL7 1VG.

The United Reformed Church *BRONZE, SILVER* and *GOLD*
The Secretary for Christian Education, 86 Tavistock Place, London WC1H 9RT.

Note: Participants wishing to follow programmes devised by other Denominations or Religions should contact the Award Office.

General Advice
Whilst appropriate service for all sections will necessarily require consultation with Diocesan and local church authorities, consideration should be given to the fact that 'Service' in the terms required by the Award Scheme is of a specified period of time. Some activities are,

SERVICE

therefore, more appropriate than others. Altar Service and Choir membership, for example, are activities or acts of service which flow from ongoing faith and Church membership which might not lend themselves to Service for a particular period of time only to achieve the requirements of the Service Section.

A new possibility of meeting the requirements of the Service section is that of participating in a Leadership course. 'Spectrum' is an inter-Church Syllabus. Details are available through either Diocesan authorities or British Council of Churches Youth Unit.

Working with people with a Mental Handicap

Training by means of a *Distance Learning Pack* and assessment to be arranged by the National Federation of Gateway Clubs. The pack can be obtained by writing to the Federation at 117 Golden Lane, London, EC1Y 0RT.

BRONZE No syllabus

SILVER Minimum age 15 years.

Theory
Details of the theory sections are contained in the Distance Learning Pack mentioned above.

Practical
1. At least 30 hours practical work to be undertaken.

2. A study is to be undertaken into the statutory and voluntary provision for people with a mental handicap in the participants' locality. The study can be prepared in any form. For details of the study see the Distance Learning Pack.

GOLD Minimum age 16 years.

Theory
Details of the theory sections are contained in the Distance Learning Pack mentioned above.

Practical
1. At least 40 hours practical service spread out over a period of 12 months.

2. Conduct a survey into the statutory and voluntary provision for people with a mental handicap in the participant's locality. Highlight in depth one particular area of the provision i.e. leisure housing, education, family support. For details of the survey see the Distance Learning Pack.

Work with the WRVS

BRONZE

1. Introduction to WRVS work—an informative talk giving story and pattern of WRVS and the work done locally, e.g. Meals on Wheels, clubs for the elderly, visiting old people, hospital work, clothing, the role of WRVS in emergencies, work with children i.e. children's holidays.

2. Clothing (including a visit and practical work in a clothing store if possible).

3. Fire Prevention.

4. Feeding in an emergency, including demonstration of equipment and a practical exercise at some point during the course.

5, 6, 7. (three sessions) On the job practical work, under supervision, in WRVS everyday work; a minimum of ten hours to be undertaken in the participant's own time but completed before assessment.

8. Work with the disabled, particularly children.

9. Revision—quiz.

10. Assessment.

SILVER

Direct entrants as Silver must cover all the work of the Bronze syllabus. All participants must complete the following syllabus.

1. WRVS work with Social Services—an informative talk followed by questions and discussion.

2. WRVS work with the National Health Service—as above.

3. WRVS work with the Home Office, Prison Department, and in Crown and Magistrates Courts—as above.

4, 5, 6. (three sessions) On the job practical work under supervision in WRVS everyday work; a minimum of 20 hours to be undertaken in the participant's own time but completed before assessment.

7. Work in Rest Centres.

8. Information Point training.

9. Revision—quiz.

10. Assessment.

GOLD

Candidates who have taken training with the WRVS for the bronze and silver Awards and wish to continue with this type of practical training for Gold, use the Gold stage of the Community Service syllabus as their training guide. The syllabus can be adapted for use with any form of practical service desired such as helping the blind, the elderly, the physically handicapped, on children's holidays or other groups for which a specialist programme is not available.

Youth Work
Award Scheme Leadership (Gold only)

This programme is designed to provide an understanding of the aim, content and conditions of The Duke of Edinburgh's Award and opportunity to gain practical experience in running the Scheme.

Note: Training, of at least 20 hours' duration, may take the form of single training sessions, or be combined with residential week-end or one-day courses.

Training

1. A briefing session on the Award Scheme as a whole—its Aim and content.

2. The personal and social needs of the adolescent and how these are provided for through the Award Scheme.

3. Overall organisation of the Scheme—Award Officers, Operating Authorities, Award Committees, Award Centres.

4. Organisation of the Scheme within a User Unit.

5. A detailed look at the Sections of the Scheme.

6. Specialist training in instructing or co-ordinating an activity or activities within a Section.

7. The theory and practice of assessment.

8.
a) Discover the facilities and opportunities available to participants in the area.

b) Prepare an introductory talk for potential participants.

c) Show how the aims of the Scheme are achieved in practice.

d) Draw up a programme of training for an Expedition on foot indicating estimated time involved, sources of assistance and approximate cost to the individual and the group.

Practical Service
For at least the balance of the 12-month period, participants should be involved in the organisation of the Scheme within a group. Such service must include at least two of the following:

a) Arranging a course from one Section—provision of Instructors, arrangement for assessment, finance, etc.

b) Assisting, after receiving appropriate specialist training, in the instruction of Award entrants in one or more activities.

c) Assisting with the assessment of participants.

d) Compiling and maintaining records of all participants in a group.

Assessment
For assessment purposes, notes should be kept along with a diary showing dates and details of practical service plus a report on the practical training exercise. Assessment should include an understanding of the **philosophical** and **educational** values of each Section of the Award. Assessment should be undertaken by the Award Officer of the Operating Authority or their nominee.

Youth Service

Many National Voluntary Youth Organisations, e.g. NABC, Youth Clubs UK, and Local Authority Youth Services organise comprehensive packages of training which provide ideal opportunities for young people to undertake this option. In such cases, this syllabus will assist participants and leaders in selecting an appropriate course. It will also indicate the requirements for each level of Award to those organisations who do not arrange their own training scheme.

In order to enable each participant to make a significant contribution within the youth organisation and to learn from their experiences, the three strands of the syllabus are:

a) Course work and a project.
b) Active leadership and participation in a group/club.
c) Personal development of the participant.

The Course work may be given as a series of single training sessions or be combined with, or given entirely at residential courses, provided that the minimum hours are undertaken.

Participants should build a portfolio to help them record and evaluate their work and show evidence of personal development. It should contain information gathered during the course work and project, a diary and record of the period of active leadership together with any photographs, letters or publicity material.

Assessment

This should be based on attendance, participation and discussion of the portfolio showing evidence of improved personal awareness and understanding. At Gold, it should be undertaken at Borough/County level.

BRONZE

Course work and project

1. Background knowledge. Basic information about the group/club, what it provides, other local youth provision.

2. Membership. The responsibilities of membership; an introduction to some of the issues affecting them; learning to take decisions; providing equal opportunities.

3. Programme and activities. How to organise and plan an evening programme in a junior club or group; the range of activities; simple group observations; use of notice boards and posters.

4. Personal Skills. Identifying personal skills and qualities; how to develop them in a youth club setting.

5. Project. Working alongside another youth worker, plan and carry out a project with a purpose such as publicising an event or organising, under close supervision an activity in a junior club.

The Course work should be a minimum of 8 hours.

Active leadership
Assisting with specific supervised activities in a junior club over a 3 month period. Participants should be given regular guidance and feedback on their performance.

SILVER
Course work and project
1. Background knowledge. The aims of the club/organisation; provisions of the local youth service; profile of the local community.

2. Principles and Practice. The basic principles of good youth work practice; concept of groups; improving participation; an introduction to issues such as equal opportunities, racism, urban and rural deprivation.

3. Programmes and Activities. Design a programme with variety to meet aims; organisation, preparation and publicity; e.g. How to arrange teams and organise simple competitive events.

4. Personal Skills. Identifying personal strengths; using them in the club/group; making decisions; taking initiative. Concept of teamwork; introduction to styles of leadership.

5. Project. Organise and evaluate an activity with a purpose for a small group of young people with the support of a youth worker.

The Course work should be a minimum of 15 hours.

Active leadership
Adopt a leadership role in a small group with the support of a youth worker over a period of 6 months. Participants should receive regular review and counselling sessions.

GOLD
Course work and Project
1. Background knowledge. The aims of the club/organisation; an evaluation of its success; the local provision for young people and the issues affecting them.

2. The Youth Work Curriculum. Aims; target groups; priorities and outcomes; techniques for evaluation; young people in society.

3. Programmes and Activities. Principles of programme planning; role of activities; promotion and publicity.

4. Leadership. Styles and functions of leadership; relationships between members and youth workers; decision making; committee work.

5. Personal Skills. Assessing personal strengths and weaknesses; devising a programme for personal development.

6. Project. Undertake and evaluate a practical project with a purpose which is related to the course work, such as: organisation of a junior club or organisations; a project integrating those with special needs; planning an Open Award night; organising an arts event.

The Course work should be a minimum of 20 hours.

Active Leadership. Adopt a leadership role in a group/club with the guidance of a youth worker for a minimum of 12 months. Participants should receive regular review and counselling sessions.

Youth Club Canteen Management

BRONZE No syllabus.

SILVER
Young people should make a study of the following:

1. The reason for a canteen in a youth organisation and the value it can be to the members in encouraging association and discussion and in the social training it can provide, in addition to its function in providing food and drink.

2. Simple business accounting, i.e. keeping records of stock, preparing a daily sales sheet and presenting a statement of income and expenditure for a canteen over a period, taking into account the value of stock brought forward and in hand and calculating the percentage profit.

3. Hygiene in the preparation and serving of food.

4. Detailed plans and costing for not less than two feature events involving the preparation and serving of simple and attractive refreshments related to the event. Such catering might be for a club supper or dance or a special guest evening; these plans should relate to the facilities available and should include allocation of duties to helpers, etc.

Practical Work

5. Assume responsibility for the management of a canteen on a minimum of one evening per week over a period of at least six months.

6. Record sales and orders during the period and produce monthly statements showing percentage profit.

7. Organise at least two special events centred around the canteen, for which detailed plans and costings have been made as in paragraph 6. A critical appraisal of the catering arrangements should be made with the Assessor.

8. Visit at least one other canteen and be able to give comments and observations on it to the Assessor.

9. Discuss with the Assessor those lines which appear most popular and whether these remain constant or change over the period of time.

GOLD

Young people should carry out a detailed study of the following, or attend a course in Canteen Management:

1. The value of canteen facilities to an organisation and the necessity for creating the most helpful conditions and atmosphere to enable maximum value to be derived from it by the customers.

2. Stocktaking and ordering procedures, the financial aspect of canteen management and the preparation of profit and loss accounts. A study should be made of the number of lines and the type of food being sold so as to maximise the profit whilst at the same time providing customers with as much variety as the size and business of the canteen warrants or can sustain.

3. Hygiene in the preparation and serving of food, including a study of the facilities and equipment needed to ensure that this is possible.

4. The design and arrangement of equipment and furnishing of an ideal canteen which the participant would wish to see provided. Such plans should consider:

a) The average numbers to be catered for.

b) The equipment necessary for the normal food to be served.

c) Whether it would be financially feasible to hire certain items of equipment, e.g. bottle coolers, ice cream freezers and coffee machines, or whether such items should be purchased.

d) The arrangements for display, serving and seating which are considered most practical.

5. Detailed plans, costings and staffing arrangements required for at least three special catering events. These should include recipes particularly appropriate to the event which might be for a programme related to a particular country, a dance, a party to commemorate a special day in the calendar, e.g. Hallowe'en, etc.

Practical Work

6. Assume responsibility for the management of a canteen over a period of at least 12 months, including keeping all necessary records of sales, orders, etc., and be able to show an increase in turnover and profit during that period.

7. Organise at least three feature evenings around the canteen, e.g. Club supper, Café Continental evening, Tramp supper or party.

8. Visit other canteens in the neighbourhood in different types of clubs, perhaps one industrial, to see how they are organised and work.

GROUP 3—SERVICE REQUIRING SPECIFIC QUALIFICATIONS

This group comprises those Forms of Service to which certificated standards are attached by the Governing Body concerned. **Additional practical service is required at all levels**.

Canoe Lifeguard

Bronze	Silver	Gold
Canoe Safety Test **of the British Canoe Union**	Assistant Lifeguard	Lifeguard

Instruction and assessment must be carried out by the Corps of Canoe Lifeguards. Details of these test and full instructions appear in the *Canoe Lifeguard Manual*, available from the Corps of Canoe Lifeguards, British Canoe Union, Adbolton Lane, West Bridgford, Nottingham NG2 5AS.

Child Care

Bronze	Silver	Gold
Caring for the Child Certificate Preliminary **of the St John Ambulance Association**	No syllabus	No syllabus
Junior Certificate **of the St Andrew's Ambulance Association**	Senior Proficiency Certificate	No syllabus
Youth Infant and Child Care Certificate	A current Youth Infant and Child Care Certificate plus proficiency	Maternal and Child Health Certificate and either a current Adult standard First Aid Certificate or a current Adult Standard Nursing Certificate
of the British Red Cross Society		
Alternate Modular **of the National Association for Maternal and Child Welfare**	Level 1	Level II

Instruction and Assessment must be carried out by approved Instructors and Examiners of the Voluntary Aid Societies listed above, to whom application should be made, and whose regulations must be complied with.

The Community Sports Leaders Award

CSLA (Preliminary)—*SILVER ONLY* (16 + years)
Higher Award in Community Sports Leadership—*GOLD ONLY*
Basic Expedition Training Award—*GOLD ONLY* (18 + years)

The **CSLA preliminary** is for those wishing to assist in the voluntary activities of a club or youth organisation. It aims to develop self confidence and organisational skills and is an ideal preparation for those wishing to pursue a national Governing Body Sports Award.

In Northern Ireland young people, at Silver level only, may undertake the 'Sport for All Leader Award' organised through the Sport for All Leader Board of the Sports Council for Northern Ireland.

The **Higher Award** is for those who wish to enhance their leadership skills (having already completed the preliminary award) and includes working with special needs groups and following National Governing Body coaching, officiating and leadership awards.

The **Basic Expedition Training Award** (BETA) is for those who wish to lead groups outdoors and focuses on the skills of leadership, caring for the countryside and living out of doors.

These voluntary schemes seek to prepare potential holders of the CSLA preliminary and higher awards and BETA to serve as leaders with any group that wishes to make use of their services as well as making them more conscious of the work in the sport and leisure industry. Further details are available from The Organising Secretary, CCPR, Francis House, Francis Street, London SW1P 1DE.

Dance Leaders in the Community (Gold only)

Recognised and funded by the Arts Council and the Sports Council and endorsed by the Community Dance and Mime Foundation, this basic course is aimed at those people working through dance within the community, wishing to extend their knowledge of movement and dance and wish to acquire confidence in working in a dance context with groups or individuals within the community.

The Sports Council
16 Upper Woburn Place
London
WC1H 0QP
Tel: 071-388-1277

Cycling Proficiency Instruction

Instruction and Assessment at the discretion of the Royal Society for the Prevention of Accidents' Cycling Organiser, to whom application should be made.

BRONZE

1. Before a candidate qualifies for the Bronze Award he or she must have obtained the Cycleway Certificate awarded by the Royal Society for the Prevention of Accidents (RoSPA) or a County Council alternative approved by RoSPA.

2. He must assist a qualified instructor, during a minimum of two training courses for child cyclists (9–12 years old approx) in the Cycleway Scheme. This will require service of not less than 15 hours during a minimum period of six months.

3. He must qualify as a trainee instructor by obtaining a minimum of 75 per cent marks in practical examinations based on paragraph 2 above.

4. RoSPA's special certificate for participants in The Duke of Edinburgh's Award will be awarded to candidates who complete the above period of service.

5. Written application for details of facilities available to enable candidates to qualify at Bronze level should be made to RoSPA.

SILVER

1. Training as an instructor in the Cycleway Scheme will require the candidate to have a knowledge of the following:

a) The Highway Code.

b) The fundamental principles of proficiency training for young cyclists.

c) Training of young cyclists as potential vehicle drivers.

d) Equipment and literature for use at indoor and outdoor training periods.

e) Projection and use of filmstrips dealing with skilful cycling in conjunction with instructor's notes.

f) Practical demonstrations of cycling skill.

2. The candidate must serve as an instructor in the Cycleway Scheme for a minimum of two training courses for child cyclists (9–12 years old approx.). This involves the organisation of at least 5 periods, both indoors and outdoors, for each complete training session—10 periods of $1\frac{1}{2}$ hours each, including time for preparation, instruction and conclusion of each period.

3. As each period will require candidates to set up, or supervise the setting up of training equipment, marking of registers, checking bicycles, etc., before actual instruction begins, and afterwards the clearing away of equipment and dismissal of child cyclists, the duration of each period will be approximately $1\frac{1}{2}$ hours. The two training courses will therefore require service as an instructor lasting for 15 hours, given during a minimum period of six months.

4. Satisfactory completion of the above will qualify the candidate to receive the Cycleway Scheme Instructor/Examiner Certificate if required.

5. RoSPA's special certificate for participants in The Duke of Edinburgh's Award will be awarded to candidates who complete the above period of Service.

6. Written application for details of facilities available to enable candidates to qualify at Silver level should be made to RoSPA.

GOLD

1. Candidates are required to undergo a period of training teaching them how to instruct children at Advanced Cycling Test level. Where the local authority does not run an Advanced Test programme, RoSPA Liaison Officers will advise on and approve other acceptable forms of service within the Cycleway Scheme (see 5 below).

2. After the appropriate course of training candidates must take and pass the RoSPA Advanced Test. Test papers, routes, etc., will be arranged through the local Road Safety Officer. Within the rules of the Gold Award candidates will be exempt from training already covered. On passing the Advanced Test they will be entitled to the Advanced Cycling Certificate and Badge.

3. After training candidates will be expected to instruct children for the Advanced Cycling Test in the following subjects, for a minimum of 12 months.

a) Practical Roadcraft
Including stopping and starting in traffic; turning right and left, vehicle parking, commonsense and courtesy; traffic signs; road markings; lights on vehicles.

b) The Highway Code
For all road users.

c) Finding the way
Map reading; direction and information signs; assessing hazards from maps; choosing the best routes.

d) Practical Cycling Maintenance
Emergency repairs; adjustment for safety; knowledge of cycle maintenance.

4. Service will be arranged in collaboration with local authorities operating the Cycleway Scheme, and in particular with their Road Safety Officers. The first approach should always be made to RoSPA.

5. Alternatively, practical service as an instructor in the National Cycling Scheme will be given at the discretion and with the approval of the RoSPA Liaison Officer. Training and practical service will together be over a minimum period of 12 months and will include not less than 40 hours as an instructor or in other forms of service. When possible, candidates will also be involved in training other instructors.

Addresses
The Royal Society for the Prevention of Accidents

1. England
National Cycling Officer
RoSPA
Cannon House
Priory Queensway
Birmingham B4 6BS
Tel: 021-200 2461

2. Scotland
RoSPA
Slateford House, 53 Lanark Road
Edinburgh EH14
Tel: 031-226 6856

3. Wales
RoSPA
23 Newport Road
Cardiff CF2 1AA
Tel: 0222 44071

4. Northern Ireland
RoSPA
117 Lisburn Road
Belfast BT9 7BS
Tel: 0232 669453

First Aid

Bronze	Silver	Gold
Essentials of First Aid	Public First Aid Certificate	Any current adult First Aid Certificate plus one of the following: Caring for the Sick Certificate–Level 1; Child Welfare Certificate; Hygiene Certificate
of the St. John Ambulance Association		
Junior Certificate	Senior Certificate	Second Senior Cert
of the St Andrew's Ambulance Association		
Youth First Aid Certificate	Adult Standard First Aid Certificate	A current Adult First Aid Certificate and either Adult Standard Nursing Certificate or Basic Welfare Certificate
of the British Red Cross Society		
Cadet First Aid Voucher	Adult First Aid Certificate	Advanced First Aid Certificate (OMAC members only) OR Adult First Aid Certificate PLUS First Aid at Work Certificate OR Adult Nursing Certificate
of the Order of Malta Ambulance Corps		

Instruction and Assessment must be carried out by approved instructors and examiners of the Voluntary Aid Societies listed above.

Participants who have completed First Aid at Silver with either St John's Ambulance or The British Red Cross Society may NOT choose the First Aid option at Gold if their adult certificate is still valid.

Life Saving

Bronze	Silver	Gold
Life Saving 3	*Bronze Medallion OR Lifeguard's Cadet Award OR Teacher's Preliminary Certificate	Award of Merit OR Lifeguard Standard Award OR Teacher's Certificate
of the Royal Life Saving Society		

*__Note:__ Any category (General, Pool, Sub-Aqua or Canoe) is acceptable, subject to the RLSS age limits. It should be noted that only the General and Pool awards are acceptable prerequisites for the Award of Merit.

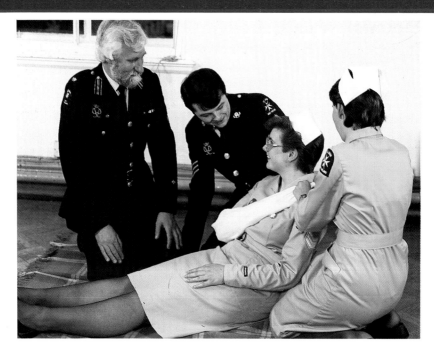

Home Nursing

Bronze	Silver	Gold
Caring for the Sick – Preliminary level	Caring for the Sick Certificate – Level 1	Caring for the Sick Certificate – Level 2
of the St John Ambulance Association		
Junior Nursing Certificate	Senior Nursing Certificate	Higher or Second Senior Nursing Certificate
of the St Andrew's Ambulance Association		
Youth Nursing Certificate	Adult Standard Nursing Certificate	A current Adult Standard Nursing Certificate and either Adult Standard First Aid Certificate OR Basic Welfare Certificate
of the British Red Cross Society		
Cadet Nursing Certificate	Adult Home Nursing Certificate	Adult Home Nursing Certificate PLUS Adult First Aid Certificate
of the Order of Malta Ambulance Corps		

Instruction and Assessment must be carried out by approved instructors and examiners of the Voluntary Aid Societies listed above, to whom application should be made, and whose regulations must be complied with.

Mountainwalking Leader Training (Gold only)

Minimum age 18 years

GOLD
This syllabus is open to participants at the Gold stage only.

Mountainwalking Leader Training Scheme participants should be aware that the standards required by the Mountainwalking Leader Training Board are very high and some enquiry, as to the detail of the syllabus, would be advisable before an attempt is made.

Full details of the Scheme are available from the Mountainwalking Leader Training Board, Crawford House, Precinct Centre, Booth Street East, Manchester M13 9RZ or the equivalent Mountainwalking Leader Training Boards of Scotland, Wales and Northern Ireland.

Occupational Safety

Minimum age 16 years

RoSPA—"Training Syllabus for Young People"

Instruction to be carried out under direct supervision of a qualified Safety Officer, assistance being provided by occupational safety groups.

Bronze	Silver	Gold
No syllabus	Basic Certificate in Health and Safety	Intermediate Certificate in Health and Safety

Assessment should be carried out by a qualified Safety Officer nominated or approved by RoSPA.

Details from RoSPA, Cannon House, The Priory, Queensway, Birmingham B4 6BS.

Rescue Coxwain

Bronze	Silver	Gold
Club Rescue Coxwain **of the Royal Yachting Association**	Fleet Rescue Coxwain	—

Royal Yachting Association RYA House, Eastleigh, Hampshire

Royal Observer Corps

Minimum age 16 years

This syllabus may be undertaken for Silver and Gold Awards only.

Instruction and Assessment must be carried out by the Royal Observer Corps to whom application should be made. Young people will be required to enrol as members of the Corps.

Headquarters' Royal Observer Corps address:
Bentley Priory, Stanmore, Middlesex HA7 3HH

SILVER. Over a minimum period of 12 months candidates are to:

1) pass the Basic Test;

2) attain a minimum of 3 current operational capabilities for Control personnel, or 6 for Post/NRC;

3) attain a minimum attendance of 30% of available exercise time;

4) attain a minimum of 50% attendance at training meetings.

These standards will allow young Observers to qualify for the Award through normal training.

GOLD. Over a minimum period of 18 months, candidates are to:

1) pass the basic test;
2) attain a minimum of 4 current operational capabilities for Control personnel, or 7 for Post/NRC;
3) attain a minimum attendance of 35% of available exercise time;
4) attain a minimum of 50% attendance at training meetings;
5) complete a period of 40 hours practical service. For this purpose each hour of exercise attendance may be counted towards the 40 hours total. Additional hours may also be acquired by service as a member of the Group social committee, involvement in the organisation of social functions or participation in recruiting/publicity displays.

Note: If the 40 hours total cannot be achieved by these means, it will be the responsibility of the participant to make arrangements for some additional form of service outside the Royal Observer Corps. This is to be drawn to the attention of potential participants **before** starting the syllabus.

Surf Life Saving

Bronze	Silver	Gold
Sea Survival: Surf Competence Certificate PLUS Beach Competence Qualifying Certificate PLUS Resuscitation Certificate	Bronze Medallion	Bronze Medallion PLUS Advanced Resuscitation Certificate
of the Surf Life Saving Association of Great Britain		

Instruction and Assessment must be carried out by the above Association, to whom application should be made. Headquarters: 13 Queens Terrace, Exeter EX4 4HR.

Welfare

Application for instruction must be made to the British Red Cross Society Branch Headquarters. Instruction will be given under British Red Cross Society regulations for these courses with the addition of a test after the course at Silver level.

Bronze	Silver	Gold
No syllabus	Basic Welfare Course	A current basic Welfare Certificate AND either Adult Standard First Aid Certificate OR Adult Standard Nursing Certificate.
of the British Red Cross Society		

Teaching of Swimming (Gold only)

ASA Preliminary Teachers Certificate plus a minimum of 40 hours of formal teaching of beginners or the handicapped.

Only work with beginners or the handicapped may count as practical service, the teaching/coaching of proficient swimmers is not acceptable.

Address: Amateur Swimming Association, Harold Fern House, Derby Square, Loughborough, Leicestershire LE11 0AL

Youth Service: Uniformed Organisations

A number of National Voluntary Youth Organisations, who have their own Leadership Training Programmes, are able to count some of these as Service Training for the Award. Details of requirements and qualifications should be obtained from the organisation concerned.

Such training may be undertaken for Silver and Gold Awards only.

Listed below are the qualifications which must be gained at Silver and Gold levels by any participant, irrespective of Operating Authority or User Unit, wishing to give service with a Uniformed Organisation.

The Community Service Programme may be used for Service within Voluntary Youth Organisations at **Bronze level only**. This Service should include supervised assistance with specific aspects or subjects such as music, craft and badgework.

For Silver and Gold level the following adult leadership training courses **must** be followed. **It is not acceptable to undertake Youth Service at Silver and Gold as Community Service.**

ORGAN-ISATION	SILVER	GOLD
ACF	Cadet: 2 Star APC (ACF) PLUS Annual Camp or Cadet Leadership Course PLUS 2 weekend camps or exercises or attachments to Regular Army	Cadet: Senior or Junior Instructor Cadre plus Cadet Corporal or Sgt. Rank for 12 months minimum *Adult*: 20 hours minimum training or approved MOD, CTT, ACF County Course plus 40 hours minimum practical service with Detachment for minimum of 12 months.
	Assessment by: Area or County Level	Assessment by: County or National Level
ATC	Cadet Corporal for 6 months minimum	Cadet Sergeant for 12 months minimum or to have been qualified as Staff Cadet for 12 months
	Assessment by: Squadron Commander or Training Officer	
BB	NCO Training Course PLUS Pre-Jnr/Junior Section Service (15+)	Brigade Leadership Training PLUS Company/Senior Service (16+)
	Assessment by: Company Captain plus Battalion/District/National Training Section	

CCF	1) Hold the rank of Corporal for at least six months OR pass the Proficiency Certificate 2) Attend Central Camp and attend two Field Days 3) Know the history of the CCF and study the history of service. In the case of Army Sections the history of the Regiment/Corps/School whose cap badge is worn	1) Attain the minimum rank of Sergeant/Petty Officer and hold the rank for at least 12 months. 2) Attend a Methods of Instruction or Special to Arms Cadre or Service equivalent and give at least 20 periods of instructions OR pass the Advanced Standard of the APC and complete at least 40 hours service for the contingent (i.e. staff cadet, storeman, office clerk, Armourer)

Assessment by: Section Commander/Contingent Commander

GB	Grade III Young Leaders Qualification	Warrant Officer Grade IV or Commissioned Rank

Assessment by:
Commissioner (Division) or Commandant (Unattached District)

GGA	Gain Young Leaders Certificate; or Ranger Camp Permit endorsed for leadership	Young Leader Certificate (if not gained for silver) OR Ranger/Young Leader Camp Permit endorsed for Leadership OR Adult Leaders Certificate OR Scheme Stage 1 and 2 If holding a warrant then Quartermasters Certificate or Campers Licence or Pack Holiday Licence

Assessment by:
Young Leader Advisor and/or the District Commissioner

Scouts	16 years–Cub Scout Instructor 17 years–Initial Training.	17+ Introductory Training OR Leadership I or Leadership II. Those below the minimum age should follow the Gold Youth Service programme (Group 2) as listed on page 87

Assessment by:
ADC (Leader Training), Personal Training Adviser, Approved Course Director

---

SCC (GNTC)	Leading Rate/Corporal including 6 months service	Cadet Petty Officer/Sergeant PLUS further 6 months service for minimum 12 months total

Assessment by:
Certified by Examining Officer and Commanding Officer on completion of service

St. J A	Cadet NCO Training plus Cadet Corporal for 6 months	Cadet: NCO Training, plus cadet sergeant or cadet leader for 12 months. Adult: Youth Leader Training, Phase I and II plus 40 hours service to Division/Set over at least 12 months.
CL & CGB	NCO Proficiency Certificate plus a minimum of 20 hours project work over 6 months under supervision of Formation Training Officer. List of projects available from HQ	Junior Leaders Training course including King George VI Leadership Training Course
	Assessment by: Formation Training Officer in consultation with NHQ	Assessed by: NHQ

Notes:

1. For Silver Service: If there is a requirement for practical service by the uniformed Organisation as part of the qualification then this must be undertaken.

2. For Gold Service: There must be a minimum of 20 hours training and 40 hours practical work spread over a minimum period of 12 months, but participants may have to give more than these minimum periods in order to obtain the necessary qualification.

3. All participants wishing to count this leadership training and practical work with a Uniformed Organisation towards their Award must notify the Assessor at the start.

ACF	Army Cadet Force
ATC	Air Training Corps
BB	Boys' Brigade
CCF	Combined Cadet Force
GB	Girls' Brigade
GGA	Girl Guides Association
SCC	Sea Cadet Corps
GNTC	Girls Nautical Training Corps
St J A	St John Ambulance
CL & CGB	Church Lads and Church Girls Brigade

Forms of Service—Index

SERVICE

SERVICE (Group One)

TITLE OF SERVICE GIVEN Help with the sick

DATES STARTED: 5/5/89 COMPLETED: 6/8/89

BRIEFING SESSIONS GIVEN BY T. Edmund ON 6/5/89

COUNSELLING SESSIONS HELD ON (1) 7/5/89 (2) 9/6/89 (3) 6/8/89

FORM OF PRACTICAL SERVICE UNDERTAKEN Hospital Radio

Assessor's report: of practical service

Although nervous at first, Tom quickly gained confidence & made lots of friends throughout the hospital. The patients appreciated his cheery manner when collecting requests from the wards.

of participant's diary and account of the service

Tom devised a clever questionnaire enabling him to compile a chart showing the most popular requests, peak listening times and a useful list of suggestions to boost the service

SIGNED Phillipa Chisnett DATE 6/8/89

QUALIFICATION / POSITION Radio Presenter

25

Silver

SERVICE (Groups Two & Three)

TITLE OF SERVICE GIVEN Rescue Coxwain

DATES STARTED: 9/6/89 COMPLETED: 7/7/90

TRAINING GIVEN BY: John Driscoll

FORM OF TRAINING COMPLETED (GROUP TWO):

OR QUALIFICATION GAINED (GROUP THREE): Fleet Rescue Coxwain

PRACTICAL SERVICE UNDERTAKEN: Safety boat at Royal Lymington YC

Assessor's report:

Nick mastered boat handling skills very quickly and having gained confidence and passed his Fleet Rescue Coxwain has become a valuable member of the safety Boat

SIGNED JA Badger DATE 15/7/90

QUALIFICATION RYA Coach

12

106

Gold

EXPEDITIONS

Aim

To encourage a spirit of adventure and discovery.

General

All ventures involve journeying in the countryside, on waterways, or at sea, conceived with a purpose and undertaken on foot, by cycle or on horseback, or in canoes or boats and without motorised assistance. The venture must present the participants with an appropriate challenge in terms of purpose and achievement.

The venture demands:

■ Enterprise and imagination in concept.

■ Forethought, careful attention to detail and organisational ability in preparation.

■ Preparatory training, both theoretical and practical, leading to the ability to journey safely in the chosen environment.

■ Shared responsibility for the venture, leadership from within the group, self-reliance and co-operation among those taking part.

■ Determination in execution.

Types of Venture

There are three types of venture:

Expeditions which have journeying as their principal component.

Explorations which involve less journeying and a greater proportion of time spent on approved, first hand investigations or other specified activities. Explorations have to be undertaken in the context of an Expedition and involve a minimum of ten hours' journeying time.

Other Adventurous Projects which are of an equally or more demanding nature but which depart from the specified conditions.

Requirements

■ At *BRONZE* participants are required to undertake an Expedition.

■ At *SILVER* they may choose to undertake either an Expedition or an Exploration.

■ At *GOLD* they may choose an Expedition, an Exploration or another Adventurous Project.

Purpose

All ventures must have clearly defined and preconceived purpose, which may range from the successful completion of a physically demanding journey to the satisfactory conduct of a practical, firsthand investigation. The purpose of the venture should receive early consideration and be related to the interests and abilities of those taking part.

Accommodation

Accommodation will be by camping. In exceptional circumstances the use of barns, bothies, mountain huts or hostels may be allowed, but if accommodation other than camping is used, then approval must be given by the Headquarters of, or at the highest level within, the Operating Authority and not at Award Unit level.

Different Camp-sites must be used each night for Expeditions but for Explorations the same campsite may be used.

In exceptional circumstances, with the approval of their Operating Authority, certain participants may have some camping equipment and food pre-positioned at camp sites. They must, however, always carry the appropriate listed emergency equipment and their own sleeping bag. In addition they should carry at least one tent, cooking gear and some food, distributed among the group to bring their pack weights up to about a quarter of their body weight.

Numbers

Minimum and maximum numbers are stipulated for different environments and modes of travel but it is not necessary for all the group to be under assessment. It is, however, necessary for all to be properly equipped and to have completed all the training requirements.

Young people who have already qualified in the Expeditions Section of the same or a higher Award must not be included in the venture.

Instruction

Instruction should be carried out by those who have the necessary skills and experience in the activity and environment in which the activity is going to take place. No specific qualifications are stipulated except in the case of preliminary First Aid training, in which instruction should only be given by one of the following:

a) An instructor in First Aid recognised by one of the Voluntary Aid Societies, the Armed Services or the Health and Safety Executive.

b) A qualified teacher or youth leader who holds a valid First Aid Certificate.

c) A State Registered Nurse or Health Visitor.

d) An instructor approved by the Operating Authority.

Before the qualifying venture, instructors must certify in *Record Books* that participants have undergone training in the required skills and have achieved a standard of knowledge appropriate to the enterprise to be undertaken.

Training

Training in safety procedures, First Aid, navigation, campcraft, country code, observation and recording must take place in addition to the skills required by the method of journeying and the environment in which the venture is taking place.

Whilst it is acceptable for some aspects of training to take place within school or works time when these subjects already form part of the curriculum, for both practice and qualifying ventures, participants are expected to show adequate evidence of voluntary effort and a substantial contribution of leisure time.

Equipment

Clothing, footwear and equipment should be suitable for the activity and the environment in which it is to be used and generally conform to current accepted practice. The equipment must be capable of resisting the worst weather for, in the event of a serious deterioration in conditions, safety may well depend on it being able to withstand the prevailing conditions.

Practice journeys provide an excellent opportunity for testing and selecting clothing and equipment for personal and group needs.

Personal Emergency Equipment

The following equipment must be carried:

Normal or Open Country

Map(s), watch, torch, First Aid kit, whistle, coins for the telephone, notebook and pencil, spare pullover and a waterproof jacket or coat.

At Bronze Level, in normal rural country, carrying a compass is optional. At Silver Level, especially in open country, compasses should be carried.

Wild Country

In addition to the equipment listed above the following additions must be made:

A Bivvy bag/large poly bag, matches, emergency rations, extra warm clothing including headgear and gloves, waterproof over clothing, spare bulb and batteries for the torch. A compass must be carried.

Ventures on Water

The list of personal emergency equipment to be carried on water, with some adjustments, is virtually the same.

Practice Journeys

Prior to the qualifying venture all participants are required to carry out practice journeys which may be accompanied by adults.

Practice journeys need not necessarily be of the same duration, and must not be over the same route, or in the vicinity of the route to be used for the assessed venture. The conditions should be as similar as possible to those anticipated for the qualifying venture and in terrain which is equally demanding. Practice journeys should include one or more nights camping. Instructors must certify in the *Record Books* that the necessary practice journeys have been completed.

Planning

Planning and organising the venture should be a joint undertaking by the group. Selecting suitable terrain to suite the purpose of the venture and finding campsites a suitable distance apart demand much forethought. The plans should be submitted through the Supervisor to the Assessor for approval. The plans should indicate details of the route, distance, check points, timings and, in wild country areas, alternative bad weather routes and escape routes. The Assessor should also be informed of the purpose of the venture and details of rations.

Supervision

All ventures, including practice journeys, are to be supervised by an experienced adult, who must accept responsibility for the safety of the group on behalf of the Operating Authority. The Supervisor must be satisfied that the participants are fully trained and properly equipped to undertake the planned venture.

Groups undertaking the qualifying venture must not be accompanied by adults except in exceptional circumstances when the Operating Authority, at Headquarters or at the highest level, may permit closer supervision. In certain circumstances, for safety reasons, it may be important that contact with an adult should be easily available at night.

The Supervisor should be present in the area of the venture. For ventures in wild country the Supervisor must be in the area.
The Supervisor should make daily contact with the group.

For ventures in coastal waters, for reasons of safety, the Supervisor should be on the water with the participants and be appropriately qualified.

Assessment

The Assessor must ensure that each participant has fulfilled the conditions of the Expeditions Section as stated in the *Award Handbook*. Before the venture the competence of individuals must be evaluated to ensure that they are properly equipped, competent and not a danger to themselves, their companions, or the environment. After the venture has commenced the participants should be regarded as a group and, provided each individual complies with the conditions and spirit of the Award, all should succeed even if they have their individual strengths and weaknesses.

The Assessor must be an adult. At Bronze Level, in normal country, the Assessor must not have trained the group. At Silver Level the Assessor should be independent and at Gold level the Assessor must be independent of the Award Unit.

For Gold assessments taking place in wild country an Assessor from the appropriate Wild Country Panel should be used or an Accredited Assessor. If the Operating Authority does not use an Assessor from a Wild Country Panel or an Accredited Assessor then the person must be of equivalent competence; ideally holding an appropriate national qualification, or approved by the Operating Authority. Every effort should be made to accredit the person at the earliest opportunity through the Award's Assessor Accreditation Scheme.

Before the Venture

The Assessor should

■ Check the application or submission to ensure that the preliminary conditions are fulfilled.

■ Scrutinise the plans and route in time to enable the group to make any essential changes.

■ Ensure that the preliminary training has been certified on the appropriate pages of the *Record Book* and then the required number of practice journeys have been completed.

■ Contact the Supervisor and arrange a meeting with the participants and the Supervisor during the familiarisation period, if appropriate, prior to setting out on the venture.

■ Check that the group is properly equipped and competent.

■ Arrange communication between the group, Supervisor and Assessor; visiting and checkpoints arrangements, the use of alternative routes in foul weather and escape routes where appropriate.

■ Arrange, or confirm, the form and nature of the report to be submitted at the end of the venture.

During the Venture

■ Visit at least one camp site to check camp craft, cooking and feeding. Inspect a camp site after the group has left.

■ Check investigatory work for Explorations.

■ Assessors, in consultation with the Supervisor, should not hesitate to require groups to modify their proposed routes for reasons of safety, weather conditions, or a greater understanding of the limited capabilities of the group.

After the Venture

■ Meet the group and confirm that the conditions have been fulfilled.

■ EITHER Receive an oral report

■ OR make arrangements to receive a written or some other form of report and, when received, check the report.

■ Sign the *Record Book* after the participants have fulfilled the requirements of the Expeditions Section.

Reports

Reports are required of all participants on completion of the venture. The report may be an oral or written account, or take some other form agreed between the group and the Assessor before the commencement of the venture, such as tape recordings or visual presentations. They may be prepared on an individual or group basis but they should reflect genuine effort from each individual member of the party.

Whatever the nature or purpose of the venture, participants are expected to be observant and, in addition to providing factual detail in their reports, they should record feelings, impressions and observations. The development of observation and recording techniques should be encouraged from the Bronze Level onwards.

Expedition Guide

Award Handbook only deals with the conditions and the syllabus. Further guidance on the conditions, supervision and assessment is to be found in the *Expedition Guide* which covers aspects in greater detail.

Trainers, participants, Supervisors and Assessors should use the *Expedition Guide* and other relevant Award literature such as *Land Navigation: Route finding with Map and Compass*, as source material and as a basis for their training programmes.

THE BRONZE EXPEDITION

Requirements

The venture must be an Expedition

Age

Participants must be between 14 and 25 years of age. Some discretion is given to Operating Authorities to permit those who are slightly under the qualififying age, to make a start with their friends.

Practice Expeditions

All participants must complete at least one practice Expedition which should correspond as closely as possible to the qualifying (assessed) Expedition and which must utilise the same mode of travel.

Duration

Two days with one overnight camp.

A minimum of six hours of planned activity must take place each day. The planned activity time will include journeying, navigation, setting up and striking camp and on tasks related to the purpose of the Expedition.

At least one simple, sustaining meal must be cooked under camp conditions each day.

Land Ventures

Distance

The following minimum distances are mandatory:

On foot   24 km   15 miles
Cycling   112 km   70 miles

Riding Expeditions must involve travelling for a minimum of 4 hours each day in addition to other planned activity.

Environment

All Bronze Expeditions should take place in normal rural country.

On Foot

Routes should make as little use of roads as is possible and every effort made to avoid villages when this is practicable.

Cycling
Routes should involve minor roads, lanes and tracks. Because of distance involved, routes may have to pass through villages. Distance cycled from home to venture area must not be included in the qualifying mileage.

Riding
Routes should involve lanes, tracks and bridle paths. Villages should be avoided where possible.

Note: Although Bronze Expeditions in more demanding surroundings are not expressly forbidden, all participants must be trained and equipped to a standard sufficient to enable them to meet any hazards which they may encounter. The requirements and syllabus of the Silver and Gold Levels, as appropriate, must be utilised if the venture takes place in more demanding country.

Numbers
The minimum number in a party is three and the maximum seven. The Award for reasons of safety and quality of experience, recommends a group of four.

Water Ventures
Distance
No fixed mileages are laid down for Expeditions on water but the following minimum number of hours must be spent in travelling, in addition to other planned activity:

Canoeing: Four hours of paddling time each day.

Rowing: Four hours of rowing time each day.

Sailing: Six hours under sail each day.

Environment
Rivers, canals and other inland waterways.

Numbers
Canoeing and Rowing: A minimum of three singles or two doubles up to a maximum of six singles or three doubles.

Sailing: A minimum of two dinghies and a maximum of three.
The Award for reasons of safety and quality of experience, recommends a group of four.

Common Training Syllabus for Expeditions on either land or water

Safety and Emergency Procedures

Choosing suitable clothing, footwear and emergency equipment and knowing how to use it.

Expedition fitness.

Travelling skills.

Keeping together.

Telling people where you are going, route cards.

What to do in the case of an accident or emergency.

Summoning help — what people need to know, telephoning for help, written message.

Fetching help, self-help and waiting for help to arrive, keeping safe and warm, helping people to find you.

Weather forecasts: knowing how, where and when to obtain weather forecasts, relating weather forecasts to observed conditions, looking for signs which will indicate changes in the weather.

Basic First Aid

The treatment of blisters, cuts, abrasions, minor burns and scalds, headaches, insect bites, sunburn, splinters, foreign bodies in the eye, nose or ear.

The recognition of more serious conditions, sprains, dislocations and broken limbs.

Stopping bleeding; treatment for shock.

Expired air resuscitation.

Country Code

Understanding the spirit and content of the Country Code. The avoidance of noise and disturbance to rural communities.

Highway Code

A thorough understanding of the content and spirit of the Highway Code with special emphasis on specific modes of travel such as riding or cycling if they are to be utilized during the venture.

Observing and Recording

Appropriate methods of recording and the preparation of records.

Navigation

At Bronze level, in normal or open country, all route finding should be based on the map alone. Using a compass in rural country, used for agricultural purposes with its hedges, meadows and fields under crops, is inappropriate and unnecessary. It may cause ill-feeling with the farmers and hinders the young people developing a "sense of direction" and retards their map reading skills. The 1:25000 scale *Pathfinder* maps, available for the whole of England, Scotland, Wales and parts of Northern Ireland, should be used wherever possible as it makes instruction and learning easier. They show the field boundaries, making it easier to locate precisely the footpaths, tracks and lanes which are utilised for travel in this type of country, so helping to reduce friction with the landowners. Participants should also be familiar with the 1:50000 *Landranger* maps.

The Preparatory Map Skills

The nature of maps.

The use of 1:25000 *Pathfinder*, 1:50000 *Landranger* and the relevant maps in Northern Ireland.

Map direction.

Scale and distance, measuring distance, distance and time.

Conventional signs.

Marginal information.

Grid references.

A simple introduction to contours and gradient if appropriate.

The ability to give a verbal description of a route linking two places.

The Practical Map Skills
Setting the map by inspection (2 methods)

Locating position from the map.

Determining geographical direction and direction of travel from the map; checking the direction of paths using the set map.

Identifying features in the country by using the map.

Locating features marked on the map in the countryside.

Planning a route, preparing a simple route card.

Following a planned route.

Compass Skills
Direction from the compass in terms of the cardinal and the four intercardinal points. Setting the map by the compass. Magnetic variation should be ignored.

Care of the compass

The introduction of the compass at Bronze should only be at a basic level. It should not be introduced until the participants have mastered the techniques of finding their way using the map alone.

Camp Craft
Choosing and caring for camping gear.

Packing a rucksack, waterproofing the contents, keeping the weight down to about a quarter of the body weight when walking.

Choosing a camp site, arrangements for water, cooking, sanitation, refuse disposal, fire precautions. Pitching and striking tents.

Cooking and the use of stoves, safety procedures and precautions which must be observed when using stoves and handling fuels. Cooking simple meals under camp conditions.

Further Training for Specific Expeditions on Land

Cycling

Training to the standard of the Cycleway Proficiency Test. Loading a cycle with Expedition equipment. Handling a loaded cycle.

Riding

Training on Pony Club "C" standard. A knowledge of tethering, picketing or hobbling. All must be competent in ensuring the well being of the horse for the duration of the venture. Recognition of dangerous going and the action to be taken in the event of accident to horse or rider.

Further Training for Expeditions on Water

For all ventures on water participants must be able to swim a distance of at least 50 metres in light clothing, either with or without a buoyancy aid.

All participants must:

a) Wear appropriate, approved buoyancy aids.

b) Be able to recognise and treat hypothermia.

c) Have an understanding of the Water Sports Code.

All craft must have adequate buoyancy and be sound, suitable and fitted out for the conditions in which they are to be used.

All craft must carry a suitable repair kit.

Canoeing

Prior to the venture, participants must:

a) present their kayak or canoe for inspection.

b) demonstrate that their equipment is adequately waterproofed.

c) satisfy the assessor as to their competence:

Kayakists — to the standard of the BCU 3 star or Proficiency Test.

Open canoeists to at least the standard of the BCU 1 star.

Rowing

All participants must undergo training based on the Award Scheme Programme for Boatwork in the Skills Section, as appropriate to the conditions to be anticipated during the Expedition, and satisfy the Assessor as to the competence to handle their craft.

Sailing

All participants must attain proficiency to the standard of the RYA National Dinghy Certificate Level 2.

THE SILVER EXPEDITION

Requirements
The venture may be an Expedition or an Exploration.

Age
Participants must be between 15 and 25 years of age. Some discretion is given to Operating Authorities to permit those who complete the Bronze Award just below the age of 15 to make a start on the Silver Award without imposing an artificial delay.

Practice Journeys
Participants who have completed their Bronze Award must complete at least one more practice Expedition which should correspond as closely as possible to the qualifying (assessed) Expedition and which must utilise the same mode of travel. Direct entrants at Silver Level must complete at least two practice Expeditions before undertaking the qualifying venture.

Duration
Three days with two overnight camps.

A minimum of seven hours of planned activity must take place each day. The planned activity will include journeying time, navigation, setting up and striking camp and on tasks related to the purpose of the Expedition.

At least one substantial meal must be cooked under camp conditions each day.

Land Ventures
Distance

The following minimum distances are mandatory:

On foot	48km	30 miles
Cycling	208km	130 miles

Riding Expeditions must involve travelling for a minimum of 5 hours each day in addition to other planned activity.

Environment
Silver ventures should take place in normal rural, or open country. The environment should make more demands on the participants than that used at Bronze Level and should represent an intermediate

EXPEDITIONS

122

stage between the normal, rural environment and wild country. Areas of open country should be included where possible.

Note: Although Silver Expeditions in wild country areas are not expressly forbidden, all participants must be trained and equipped to a standard sufficient to enable them to meet any hazards which they may encounter. The requirements and syllabus of the Gold Level must be utilised if the venture takes place in wild country. Wild Country Panels must be notified.

On Foot
Routes should make as little use of roads as possible and every effort made to avoid villages when this is practicable.

Cycling
Routes should involve minor roads, lanes and tracks. Routes may have to pass through villages out of necessity. The distance cycled from home to the venture area must not be included in the qualifying mileage.

Riding
Routes should involve lanes, tracks and bridle paths. Villages should be avoided where possible.

Numbers
The minimum number in a party is three and the maximum is seven. The Award for reasons of safety and quality of experience, recommends a group of four.

Water Ventures
Distance
No fixed mileages are laid down for Expeditions on water but the following minimum number of hours must be spent in travelling, in addition to other planned activity:

Canoeing: Five hours of paddling time each day.

Rowing: Five hours of rowing time each day.

Sailing: Seven hours under sail each day.

Environment
The water must present an appropriate challenge to the participants and must be unfamiliar to them.

Canoeing: rivers, canals, or other inland waterways and lakes in rural areas should be used.

Sailing: inland waters, sheltered estuaries or coastal waters.

Numbers

Canoeing and Rowing: A minimum of three singles or two doubles up to a maximum of seven singles or three doubles.

Sailing: A minimum of two dinghies and a maximum of three.

The Award for reasons of safety and quality of experience, recommends a group of four.

Explorations

All Explorations must take place within the context of an Expedition and must involve a minimum of 10 hours' journeying time.

Participants are required to complete the same preparations and training, including practice journeys, as if they were undertaking an Expedition.

The same camp site may be used on both nights.

The Exploration Environment

Normal rural or open country should be used and the environment must be appropriate to the venture and unfamiliar to the participants. Roads must be avoided as much as possible and both the site(s) of the Exploration and the camp site(s) should be relatively remote to the extent that the group should feel the need to be self-reliant and dependent on their own resources.

Common Training Syllabus
For all ventures whether Exploration, Expedition on land or water.

Safety and Emergency Procedures

Choosing suitable clothing, footwear and emergency equipment and knowing how to use it.

Expedition fitness.

Travelling skills.

Keeping together.

Telling people where you are going, route cards.

What to do in the case of an accident or emergency.

Summoning help – what people need to know, telephoning for help, written message.

Fetching help, self-help and waiting for help to arrive.

Keeping safe and warm, helping people to find you.

Weather forecasts: Knowing how, where and when to obtain weather forecasts, relating weather forecasts to observed conditions, looking for signs which will indicate changes in the weather.

Basic First Aid

The treatment of blister, cuts, abrasions, minor burns and scalds, headaches, insect bites, sunburn, splinters, foreign bodies in the eye, nose or ear.

The recognition and the immediate treatment of more serious conditions, sprains, dislocations and broken limbs.

The emergency transport of casualties. Treatment for shock. Expired air resuscitation.

Country Code

Understanding the spirit and content of the Country Code. The avoidance of noises and disturbance of rural communities.

Highway Code

A thorough understanding of the content and spirit of the *Highway Code* with special emphasis on specific modes of travel such as riding or cycling if they are to be utilized during the venture.

Observing and Recording

Appropriate methods of recording and the preparation of records.

Navigation

In normal or open country, at Silver Level, navigation should be based on the map alone. Using a compass in rural country, used for agricultural purposes with its fields, hedges, meadows and fields under crops is inappropriate and unnecessary. It may cause ill-feeling with the farmers and prevents young people developing a 'sense of direction' and retards their map reading skills. The 1:25000 scale *Pathfinder* maps, available for the whole of England, Scotland, Wales and some parts of Northern Ireland, should be used wherever possible as it makes instruction and learning easier. They show the field boundaries, making it easier to locate precisely the footpaths, tracks and lanes which are utilised for travel in this type of country, so helping to reduce friction with the landowners.

The Preparatory Map Skills

The nature of maps.

Use of the 1:25000 *Pathfinder* and the 1:50000 *Landranger* maps or the appropriate maps in Northern Ireland.

Map direction.

Scale and distance, measuring distance, distance and time.

Conventional signs.

Marginal information.

Grid references.

Understanding contours, recognition of major landforms such as hills, valleys, spurs, gradients.

The ability to describe a route linking two places from the map.

The Practical Map Skills

Setting the map by inspection (2 methods).

Locating position from the map.

Determining geographical direction and direction of travel from the map; checking the direction of paths using the set map.

Identifying features in the country by using the map.

Locating features marked on the map in the countryside.

Relating the map to the ground and estimating speed of travel and arrival times.

Planning a route, preparing a route card.

Following a planned route.

Compass Skills

Measuring direction in degrees.

Direction from the compass in terms of the cardinal and the four intercardinal points. Setting the map and checking the direction of paths by the compass ignoring magnetic variation.

Obtaining a Grid bearing from the map, allowing for magnetic variation, practical experience of travelling on a bearing.

Care and protection of the compass.

The influence of ferrous objects. Magnetic variation and the relationship between True, Magnetic and Grid Norths.

The compass should not be introduced until the participants have mastered the techniques of finding their way using the map alone.

Camp Craft

Choosing and caring for camping gear.

Packing a rucksack, waterproofing the contents, keeping the weight down to about a quarter of the body weight when walking.

Choosing a camp site, arrangements for water, cooking, sanitation, refuse disposal, fire precautions. Pitching and striking tents.

Cooking and the use of stoves, safety procedures and precautions which must be observed when using stoves and handling fuels. Using dehydrated foods under expedition conditions. Cooking a substantial meal under camp conditions.

Further Training for Specific Expeditions on Land

Cycling

Training to the standard of the Cycleway Test. Loading a cycle with expedition equipment; handling a loaded cycle.

Riding

Training to Pony Club "C" or "C plus" Standard. A knowledge of tethering, picketing, or hobbling. All must be competent in ensuring the wellbeing of the horse for the duration of the venture.

Recognition of dangerous going and the action to be taken in the event of accident to horse or rider.

Further Training for Expeditions on Water

For all ventures on water participants must be able to swim a distance of at least 50 metres in light clothing, either with or without a buoyancy aid.

All participants must:

a) wear appropriate, approved buoyancy aids.

b) be able to recognise and treat hypothermia.

c) have an understanding of the Water Sports Code.

All craft must have adequate buoyancy and be sound, suitable and fitted out for the conditions in which they are to be used.

All craft must carry a suitable repair kit.

Canoeing

Prior to the venture, participants must:

a) present their kayak or canoe for inspection.

b) demonstrate that their equipment is adequately waterproofed.

c) satisfy the assessor as to their competence:

Kayakists – to the standard of the BCU Proficiency Test.
Open canoeists – to at least the standard of the BCU 2 Star Test.

Rowing

All participants must undergo training based on the Award Scheme Programme for Boatwork in the Skills Section, as appropriate to the conditions to be anticipated during the expedition, and satisfy the assessor as to their competence to handle their craft.

Sailing

Sailing dinghies or Keelboats.

All participants must attain proficiency to the standard of the RYA National Dinghy Certificate Level 3 or the RYA National Keelboat Certificate Level 3.

THE GOLD EXPEDITION

Requirements

The venture may be an Expedition, an Exploration or an Other Adventurous Project.

Age

Participants must be between 16 and 25 years of age. No activities may count for the Gold Award below the age of 16.

Practice Journeys

A minimum of three practice journeys are required prior to the qualifying venture. Those who have completed a Bronze Expedition using the same mode of travel are exempt from one practice journey while those who have completed a Silver venture of a similar nature are exempted from two practice journeys.

Duration

Four days with three overnight camps.

A minimum of eight hours of planned activity must take place each day. The planned activity will include journeying time, navigation, setting up and striking camp and on tasks related to the purpose of the expedition.

At least one substantial meal must be cooked each day.

Land Ventures

Distance

The following minimum distances are mandatory:

| On foot | 80 km | 50 miles |
| Cycling | 320 km | 200 miles |

Riding expeditions must involve travelling for a minimum of 6 hours each day in addition to other planned activity.

The Land Environment

The environment must be appropriate to the purpose of the venture and the route and the surrounding area must be unfamiliar to the participants.

On Foot: Wild country, remote from habitation with the use of roads limited to that necessary to move between areas of open country.

Cycling: Wild country, including upland and unpopulated areas. Minor lanes and tracks should be used to the fullest extent.

Riding: Remote country lanes, tracks and bridle paths as necessary in open or wild country.

Wild Country: Wild country is defined as being areas remote from habitation in which all ventures for reasons of safety must be completely self-sufficient. The areas of wild country authorised for Gold foot and cycle expeditions should be defined by each National Award Authority.

Journeys should be through, rather than over, Wild Country.

The United Kingdom: The following areas are defined as wild country: Dartmoor, Brecon Beacons and Black Mountains, Mid-Wales, Snowdonia, Peak District (northern moors or Dark Peak), Isle of Man (parts), Cheviots, Durham Dales, North Yorkshire Pennines. North York Moors, Lake District, Yorkshire Dales, Mourne Mountains, Sperrin Mountains, North Antrim Hills, Scottish Borders, Lowther Hills, Galloway Hills, Central Highlands, Western Highlands, Northern Highlands, Isle of Skye, Isle of Arran, Isles of Harris and Lewis. In each area there is a voluntary Wild Country Expedition Panel to advise on all aspects of ventures being undertaken there. Names and addresses of all the Panel Secretaries are published in the Award Scheme staff list circulated every January with the Award News Section in the *Award Journal*.

Advance notice, in duplicate on the standard *Expedition Notification Form* available from all Operating Authorities, must be given of all ventures, including practice journeys, which go into wild country areas. This notice, addressed to the appropriate Panel Secretary, must be given at least six weeks in advance, or four weeks in advance if an Assessor is not required. A Notification Reference Number will be allocated to each venture.

Certain Award Operators, e.g. those who are based in a wild country area may, however, negotiate blanket agreements with the appropriate panel on an annual basis to avoid the need to render forms for each individual expedition, practise journey or training exercise. Further details are available from the Award Office.

Wild Country Expedition Panel Areas in Scotland

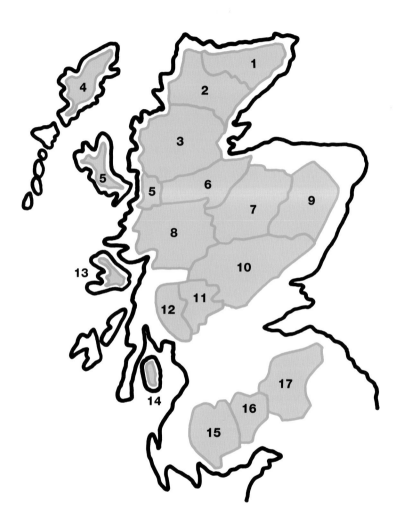

1. Caithness & North Sutherland
2. Sutherland South;
3. Wester Ross–Easter Ross;
4. Western Isles;
5. Skye & Lochalsh;
6. Inverness;
7. Cairngorms;
8. Lochaber & Glencoe;
9. Grampian;
10. Tayside;
11. Trossachs & Crianlarich;
12. Lomond & Argyll;
13. Isle of Mull;
14. Isle of Arran;
15. Galloway Area;
16. Lowther Hills;
17. Borders.

Wild Country Expedition Panel Areas in England, Wales and Northern Ireland.

EXPEDITIONS

1. Cheviots;
2. Cumbria (Lake District);
3. North Yorkshire Moors (North York Moors and Cleveland Hills);
4. Durham Dales (Teesdale, Weardale, Allendale and west to Crossfell);
5. North Yorkshire Pennines (Teesdale to Wensleydale);
6. Yorkshire Dales;
7. Isle of Man;
8. Peak District (Northern Moors);
9. Dartmoor;
10. Snowdonia;
11. Mid-Wales;
12. Brecon Beacons and Black Mountains;
13. North Antrim Hills;
14. Mourne Mountains;
15. Sperrin Mountains.

Familiarisation

All participants should make every effort to improve their physical fitness before embarking on a venture in wild country. They should spend 48 hours in the wild country area prior to their departure on the qualifying venture if they have not carried out at least one recent practice venture in the terrain and conditions which are at least as demanding.

Participants should always arrive in the wild country area the day before the venture to facilitate the initial meeting between the participants, the Supervisor and the Assessor.

Winter Expeditions

The expedition season is between the end of March and the end of October. For very experienced older participants, approval may be given for out of season expeditions but approval must be given, in writing, by headquarters or at the highest level within the Operating Authority and the plans must be agreed by the wild country expedition panel for the area being visited. The supervisor must hold the Scottish Winter Mountain Leader Award or have equivalent experience. For details see Expedition Guide.

Numbers

In wild country the minimum number in a party must be four and the maximum seven.

Explorations

All exploration must take place within the context of an expedition and must involve a minimum of 10 hours' journeying time.

Participants are required to complete the same preparations and training, including practice journeys, as if they were undertaking an expedition. The same camp site may be used on both nights.

The Exploration Environment

Wild country. Open country or coastal areas, isolated or remote from habitation should be used and the environment must be appropriate to the venture and unfamiliar to the participants. Roads must be avoided as much as possible and both the site(s) of the exploration and the camp site(s) should be remote to the extent that the group should feel the need to be self-reliant and dependent on their own resources. Both inland and sheltered coastal waters, canoes, sailing or rowing are often ideal for explorations.

Other Adventurous Projects

Other Adventurous Projects are of an equally or more demanding nature than a Gold venture but depart from the specified conditions of the expedition. Full details of such proposed projects, including the necessary training, should be submitted by the Operating Authority to the National Award Office for approval at least three months before the intended starting date. Notes on the format of such submissions are contained in *Expedition Guide*. Projects should not normally relate to solo ventures, but any truly enterprising venture will be considered, providing that the Operating Authority has approved and accepted responsibility for the venture.

The projects should take place within the context of an expedition and be conceived and initiated by the participants themselves. The removal of certain conditions relating to the expedition section should provide the participants with even greater scope for enterprise and imagination in the concept of such projects. This form of venture provides the opportunity for more ambitious undertakings and it should never be utilised to circumvent the conditions of the expedition or exploration. During the project participants must be self-reliant and dependent on their own resources and the environment in which the project takes place should emphasise this independence. The submission must show the extent to which the participants are involved in the planning and preparation of the project and the same training and preparation must take place as for Gold ventures. A project which only modestly exceeds the expectations of the Gold expedition, entirely conceived and executed by the participants, is better than the participants being part of a much more ambitious scheme which has been initiated and planned by adults.

Water Ventures

Distance

No fixed mileages are laid down for expeditions on water but the following minimum number of hours must be spent in travelling, in addition to other planned activity:

Canoeing: 6 hours of paddling per day.

Rowing: 6 hours of rowing per day.

Sailing: 32 hours under sail averaging eight hours per day.

The Water Environment

The water must present an appropriate challenge to the participants and must be unfamiliar to them.

Canoeing – rivers, certain inland waterways and lakes should be used but sheltered coastal waters may also be used.

Sailing – inland waters such as the tidal areas of the Norfolk Broads, lochs, estuaries or sheltered coastal waters. Yachts may use open sea areas.

Supervision of Ventures in Estuaries, Sheltered Coastal Waters and Open Sea Areas.

Canoeing – the supervisor should accompany the expedition in a kayak or a powered craft.

Sailing – the supervisor should accompany the expedition in a powered craft and should be dinghy sailors or yachtsmen or women having considerable experience of the venture area.

For yachts in open sea areas the supervisor should be aboard and hold the RYA/DTp Yachtmaster Offshore Certificate.

Contact should not be made with the group during the journey except for the purposes of safety.

Numbers

Canoeing and Rowing: A minimum of three singles or two doubles up to a maximum of six singles or three doubles.

Sailing: A minimum of two dinghies and a maximum of three. One keelboat or yacht of suitable size may be used.

Common Training Syllabus
For all types of venture whether Expedition, Exploration or Other Adventurous Projects on land or water.

In coastal waters some aspects of this common syllabus should be replaced by the appropriate water syllabus.

Safety and Emergency Procedures

Choosing suitable clothing, footwear and emergency equipment and knowing how to use it.

Expedition fitness.

Travelling skills.

Keeping together.

Informing people where you are going, route cards.

What to do in the case of an accident or emergency.

Summoning help – what people need to know, telephoning for help, the written message.

Fetching help, self-help and waiting for help to arrive, keeping safe and warm, helping people to find you.

A knowledge of the safety precautions which must be observed in wild country, as laid down in the handbook "*Safety on Mountains*".

Weather Forecasts: knowing how, where and when to obtain weather forecasts, relating weather forecasts to observed conditions, anticipating weather changes from observed conditions.

Basic First Aid

The treatment of blisters, cuts, abrasions, minor burns and scalds, headaches, insect bites, sunburn, splinters, foreign bodies in the eye, nose or ear.

The recognition and the immediate treatment of more serious conditions, sprains, dislocations and broken limbs.

The emergency transport of casualties. Stopping bleeding, treatment for shock.

Expired air resuscitation.

The recognition, treatment and prevention of hypothermia and heat exhaustion/heatstroke.

Country Code

Understanding the spirit and content of the Country Code. To have an awareness of conservation and access and the problems brought about by over use of some Wild Country areas. The avoidance of noise and disturbance to rural communities.

Highway Code

A thorough understanding of the content and spirit of the Highway Code with special emphasis on specific modes of travel such as riding or cycling if these are to be utilized during the venture.

Observing and Recording

Appropriate methods of recording and the preparation of records if these are to be utilized during the venture.

Navigation

The Preparatory Map Skills

The nature of maps.

Use of the 1:25000 *Outdoor Leisure* or *Pathfinder* maps and the 1:50000 *Landranger* maps.

Map direction.

Scale and distance, measuring distance, distance and time.

Conventional signs.

Marginal information.

Grid references.

Understanding contours, recognition of major landforms such as hills, valleys, spurs, interpretation of contours into mountain landforms and relief; slopes and gradients.

The ability to describe a route linking two places using the map.

The Practical Map Skills

Setting the map by inspection (2 methods).

Locating position using the map.

Using the set map to determine geographical direction, direction of travel and the direction of paths. Identifying features in the country by the map and locating features marked on the map in the countryside.

Relating the map and contours to the ground; estimating journey times in wild country.

Navigation in restricted visibility;
action to be taken in the event of being lost.

Planning a route, preparing a route card, following a planned route.

Compass Skills

Measuring direction in degrees and the relation with the cardinal and intercardinal points. Setting the map and checking the direction of paths by the compass ignoring magnetic variation.

Obtaining Grid bearings from the map, allowing for magnetic variation. Practical experience in travelling on a bearing under realistic conditions.

Care and protection of the compass

The influence of ferrous objects on the compass. Magnetic variation and the relationship between True, Magnetic and Grid Norths.

The compass should not be introduced until the participants have mastered the techniques of finding their way using the map alone.

Camp Craft

Choosing and caring for camping gear.

Packing a rucksack, waterproofing the contents, keeping the weight down to about a quarter of the body weight when walking.

Choosing camp sites in wild country, arrangements for water, cooking, sanitation, refuse disposal, fire precautions. Pitching and striking tents in all weather conditions; the provision of emergency shelter or bivouacs.

Cooking and the use of stoves, safety procedures and precautions which must be observed when using stoves and handling fuels. Using dehydrated foods and an elementary understanding of dietary needs for expeditions. Cooking substantial meals under camp conditions.

Further Training for Specific Expeditions on Land

Cycling

Training to the standard of the Cycleway Proficiency Test.

Loading a cycle with expedition equipment; handling a loaded cycle.

Riding

Training to Pony Club "B" Standard. A knowledge of tethering, picketing, or hobbling. All must be competent in ensuring the wellbeing of the horse for the duration of the venture. Recognition of dangerous going and the action to be taken in the event of accident to horse or rider.

Further Training for Expeditions on Water

For all ventures on water participants must be able to swim a distance of at least 50 metres in light clothing, either with or without a buoyancy aid.

All participants in open boats must wear appropriate, approved buoyancy aids.

All open craft must have adequate buoyancy. All craft must be sound, suitable and fitted out for the conditions in which they are to be used and carry the appropriate safety equipment.

All craft must carry a suitable repair kit where appropriate.

Canoeing
Prior to the venture, participants must:

a) present their kayak or canoe for inspection.

b) demonstrate that their equipment is adequately water proofed.

c) satisfy the assessor as to their competence:

Kayakists – to the standard of the BCU Proficiency Test.

Open canoeists (canadian) – to at least the standard of the BCU 2 Star Test, plus, rescue of capsized canoe.

Further details are available from the BCU.

Rowing
All participants must undergo training based on the Award Scheme Programme for Boatwork in the Skills Section as appropriate to the conditions to be anticipated during the expedition and satisfy the assessor as to their competence to handle their craft.

Sailing
Sailing dinghies or keelboats.

All participants must attain proficiency to the standard of the RYA National Dinghy Certificate Level 5 or the RYA. Day Skipper Shorebased and Practical Certificates as appropriate to the type of boat. For offshore ventures it is mandatory to hold the award.

For Expeditions in yachts involving overnight passages in open sea areas, at least one crew member must hold the RYA/DTp Coastal Skipper Certificate of Competence.

Qualifying Expedition

TYPE OF EXPEDITION / EXPLORATION / OTHER ADVENTUROUS PROJECT

FOOT EXPEDITION

EXPEDITION NOTIFICATION NO. Cu/17/90/A/G   OAP REF NO: —

AREA   LAKE DISTRICT

DATES STARTED: 11th JUNE 90   COMPLETED: 14th JUNE 90

PURPOSE FOLLOWING THE FOOTSTEPS OF COLERIDGE

Assessor's report of expedition:

The group made good use of their two days acclimatisation by visiting Dove Cottage collecting information on Coleridge. The demanding route was very well planned and their route finding and navigation skills were excellent. I am most impressed with their campcraft skills, every site was left clean and tidy. Tejinder was largely responsible for the

17

Gold

high morale of the group. His determination and cheerful personality kept everyone in high spirits despite the poor weather. A marvellous team effort.

Assessor's report of participant's account of the venture:

Each member of the group contributed different aspects to an illustrated lecture at a presentation evening. Tejinder was responsible for producing an excellent slide show from the many photographs he took on the venture. The presentation was such a success that they have been invited to give the talk at several local schools. Well done!

SIGNED Bethan Halstery   DATE 5th July 90

QUALIFICATION Assessor, Cumbria Panel.

18

Aim

To encourage the discovery and development of personal interests and social and practical skills.

General

■ The object is to stimulate young people to take up and persevere at satisfying and purposeful pursuits within a wide range of practical, cultural and social activities.

■ The choice can be either a continuing and progressive interest in an activity (such as stamp collecting or playing a musical instrument) or the study of a topic of personal interest to the participant (such as fashion, relationships or money matters) or a definite task to be completed (such as making simple pieces of furniture, building a boat or producing plays).

■ In addition to developing skills, participation is intended to lead to contact with experienced people. This may be through membership of a club or group, or through the wealth of individual expertise available in the community.

Requirement

■ Individual progress and sustained interest over a period of time, leading to a deeper knowledge of the subject and the attainment of a reasonable degree of skill.

Types of Skills Programmes

For convenience the Skills Programmes are listed under the following group headings:

A complete list of Skills Programmes currently available is given in the index on pages 149–151.

Conditions

1. Choose a Skills programme from the Skills Index on pages 149–151 with a view to following it for a minimum period of:

BRONZE—6 months

SILVER—6 months for those who have completed this Section at Bronze

or

12 months for Silver direct entrants

GOLD—12 months for those who have completed this Section at Silver

or

18 months for Gold direct entrants

It is recognised that there may be periods when participants are forced through circumstances, such as examinations, to defer active participation in their programme for an interval.

2. The Skill may be an existing interest or something entirely new to the participant. Under certain circumstances such as an unsatisfactory choice, lack of facilities, or movement of the instructor or participant away from the area, the Skill may be changed once at any time during the period of an Award, but if two activities/topics are taken, they are to be followed one after the other, with as short an interval as is reasonable, not together.

3. Skills acquired in formal education, training and employment are not excluded, but participants must show adequate evidence of additional voluntary effort in their own leisure time.

4. The number of hours to be spent on the chosen Skill is not specified but regular effort during leisure time is required throughout the period.

5. The Skill may be followed independently or as a member of a group. Knowledge and experience may be acquired by attending a course or by individual enquiry, being in both cases associated with further investigation and/or practical work.

Guidance and Programmes

6. Outline Programmes for the more popular activities and topics are given on pages 152–233. Programmes for these and all other activities listed are also available in loose-leaf form.

7. All Programmes are for the guidance of participants and the adults helping in this Section but they need not be taken as rigid syllabuses to be followed. **Safety requirements** for any Skill are, however, printed in bold type in the programme and must be followed.

8. To indicate the content appropriate to young people with varying degrees of knowledge and experience, most Programmes are set out in three parts—**For beginners, For those with some knowledge** and **For the more advanced.** The Programme for beginners will not necessarily be appropriate at Bronze if the young person is already well acquainted with the activity chosen. Conversely, a participant at Gold tackling an unfamiliar subject might start with the beginners programme.

9. There is no need to limit young people to one part of the programme only. Starting at their own level of knowledge and experience, participants are free to select as broad or as restricted an aspect of their chosen Skill as they wish, but appropriate social and cultural aspects are to be covered.

10. Whilst participants are encouraged to make their own choice of activities, some advice may be needed on this or on changing to a different Skill whilst working for an Award. Those who have completed Bronze or Silver may also need guidance as to whether to change their Skill for the next higher Award. Award Leaders will be in the best position to advise on this matter, and where young people are likely to benefit by taking up a new activity, they should be encouraged to do so.

Instruction

11. Instruction should be undertaken by persons suitably qualified or experienced in the chosen activity or topic. The essence of this Section is to find people with expertise and enthusiasm to guide and encourage participants in their efforts.

Assessment

12. Each individual is to be assessed throughout the required period on effort, perseverance and progress, as well as on an understanding of the practical, cultural and social aspects of the chosen activity or topic.

13. The person who is guiding the work may well be in the best position to undertake assessment but in some cases it will be desirable to bring in an independent Assessor.

14. Group activities are to be assessed in regard to each individual's contribution to the planning, execution and completion of them.

15. A young person qualifies in this Section if the Assessor, after consultation with the Instructor where applicable, is satisfied that:

a) There has been a substantial commitment of genuine leisure time.

b) The skill has been consistently followed for the required time.

c) Genuine effort and individual progress have been made within the young person's capability. Any written work should be assessed on content rather than on style or spelling.

16. Dates of starting and of successful assessment are to be entered in *Record Books*. No report should be made until participants have satisfied the Assessor. Those failing to do so should be encouraged to continue. Examples of typical *Record Book* entries are given on page 234.

17. Assessors should ensure that the date entered in the *Record Books* is the actual date on which the assessment was carried out, stating clearly that any safety requirements have been met and giving remarks which are positive and encouraging to the individual.

How to Find your Programme

When looking for a Programme in the index remember to look under alternative headings. Every effort has been made to cross reference Skills. You will find, for example, that Bell ringing is not listed but Handbell ringing and Campanology (church bell ringing) are both listed.

Where there is no Programme available for the Skill that you wish to do, decide which group, listed on page 144, your activity fits into and look for a General Programme printed in that sub-section. Remember that there may be more than one General Programme printed in any group and so you need to find one that is relevant to your chosen activity. Using the General Programme for guidance you should draw up a brief outline Programme for your chosen activity and forward it to your Operating Authority for it to approve. If in doubt send it to your Regional Award Office (a list of addresses is on the inside back cover). **You must not start on any activity that is not listed in the book until you have received written approval from your Operating Authority or your Regional Award Office.**

It would be helpful if the usual Skills format is used when submitting a Programme for approval, this divides the Programme into three sections for convenience: **For beginners, For those with some knowledge, For the more advanced.** (See page 146 paragraph 8).

Skills—Index

Included in this list are a number of activities indicated by *, the Programmes for which are not printed in the Award Handbook, but single copies of which can be obtained, free of charge, by sending a stamped addressed envelope to the Scottish Award Office, 69 Dublin Street, Edinburgh EH3 6HS.

Note: Those living in Northern Ireland or Wales should apply to The Duke of Edinburgh's Award, 593 Lisbon Road, Belfast BT9 7GS or 17 Cathedral Road, Cardiff CF1 9HA.

SKILLS

SKILLS

Note: This list is not exhaustive, but any proposed additions must first be submitted through Operating Authorities or Award Regional Offices, to the National Award Office for approval.

COLLECTIONS, STUDIES AND SURVEYS

Archaeology/Astronomy/Bible Study/Collections—General/Librarianship/Local and Historical Survey/Natural History/Philately (Stamps)/You and the Commonwealth/Anthropology/Chemistry/ Civics/Computers/Costume Study/Criminology/Entomology/Forces Insignia/Genealogy/Geology/Geometrical and Technical Drawing/ Heraldry/Herpetology/Map Making/Meteorology/Microscopy/Model Soldiers/Numismatics (Coins)/Palaeontology/Phillumeny (Matchboxes)/Practical Mathematics/ Relief Modelling/Religions of the World/War Games/Zoology/Fine and Applied Arts and Design/ Architectural Appreciation/Ballet Appreciation/Church Architecture/Period Furniture/Theatre

Introduction

Collections, Studies and Surveys provide an excellent opportunity for those who show little interest in creative activities or handicraft Skills to take up and develop a worthwhile pursuit from a very wide range of choice.

Any one of these activities should give a balance between academic interest and the practical work necessary to present the work done. In this way, the participant's understanding of the historical, social and cultural development of our society can be helped.

Although the opportunity for group work may occur less frequently than in other Skills, in many cases both progress and understanding can be best achieved by group practice.

Collections—General Guidelines

Many different types of collection are acceptable for all stages of the Award Scheme. In each case a Programme should be worked out on the following general outline:

a) Any collection should have a defined object and a defined field of interest. It should not be a haphazard collection of specimens which bear no relation to each other or the rest of the work the young person is undertaking concerning the object to be collected.

b) Any worthwhile collection should involve effort and imagination during the whole period the activity is to be followed. (The mere physical collection of objects on its own is not sufficient and such collections as birds' eggs, autographs and car numbers are not acceptable).

SKILLS

c) The work to be covered should include the reading of books and visits to museums and places of interest connected with it. Suitable contact should be made with other enthusiasts (in addition to those giving instruction or assessment), wherever possible in a group or society.

d) At some time during each stage, the young person should give a short talk illustrating the purpose of the collection. Something of the history of the subject should certainly be studied, together with any geographical, social or scientific aspects it may have.

Studies and Surveys—General Guidelines

Many different topics lend themselves to a Study or Survey and some suggestions are given below. In each case a Programme should be worked out on the following general guidelines:

a) The objects and field of interest of the Study or Survey should be clearly defined before commencing this activity.

b) In each case clear evidence of thorough research with a reasoned approach should be given.

c) The collection of data or information should not be considered sufficient on its own and some attempt should be made to interpret or summarise the information collected.

d) The results of the Survey or Study should be in some form of report or guide.

The work should not be taken solely from existing books and wherever possible evidence of some original work should be given.

e) Throughout the required period of activity regular effort must be made and close contact with the Instructor and Assessor is recommended.

Studies—suitable study topics might include

a) The history of a sport, a sports club.

b) The study of a type of music e.g. classical, folk or popular, or dance e.g. ballet.

c) The life and times of a famous person (i.e. politician, sportsperson, dancer, musician etc).

d) A period in history such as the Industrial Revolution, The Great War, or a study of the architecture or furniture of a period.

e) Developing Countries of the Third World, The Commonwealth, The European Community.

f) Charitable organisations. Etc. etc.

Surveys—suitable subjects might include

a) Local village/town survey.

b) Survey of a local historical site(s).

c) Tourist attractions in an area.

d) Local language/dialects.

e) Local customs, songs, dances etc.

f) Job opportunities for school leavers.

Astronomy

(See also Introduction on page 152).

For beginners

Young people starting this activity should have a good knowledge of:

1. The night sky as seen with the unaided eye from their home area.

2. The recognition of the main classical constellations, and their use in identifying the main star groups and the brighter fixed stars.

3. Finding directions by the stars.

4. The seasonal change in appearance of the night sky. The apparent motion of the sun, moon and planets.

5. The earth-moon system and the solar system. The sun as a moving star and member of the Milky Way system or Galaxy. The domain of the galaxies.

For those with some knowledge

6. Young people should compile a record of regular observations made over the stipulated period. This can be of a general nature, but must include reference to at least **one** of the following:

a) The motion of the moon against its background of stars and its change in phase. The seasonal change in the apparent height of its path.

b) The observed change in position of one of the planets at regular intervals during this period.

c) The apparent tracks of bright meteors.

d) The observed tracks of artificial satellites and other man-projected bodies.

e) Sunspot positions obtained by projection through a small telescope, and aurorae in districts where appropriate.

7. In each case young people should submit suitable charts. They may:

a) Make and use simple pieces of apparatus, e.g. a home-constructed clinometer, simple two-lens telescope, or other forms of sighting device.

b) Observe and record in a systematic manner any adventitious object, e.g. a comet which may be visible during this period.

8. Those taking part should have some knowledge of the historical and scientific development of the study of astronomy.

For the more advanced

9. Young people should make regular observations with a simple telescope and produce a written record, in diary form. They should produce a written paper on some aspect of astronomy which has appealed to them from their own observations, involving further reading in books dealing with the subject chosen.

10. Those taking part should have further knowledge of the historical and scientific development of the study of astronomy.

The London Planetarium Company Ltd.

Librarianship

(See also Introduction on page 152)

General

At all stages, there should be some knowledge of the history of printed books.

For beginners

Young people should undertake practical work in a school library or some other library regularly during the stipulated period, and should become familiar with the following:

1. The purpose of the library.

2. The arrangement of the books in proper order on the shelves.

3. The use of the catalogues.

4. The method of recording loans.

5. The procedure for obtaining a book on loan which is not in the library and which is unlikely to be acquired for it.

6. Elementary fact-finding, i.e. use of telephone book, dictionary, encyclopaedia.

7. In addition, they should write a brief account of the library, giving specimens for catalogue, stock record, etc.

For those with some knowledge

Those taking part should continue regular practical help with a library and in addition undertake the following:

8. Visit by arrangement with the librarian, a public library, and find out what services are given there, i.e. Lending and Reference Libraries, Children's Library, and so on.

9. Write a brief account of item **8** above.

10. Undertake practical work of not less than twenty-five hours, to include:

a) Helping for an hour or two, if this can be arranged, at a library counter.

b) Making a list, with author, title, publisher and, when possible, price of ten books on a particular subject.

c) Finding information on a specific subject or subjects, by using books in the reference library.

11. Write short appreciations of five books read by them (not more than two of which should be fiction). Make author and alphabetical subject cards for the non-fiction books.

12. Show some awareness of the impact of books on the social and cultural development of civilisation.

For the more advanced
Participants should:

13. Have regular practical experience during the stipulated period in a library, which may be a public (municipal or county) or a non-public (industrial, academic or other) library.

14. Study the different kinds of libraries (public and non-public); their purposes and their place in the national library service.

15. Become familiar with the methods of obtaining for readers, books which are not in the stock of a given library.

16. Give a brief account of one of the following:

a) The history of Public Libraries in a given country.

b) A description of methods of co-operation between libraries.

c) What the library (public or special) can do for you.

17. Make a study of the parts of books and the periodicals (i.e. title-page, contents page, preface, text, illustrations, index, etc.) and their functions.

The Library Association.

Philately (Stamps)

(See also Introduction on page 152)

General

1. At all stages, there should be some knowledge of "stamps in use" in addition to "stamps in collection". Young people should also be aware of the increase of personal and business contacts and of the political significance, brought about by the introduction of a universal postal system. Wherever possible young people should be encouraged to join a stamp club and to visit National or local exhibitions.

For beginners
Those starting this programme should:

1. Be able to look at a cover and distinguish any interesting postal markings which make it worth keeping in its entirety. Be able correctly to wash stamps off paper and remove surplus gum.

2. Be able to mount stamps on album leaves correctly, i.e. to use care in the use of hinge.

3. Be able to recognise the differing qualities of hinge, avoiding those which cause too permanent an adhesion.

4. Be able to use pattern, i.e. symmetry in placing stamps in album pages.

5. Develop colour sense i.e. be able to recognise colours and distinguish shades.

6. Be aware that catalogue prices are not those at which the collections can be sold.

7. Be able to give a five-minute talk on any six sheets of their own stamps.

8. Be able to detect watermarks.

9. Submit a well-arranged collection of stamps, which should show that the collector has a planned collection with an objective:

a) Collection of one particular country.

b) Collection of a group of countries, e.g. British Commonwealth.

c) Collection of a particular type of stamp, e.g. Air Mails.

d) A thematic collection.

For those with some knowledge
Young people should:

10. Be able to understand the perforation measurements.

11. Be able to name two types of separation.

12. Be able to use stamp catalogues intelligently, i.e. by studying the indices, be aware of Russian, Greek, etc. stamps on which English does not appear.

13. Be able to recognise countries, geographical positions from the maps which appear on many stamps.

SKILLS

14. Be able to recognise the theme in the stamp designs, i.e. industrial or agricultural products, poets and peasants, the rise and fall of governments and so on.

15. Be able to talk for 5 minutes on sixteen sheets of their own stamps.

16. Have developed a neat style in connection with the write-up of their album leaves.

17. Be able to distinguish different watermarks.

18. Know the broad purpose of the Universal Postal Union.

19. Identify by catalogue, 20 stamps already mounted on a plain sheet of paper.

20. Submit for inspection a general collection of not less than 500 stamps mounted in an album, all stamps being mounted in date order under the appropriate country heading.

For the more advanced
Those taking part should:

21. Own their own catalogue and take a stamp magazine.

22. Be able to talk on the articles of general philatelic interest which appear in item **21** above and in the daily press.

23. Know something of stamp auctioneers and how they work. Information can be obtained through general reading.

24. Know something of Dockwra (contractor of pre-stamp era), Rowland Hill, and Archer who invented the perforating machine, and the background history of stamps.

25. Be familiar with the name of Heinrich von Stephan, Postmaster General of the German Empire and his work in connection with Postal Reforms.

26. Be able to describe how posts were conducted before 1840 when postage stamps were first used.

27. Know why some stamps show more than one currency and why stamps are issued in particular denominations.

28. Know the technical terms for the different kinds of British water-mark and recognise them.

29. Know how the postage due system differs between the countries.

30. Know what is meant by a "Thematic" collection.

31. Name three processes by which stamps are produced and be able to recognise the different methods.

32. Be able to name at least four stamp printing firms.

33. Be able to talk for ten minutes on the stamps of one country, or for fifteen minutes on a general collection.

34. Be able to write up and prepare stamps for display.

35. Submit for inspection one of the following collections mounted on quadrille ruled leaves used in the normal loose-leaf albums.

a) Great Britain—not less than 150 stamps.

b) Any one foreign country, e.g. France, Germany, Italy, USA, etc.—not less than 150 stamps.

c) Any one group of British Colonial Territories.

d) Any subject ("thematic") collection, e.g. flowers, historic buildings, aircraft, animals, etc.—not less than 100 stamps. In this group special note would be taken of brief informative notes written on the album sheets.

36. If possible, visit a local Sorting Office.

COMMUNICATION

Committee Procedure/Debating/Drama and Stagework/Languages/
Public Speaking/Reading/Writing/Braille/Casualty Simulation/
Conjuring and Magic/Film Production/Magazine Production/
Puppetry/Short-wave Radio Listening/Signalling/Speech/Sound
Appreciation/Computing/Amateur Radio/Total Communication
(Signing).

Introduction

These activities provide vehicles by which individuals
express themselves, their beliefs, and communicate with
others. They call for an understanding of the various media
as well as for an awareness of their potential and effects.
They are skills which influence human relationships and
societies and it is required that such aspects be regarded as
integral parts of the subject undertaken. It is considered
that group discussions should be included in the work of
participants.

Some of the activities—especially those involving verbal
and written modes of communication—call for a high degree
of personal involvement. Acquisition of technical skills are
to provide the basis upon which the ideas and creativity of
participants can be expressed. Each individual is to produce
evidence of regular application over the required period and
to supply diary, or tape recording or appropriate logs for
assessment. This may be an ideal way of using such skills
as typing, word processing and handwriting.

Committee Procedure

(See also Introduction above)

Note: Attention is drawn to *Award Handbook* Chapter 4, paragraph
10, and Skills Section, paragraph 3 in relation to this subject.

For beginners

Those taking part should:

1. Where possible join a Committee or attend at least 3 meetings of
a Committee of your choice.

2. Know the usual form of a Committee and the function of the
Chairman, Secretary, Treasurer and members.

3. Discuss some of the difficulties of Committee work from the point of view of timing, conduct and personalities.

4. Be able to propose and speak to a point on an Agenda.

5. Learn something about a Skill connected with the role of an Officer of the Committee:

- Committee procedure/Chairman
- Simple accounting/Treasurer
- Typing/Secretary
- Speed writing or Shorthand/Minutes Secretary
- Use of cassette recorder or other audio equipment/Secretary

For those with some knowledge
6. Continue as a member of a Committee or attend at least 3 Committee meetings of your choice.

7. Draw up an agenda for a meeting.

8. Understand the purpose of an Annual General Meeting.

9. Have a knowledge of the constitution of a committee attended.

10. Study the role of the Committee in local government and where possible attend at least 1 Local Government committee meeting.

11. Continue to learn at least one Skill connected with the role of an Officer of the committee:

- Committee procedure/Chairman
- Simple accounting/Treasurer
- Auditing/Treasurer
- Typing/Secretary
- Speed writing or Shorthand/Minutes Secretary
- Use of audio equipment/Secretary

Wherever possible the chosen skill should be put into practice, i.e. by taking minutes, typing up the minutes, drawing up agendas and sending out notices, keeping the books or auditing accounts.

For the more advanced
12. Participants should join a Committee and wherever possible serve as an Officer of the Committee.

13. Submit a written report on at least one meeting to the local press.

14. Study the history of English Committees and their use since early times.

15. Study the role of the Committee in National Government and where possible attend at least one session of Parliament and/or read a report prepared by a Government Committee, The United Nations, The EEC or some other similar body.

16. Continue to learn at least one Skill connected with the role of an Officer of a Committee, or choose a new Skill if a satisfactory standard has been reached in a Skill at a previous level of Award:

- Committee procedure/Chairman
- Simple accounting/Treasurer
- Auditing/Treasurer
- Typing/Secretary
- Speed writing or Shorthand/Minutes Secretary
- Use of audio equipment/Secretary

Wherever possible the chosen skill should be put into practice, i.e. by taking minutes, typing up minutes, drawing up agendas and sending out notices, keeping the books or auditing the accounts.

Drama and Stagework

(See also Introduction on page 161)

General
1. This programme seeks to underline the corporate practical and creative aspects of the art of theatre, and to offer the possibility of a general interest in theatre developing into a specialised one. It is expected that specialisation will take place in one of the following: Acting; Stage Management; Design; History of the Theatre; Production; Stage Lighting; Wardrobe; Make-up; Dance-Drama.

Young people are, however, encouraged to experiment and develop their knowledge in any other aspect which they may find worthy of study and practice.

Throughout, there is scope for those taking part to deepen their knowledge of one side of theatre, and to give practical demonstrations of an increasing knowledge or ability. Thus an actor as a beginner may play a small part, with some knowledge may play an important part, whilst a more advanced actor would demonstrate in a particular part an increased ability and range of experience. A stage electrician as a beginner may take part in a play or help with stage lighting, with some knowledge may be responsible for the lighting of a production, whilst a more advanced participant would give evidence of considerable knowledge of the use of colour lighting control, and would have put this knowledge to use in a production. Similar developments should be expected in the other departments.

2. Further notes on this programme may be had from the County or County Borough Drama Adviser, who will also be able to give advice.

For beginners
Those taking part should:

1. Show evidence of continuous study, effort and achievement with a group under adequate guidance of one aspect of practical dramatic activity, including participation in a theatrical presentation.

2. Keep a scrapbook or log devoted to one aspect of the theatre.

3. Have seen at least **four** plays and produced a written or oral critical comment on one of them.

For those with some knowledge
Young people should:

4. Show evidence of further study, effort and achievement with a group under adequate guidance, giving final evidence of responsibility for one aspect of a production.

5. Show evidence of regular reading on the subject, and produce a written or oral critical comment on at least **two** books on theatre.

6. Have seen at least **four** plays and produced a written or oral critical comment on two of them. One of these criticisms should consider the play from the aspect of the theatre chosen for special study.

For the more advanced
7. Show evidence of further study, effort and achievement under adequate guidance of one particular aspect of theatre. Specialise in some specific aspect of drama, and show clear evidence of considerable knowledge and/or ability in it.

8. Have seen at least **four** plays and produced a comparative analysis of three of them with reference to the aspect chosen for special study.

9. Have some knowledge of the major historical developments of the theatre, e.g. Greek, Medieval Elizabethan, Restoration, 19th Century, Contemporary or examples of contemporary African, Asian or Caribbean dramatic influence, e.g. Carnival, and demonstrate this knowledge in some literary form.

Note: Since it is not always easy to integrate a drama group into a youth club—especially the smaller rural clubs—it may become necessary to establish area drama groups, so that those doing the Award may follow their chosen interest; or alternatively, to recommend that they should join an existing theatre group or drama class. The way chosen will, of course, depend upon the number of young people taking the Award, the number and type of clubs or groups, and the nature of the area.

National Association of Drama Advisers.

Languages

(See also Introduction on page 161)

1. Before starting this interest, at any level, young people must give their tutor, or an expert assessor appointed by him, reliable evidence of any existing proficiency in speaking, reading and/or writing the language and of any knowledge they may possess of the people and country concerned. No initial proficiency or knowledge is stipulated; assessment should be based on progress made rather than on the standard reached, and the tutor or assessor should compare the individual's initial proficiency (if any) with that shown at the end of the prescribed period for the stage attempted.

2. Young people should show evidence of improved pronunciation, wider vocabulary, greater grammatical accuracy and increased knowledge of the country and people.

3. They should show that these have been achieved by individual enterprise such as attendance at voluntary classes, using recorded courses at home and private reading and study. Progress in learning a language being studied as part of full-time education will not be recognised as qualifying for the Award.

4. Those taking part should produce evidence of sustained correspondence with someone in the country whose language they are learning and to whom they themselves should have written an average of at least one letter per month. Copies of these letters and of any replies received should be produced. Letters written by participants may be partly in English but should contain some attempt to write the language being learnt.

5. More advanced participants studying any of the West European languages should, if possible, give evidence of at least two weeks' travel or residence in the country whose language is being learnt.

Note: In the event of any difficulty in finding expert assessors or correspondents, applications may be made to the Honorary Secretary, The Modern Language Association, 2 Manchester Square, London W1.

The Modern Language Association.

Computing

General

1. At all stages there should be an appreciation of the roles that computers play in society, and of the effects that their introduction into an increasing range of situations may have on that society.

2. All those taking part should become familiar with microcomputers, and should be able to make constructive use of them.

3. Participants should be familiar with the widest possible applications of computing including video games, word processors and data retrieval. An awareness of the limitations of computers is also important.

For beginners
Young people should be able to:

1. Use existing programs to store, interpret and recall suitable information in a useful form.

2. Keep such a system up to date over a period of time.

3. Suggest improvements to the system, or make simple modifications to it.

For those with some knowledge
They should have a working knowledge of:

1. The elements of developing and writing a program to achieve a defined goal, using a suitable high-level language.

2. The difference between microcomputers, and the extent to which programs written for one machine can be adapted to another machine.

3. The use to which computers of all types are put in business, leisure and other fields.

For the more advanced

Those taking part should:

1. Devise, write, run and debug a user-friendly and useful program.

2. Use advanced programming techniques in one high-level language to produce software.

3. Have some knowledge of at least a second high-level language.

4. Be aware of low-level codes and their uses.

5. Appreciate the differences of design and application between micro and mainframe computers.

CRAFTS—GENERAL

Brass Rubbing/Cookery/ Electricity and Electronics/Floral Art/ Wine-making/Confectioners' Decoration/Construction of Camp and Outdoor Equipment/Radio Construction/Taxidermy/Glasswork

Introduction

These activities should include as much practical work as possible, preferably undertaken with others through a group or club. The emphasis should be on real improvement of skill together with an understanding of the social and cultural significance of the activity.

For assessment, each individual is to produce evidence of regular application to the activity over the required period, which may take the form of finished articles, notebook, diagrams etc.

General Programme

The following guidelines should be used to draw up a programme for a craft that does not have a particular programme listed, but which a participant wishes to follow. Before embarking on this programme it should be approved by the participant's Operating Authority.

Participants would need to have knowledge and experience of:

a) Range of materials available, their cost and characteristics and storing/keeping qualities.

b) The tools available and how they are used, together with safety precautions required when using cutting tools and electrical or mechanical tools.

c) The ability to follow plans, diagrams, instructions, menus etc.

d) The production of a finished article, initially under supervision but eventually on their own.

e) The use of different techniques/materials in order to produce a balanced range of items in the craft concerned.

f) The historical development of the craft and perhaps international variations, or a knowledge of related crafts.

g) An opportunity to display finished items should be found at least once during the period of participation.

h) For the more advanced it is important that they have the opportunity to design, plan and produce their own product without relying on others.

i) Instruction should be given in the safe use of glues and precautions required when working with other materials where face masks or good ventilation may be required.

Brass Rubbing

(See also Introduction on page 168).

General
Young people are advised to seek permission before taking rubbings.

For beginners
1. Make a collection of Brass Rubbings, aiming at a minimum of twelve, with notes giving:

a) The identity and date of death of the individuals commemorated. Where these are unknown, insert the approximate date.

b) The position of the brass in the church. Say whether relaid, mural, etc.

c) The dedication of the church, the name of the village or town and the county.

d) Any other details of interest.

e) State whether there are any parts of the brass lost, or any that exist but do not appear on your rubbing for any reason.

f) A certain amount of biographical information about the people, stating in addition to a) the age of the individual, station and/or trade, relation to any other brasses or monuments, unusual points in brass, e.g. (as in Cornwall) flowers between feet.

g) List of sources consulted should be given.

For those with some knowledge
2. Make a collection of all the brasses in a given area, including the indents of lost brasses.

3. Make a collection to show an elementary knowledge of the development of:

a) Military brasses.
b) Ladies' costume.
c) Civilian costume.
d) Religious vestments.

4. Study heraldry on brasses.

For the more advanced
5. Make a more advanced study of item 3 above, or a particular study of some feature, e.g. ladies' head-dress, knights' helmets.

6. Make a survey of:

a) A family, with a genealogical tree.
b) Religious symbolism on brasses.
c) The merchants' mark and the rebus on brasses.
d) Chalice brasses, etc.
e) Skeletons, shrouds, heart and chrysom brasses.

Cookery

(See also Introduction on page 168)

For beginners
Theory

1. Have a general knowledge of foods and know which ones to eat and why.

2. Know how to maintain cleanliness in the kitchen, and how to use and maintain utensils and equipment, including a gas or electric cooker, microwave, etc.

3. Know how to lay tables and trays.

Practical work

4. Prepare simple meals for the day, e.g.:

a) Breakfast—Porridge, fried bacon and bread, boiled eggs, stewed apples and the like to serve with cold cereals. Toast, tea, coffee.

b) Lunch—Simple two course menus, both hot and cold, e.g. Brown stew, Irish stew, root and green vegetables, grilled sausages and chops, salads. Steamed or baked puddings with sauces or custard. Comparable menus will be selected by participants with the help of the instructor. Cost should be borne in mind and kept reasonably low.

c) Tea—Brown and white scones, Small and large cakes and biscuits.

5. Make sweets such as fudge, toffee apples, etc.

For those with some knowledge
Theory

6. Assuming that young people know their kitchen and how to take care of everything in it, they should now learn to use and look after a second kind of cooker; to know how and where to store different kinds of food at home, and how to use and take care of a refrigerator and other mechanical kitchen equipment.

SKILLS

7. Those taking part should have a knowledge of food values and be able to plan a well-balanced menu for a family for a week.

Practical work — This should include:

8. Breakfast — Scrambled and poached eggs, kippers and other breakfast dishes that are quick to prepare.

9. Lunch — more complex menus to include roast meat, meat pies and puddings, soups of the broth variety, savoury and sweet sauces, the use of savoury and sweet left-overs, short crust pastry. Fish pie, fish cakes, grilled herrings.

10. Tea — Cakes from creaming method recipes. Glace icing.

11. Buffet meals — Sandwiches and fillings, sausage rolls, patties, etc.

12. Supper dishes — Use of cheese, sardines, left-overs, etc.

13. Experimental dishes, e.g. recipes from women's magazines.

For the more advanced
Theory

14. By now those taking part should be able to plan, prepare and serve meals for four people for ordinary daily occasions and have some idea of how much time they will require for whatever meals they propose to make, what it will cost and the order in which they will do the necessary work. They will now want to add a few frills to their basic skills.

15. Young people should know something of the use of modern equipment for cooking, e.g. electric mixers, rotary spits, trying different ways of using them, and assessing advantages, disadvantages and the main points in using them wisely.

Practical work — This should now include:

16. Sweet and savoury dishes with rough puff pastry. Bread making. The making of one kind of jam. Any boiled icing.

17. Use and adaptation of convenience foods, e.g. frozen, tinned or dried foods.

18. Experimental work on foods suitable for expeditions, including the production of a recipe book suitable for inexperienced cooks.

19. Experimenting with old traditional or foreign recipes. Tracing old recipes and trying them.

20. Experimenting with interesting but simple recipes suitable for use in clubs.

Electricity and Electronics

(See also Introduction on page 168)

General
Instructors should ensure that power for working models and experimental work is provided from batteries or low-voltage units.

For beginners
Those starting this activity should attempt at least **three** of the following:

1. Take an old torch to pieces. Examine each part carefully. Make a detailed sectional drawing labelling all the parts.

2. Find out all they can about an accumulator. Draw a circuit showing one being charged. Draw a sectional diagram labelling the parts. Know how to check it.

3. Keep a daily check on their electric meter. Read it at set times and make a table which shows clearly the consumption of electricity in their home. After two months calculate the cost at rates in force.

4. Make a two-pole electric motor.

5. Make an electro-magnet.

6. Make a two-way switch.

7. If they have a bicycle with a dynamo make a drawing showing the path of the current.

8. Show by means of a large diagram the lighting system of their house.

9. Know how an electric bell works, and try to make one.

10. Make transistorised AND, OR and NOT gates. Combine these to form NAND and NOR gates.

11. Make a circuit to demonstrate the operation of a NAND or NOR gate in an integrated circuit, e.g. TTL 7400 or TTL 7402.

For those with some knowledge
Young people should attempt at least **five** of the following:

12. Keep a daily check on their electric meter. Read it at set times. Show the amount of electricity consumed clearly in form of a table. Compare the consumption for two different quarters.

SKILLS

13. Use an integrated circuit with NAND or NOR gates to make a bistable or flip flop.

14. Make a current detector.

15. Make a condenser.

16. Make a binary counter with at least four bits indicated by light emitting diodes.

17. Make an electric bell.

18. Make a transistorised fire alarm and burglar alarm (the indication need only be an LED or other low current device).

19. Make a reversing switch.

20. Think of a topic concerned with electricity, find out from books all they can about it and write an article summing up their findings.

21. Combine NAND or NOR gates (e.g. in the TTL 7400 or TTL 7402 chip) to form all five basic logic gates.

For the more advanced

Those taking part should attempt at least **eight** of the following:

22. Keep a weekly check on electricity consumed in their own home. Find out the cost per unit and find by calculation the cost per quarter. Know which quarter is the most expensive.

23. Find out all they can about Faraday. Set down their findings on paper.

24. Make a three-pole electric motor.

25. Make a hot wire ammeter.

26. Make an electric bell.

27. Make a simple chip controlled electronic organ.

28. Make a microchip radio.

29. Find out all they can about an accumulator. Draw diagrams and explain why it has to be charged.

30. Make a transistorised fire alarm or burglar alarm with adequate amplification to operate a buzzer.

31. Make a current detector.

32. Make an 8 bit binary counter with the output connected to two 7-segment displays.

33. Write a history of one great man in the world of electricity (not Faraday).

34. Find out all they can about the Grid System. Write an article about it well supplied with labelled diagrams.

35. Study a topic such as radio, television, microprocessors or any other topic of their choice and write an article about it.

36. Make a shift register with at least 8 bits.

37. Make a microchip controlled model traffic light system or model railway signal set.

GRAPHIC ARTS
Cinematography/Drawing/Painting and Design/Photography/Fabric Printing/Handwriting/Calligraphy and Lettering/Mosaics/Printing/Screen Printing

Introduction
These activities should include as much practical work as possible, preferably undertaken with others through a group or club. Some form of sketchbook or log book should be compiled, or a folio of work kept. Wherever possible, young people should be encouraged to apply their practical work to extend the social possibilities of these skills—for example, youth club notices would be a suitable exercise for lettering and printing.

Calligraphy and Lettering
Introduction
This activity should include as much practical work as possible, preferably undertaken with others through a group or club. Some form of sketchbook or log book should be compiled, or a folio of work kept. Wherever possible, young people should be encouraged to apply their practical work to extend the social possibilities of this skill.

General
1. This programme comprises practical work in Lettering (drawn with pencil or pen or painted with a brush) and Calligraphy (formal penmanship using the edged-pen). The aim should be towards a good all-round standard in practical work and an awareness and appreciation of good lettering and calligraphy of the past and present and their use today for a variety of purposes.

2. Study of the Proportion and Arrangement of Letters. In all aspects of this programme young people must be aware of the need for well designed work, the important factors being:

a) The proportion of individual letters.

b) The spacing between letters, between words and between lines.

c) The weight and density of the lettering and the balance of one area of writing with another.

d) The arrangement, or layout, of the writing in relation to the margins and the blank spaces.

e) The use of colour in writing.

f) The interpretation of illustration or decoration with the other elements.

3. In each level young people should select and present for assessment from the following, the choice being appropriate to the level reached by the individual:

a) Practice sheets in brush and pen, or drawn lettering, and one fair copy of the alphabet showing related letters in their groups; or a complete alphabet after group study has been made.

b) A poem of not less than 14 lines written with an edged-pen in the italic hand.

c) In painted Roman lettering an inscription including a date, or a poster for an exhibition (light letters on a dark ground or light and dark letters on a medium ground).

d) One example of prose, of approximately 200 words, written with the edged-pen for a double page opening of a manuscript book, and including decorative capitals and a heading, or an illustration.

e) In sans-serif block letters a suitable example of public notice, e.g. SILENCE PLEASE.

f) Four varied examples from the following: a greetings card; a Christmas card; invitation to a party; recipe for a cake or other foods; menu for a Steak House, Fish Restaurant or Snack Bar; notice for a sale of work at a local school; advertisement for a fountain pen; monograms; design for a wrapping paper, or paper bags, incorporating the name of a firm and reflecting the nature of the shop and the goods sold.

g) A book of mounted examples and notes, as outlined in the section (appreciation of lettering and calligraphy past and present).

4. Young people should choose the size of paper and scale of layout. The work should be presented in a folder, or mounted in a sketch-book, or in a loose-leaf book, each piece being clearly labelled.

For beginners
Lettering—young people should:

1. Study and practise the skeleton alphabet in groups of letters. Paint with a brush the Roman alphabet in related groups of letters. Start with the capital letter, follow with the lower-case letters and numerals.

2. Study and practise a formal italic alphabet.

3. Draw and paint sans-serif letters, not less than 5cm high, or draw and cut out sans-serif letters 5cm, 7.5cm or 10cm high, in white paper and arrange in words on black or coloured paper for practice in experimental spacing and layout.

Calligraphy—Those taking part should:

4. Start with the alphabet in skeleton form. The letters and their relative proportion to the circular "O" should be studied and practised in groups, i.e. rectangular groups of letters, round letters, wide letters, narrow and very narrow letters.

5. Writing with the edged-pen should be practised, beginning with the lower-case letters, followed by simple capital letters and numerals and starting with a nib that is not less than Nib Size No. 1 (2.5mm) across its writing edge. A Formal Hand (the Foundational Hand) based on the circular "O" should be used, also a formal italic hand made from a number of pen strokes.

6. Versal letters and flourished and swashed capitals, used for leading into the text, or for adding to it, may now be practised.

7. Monograms: emblems for chapter headings and chapter endings; and decorative borders related to the writing, and made in themselves with edged-pen, may be included.

8. The writing may be suitably illustrated in any medium, provided it is related to the writing in scale and weight.

For those with some knowledge
9. Young people should continue the practice of lettering and calligraphy on the lines suggested above. Finished examples of work should show evidence of an understanding of layout and design and the choice of good model alphabets.

10. They should collect and mount in a sketch-book, or on sheets in a folder examples of past and present day lettering and calligraphy, which appeal to them, and give reasons for the choice. Young people should collect examples from newspapers, magazines, journals, book jackets, and draw or take photographs of shop signs, street names, inn signs and the like.

For the more advanced

11. In addition to completed examples of lettering and calligraphy for practical purposes, young people should make a study of lettering from the past, and historical manuscript writing. Churches should be visited for lettering on memorials; and museums to see early manuscripts and historical documents. Rubbings can be made from slate or stone incised inscriptions, on detail paper bought in a roll, the rubbing being done with a cobbler's heel ball.

Drawing

(See also Introduction on page 175)

For beginners
Suggested scale—A4 to A3 or $\frac{1}{4}-\frac{1}{2}$ Imperial.
Those taking this programme should show evidence of regular work done during the stipulated period, and should submit samples of work in monochrome and/or colour, in the following range:

1. Natural Forms—Human, animal, trees, plants, rocks, stones, bones, feathers, etc.

a) Four life studies.
b) Three other studies.

2. Inanimate objects—Man-made and all sizes: buildings, bridges, bicycles, bottles, etc.

a) Two group studies.
b) Three single studies.

3. Landscape—Countryside, seashore, town scene. Three of any type, either made on the spot or from sketches.

4. Composition—Representational or abstract. Three studies from everyday life either from imagination or from memory.

5. Other work—Patterns, using brush, potato or lino cuts. Two designs (repeat, regular or geometric).

For those with some knowledge
Suggested scale—A4 to A3 or $\frac{1}{4}-\frac{1}{2}$ Imperial.
Young people should show evidence of regular work done during the stipulated period, using a sketchbook, in monochrome and/or colour, in the following range (suggested examples as for beginners):

6. Natural Forms:

a) Three figure studies.
b) Two portraits.
c) Two other studies.

7. Inanimate objects:

a) Three group studies.
b) Three single studies.

8. Landscape: Four—suggested that two be taken from each of two types.

9. Composition. Four from such fields as:

a) Everyday life.
b) A poem.
c) A legend.

10. Other work:

a) Patterns—two regular and two free.
b) A series of studies of a particular topic, e.g. a theme from nature—animals, birds, flowers, etc.—or architecture, or period furniture.

11. Give evidence of some knowledge of the history of drawing (e.g. a brief study of a particular period, artist or illustrator).

For the more advanced
Suggested scale—A4 or $\frac{1}{4}$ Imperial minimum.

12. Those taking part should show evidence of regular work done during the required period, using both monochrome and colour. All work should be presented in an A3 or $\frac{1}{2}$ Imperial folder mounted together with the accompanying sketches. A full and varied sketchbook of the individual's work should also be submitted.

13. Young people should have used and be familiar with a wide range of media. Examples of these, exploiting their individual techniques, should be included in the folder (participants should have the choice of subjects).

In addition they should:

14. Present a pen and wash study, in a suitable medium, of a landscape, seascape or townscape, using a suitable paper, together with the accompanying sketches. This work should show command of perspective and suggestion of mood.

15. Illustrate two widely divergent authors in a suitable manner. These studies should have the accompanying text, and the drawing should enhance the character of the individual work.

16. Make a study using one of the following suggested techniques:

a) Collage.
b) Montage.
c) Stencilling.
d) Paper mosaic.

Young people should make the choice of subject.

17. Give an illustrated account of any artist/illustrator whose work they have studied.

18. Give evidence of further knowledge of the history of drawing.

Photography

(See also Introduction on page 175)

General
1. All taking part should understand the potential hazards of the chemicals used.

2. At all stages, some study of the history of photography should be included, together with an appreciation of the social and cultural implications of this art, (e.g. use by press, in advertising).

For beginners
Young people should be able to:

1. Load and develop a film in a "daylight" tank.

2. Make contact prints from normal negatives and glaze or flat dry the prints.

3. Take a series of twelve photographs of animals or children. Mount them in a loose-leaf album. Prints should not be less than $2\frac{1}{4}$in. square. Enlargements, if necessary, may be processed professionally.

For those with some knowledge
Those taking part should:

4. Prepare a series of twelve landscapes—seascapes or commercial or industrial subjects, mounted in a loose-leaf album, e.g. pastoral scenes, roof tops, architecture—varying angles, grouping of proprietary articles, photographs of machinery.

5. Make a photo study. A maximum of twelve photographs (not necessarily the same size) or 50′ of 8mm, 100′ of 9.5mm or 16mm film (sub-titles may be added if required) illustrating, for example, a club activity, the history of a village/town or an industrial process.

6. Study the full process from taking a photograph through to enlargement of any subject (Young people should be responsible for taking the photograph, developing the film or plate and printing the picture. The enlargement itself—not more than $8\frac{1}{2}''$ by $6\frac{1}{2}''$—may be processed professionally).

Exposure tables and calculators should be used to give correctly exposed negatives from outdoor subjects.

For the more advanced
Young people should have a working knowledge of:

7. Lighting and use of filters for special effects by day, artificial lighting and flash.

8. Shading and retouching of enlargements made from any negative.

9. Basic rules of composition in general and lighting for portraiture.

10. Action of chemicals in developers and fixers in black and white photography.

11. The basic principles of colour processes. Two samples should be produced.

12. They should also prepare a log book on the history of photography and the care and maintenance of a camera.

Photographic Information Council.

HANDICRAFTS

Basketry (Canework)/Clay Modelling and Sculpture/Model Construction—Aircraft; Cars; Railways; Ships/Bookbinding/ Candlemaking/Corn Dollies/Fancy Lampshade Making/Origami/ Woodcarving.

Introduction

These activities should include as much practical work as possible, preferably undertaken with others through a group or club. Practical application in learning the basic skills, right choice of materials, etc., is of primary importance in these programmes. It is also hoped that young people will be encouraged to be creative in making their own designs, especially at the more advanced stages.

Some of these activities lend themselves to study of their social and cultural significance and historical aspects.

For assessment, each individual is to produce evidence of regular application to the activity over the required period, which may be in the form of a certificate of attendance at instruction classes, finished articles, notebook or log.

General Programme

The following guidelines should be used to draw up a programme for a handicraft that does not have a particular programme listed, but which a participant wishes to follow. Before embarking on this programme it should be approved by the participant's Operating Authority. Participants would need to have knowledge and experience of the following:

a) Range of materials available, their cost and characteristics and storing/keeping qualities.

b) The tools available and how they are used, together with safety precautions required when using cutting tools and electrical or mechanical tools.

c) The ability to follow plans, diagrams, instructions etc.

d) The production of a finished article, initially under supervision but eventually on their own.

e) The use of different techniques/materials in order to produce a balanced range of items in the handicraft concerned.

f) The historical development of the craft and perhaps regional or national variations, or a knowledge of related crafts.

g) An opportunity to display finished items should be found at least once during the period of participation.

h) For the more advanced it is important that they have the opportunity to design, plan and produce their own product without relying on others.

i) Instruction should be given in the safe use of glues and precautions required when working with other materials where face masks or good ventilation may be required.

Candlemaking

Great care should be taken when hot wax is being used—this should only be used when an instructor/assessor is present.

For beginners

1. Have a knowledge of materials and equipment necessary for candle making.

2. Know methods for making a simple straight candle, a twisted candle and other shapes.

3. Know the origin and use of candles and the sources of wax and types available.

4. Use a kit to make at least five candles to show to the Instructor.

5. Using improvised moulds, experiment with different colours and textures to make candles of various shapes and colours.

6. Show how to make a simple candle from start to finish.

7. Produce an illustrated loose-leaf notebook showing various uses of candles and methods of making.

For those with some knowledge

8. Display at least four different types of candles they have made using a kit and improvised moulds, e.g. twisted, ball-shaped, pear-shaped.

9. Show candles which they have made for a special occasion, e.g. to match a Birthday cake, for a Dinner Party, for a children's Christmas party table, etc.

10. Demonstrate how to make a candle from start to finish using an original idea for colour and/or texture.

11. Continue the notebook showing a wide range of miniature samples together with methods and illustrations of wider uses of candles for decorative purposes.

For the more advanced
Participants should:

12. Continue the loose-leaf notebook as in (11), showing more advanced methods such as multi-mould, imprinted and pebbled candles.

13. Display candles made using Sand, Ice, two colours and two moulds.

14. Show candles which they have carved or sculptured themselves.

15. Demonstrate a technique which you have invented.

16. Design and make at least three pairs of candles, some 25cm long, differing in shape and colour.

Corn Dollies

For beginners
Those taking part should:

1. Know something of the history of corn dollies and see a variety of traditional dollies.

2. Know:
a) What materials can be used, and when to collect them.
b) How to prepare the selected material, and how to clean, strip, and grade it.
c) How to start work by (i) using a head, with and without a core, (ii) using a core without a head, (iii) using a square cut.
d) How to carry out feeding.
e) How to increase and decrease, with and without the use of a core.
f) How to do
i) a Tail finish
ii) a dressed square cut finish
iii) a Bell end
g) How to dress and join finished work.
h) How to store material for use later, and how to temper the straw.

3. Have some knowledge of:
a) How corn is planted and grown

b) Suitable types of cereals, the best varieties of straw and other materials that can be used, e.g. rye, grasses, reeds, manmade fibres.

4. Be able to make a corn dolly, up to the standard of at least two of the following:

a) The Traditional
b) A Bell
c) The Cambridge Umbrella
d) A Rattle

5. Be able to make a flat braid (Plait) using between 4–7 straws and be able to make a dressed sheaf.

For those with some knowledge
Young people should:

6. a) Have some knowledge of the history of the corn dolly, the pagan and religious connections, and the customs of the harvest field and the harvest supper.
b) Have some knowledge of the various country and county names for the corn dolly, and some of the types of dolly associated with these names.

7. Be able to make a corn dolly, up to the standard of at least two of the following:

a) The Cross
b) The Double Twist
c) The Spider's Web
d) The Cornucopia

8. Be able to make a Buttonhole Favour, and know the reason why these were made.

9. Be able to make a corn dolly of their own design, incorporating at least three identical parts.

For the more advanced
Participants should:

10. Show some knowledge of the historical progress, up to modern times, of corn production, both in the method of planting and in harvesting.

11. Make a corn dolly, up to the standard of at least two of the following:

a) A Crown and Anchor
b) A Lantern
c) A Welsh Border Fan
d) Horseshoe and Stock
e) Mother Earth, or the Man in Armour

12. Be able to make a Rick Final or a Stack Ornament, and one of the foreign corn dollies.

13. Make either a pattern or picture in straw marquetry.

Model Construction—General Programme

There are many sorts of model making but generally speaking they fall into two types: **a**) commercially produced kits/parts, **b**) models constructed from parts made by the modeller. Models may be powered or non-powered, working models or static.

Specific programmes have been produced for some types of modelling but where there is no programme or another type of model making is being offered then the group programme given below should be used as a guideline.

a) Acquire a general knowledge of the history of the items being modelled.

b) Investigate the availability of model kits and/or published plans for making up their own models.

c) If possible join a model club or try and obtain relevant model magazines.

d) Decide in conjunction with the assessor on a project which might involve making either one or a series of models depending on size/ difficulty and whether they are using a commercially produced kit or making up the parts themselves.

e) Have a knowledge of the materials they will be using in the model.

f) **Where power models are constructed the participant should display knowledge of the type of motor used and of any necessary safety precautions.**

g) **Instruction should be given in the use of sharp cutting tools and precautions necessary when using glues or working with other toxic materials.**

h) Assessment should be on the basis of regular application, an increasing knowledge of the type of modelling concerned and an improvement in the quality of workmanship displayed.

Wood Carving

For beginners

Work submitted can be undertaken under the guidance of an adult.

The work should embody some of the principles mentioned below, be well constructed, of good design, correctly finished, and well suited for its particular purpose, i.e. an art form.

Those undertaking this programme should:

1. Have some knowledge of the types of wood best suited for carvings, taking into account grain and colour to suit the design.

2. Have studied carvings in exhibitions, churches, museums, and made a sketch book record of what he has seen.

3. Have a thorough knowledge of the tools used in the preparation of the block, in the actual carving, and in the finishing process, and watched an experienced woodcarver at work.

4. Submit one item only which should embody a good knowledge of design and use of various tools.

5. Submit a signed and witnessed statement with the work, stating the amount of assistance given to the participant.

For those with some knowledge

Young people should:

6. Continue the sketch book to include carvings from different periods.

7. Submit work made individually and to the participant's own design, embodying a higher standard of design and workmanship and finish, and making use of a free choice of design and expression.

8. Submit a signed and witnessed statement that the work has been completed entirely by the participant.

For the more advanced

Those taking part should:

9. Continue with the sketch book including well known carvings of different cultures.

10. Design at least two pieces of work which are different in expression, one from the other, i.e. the first piece of work could be of a formal nature, e.g. a wild animal, whilst the second piece could be an art form in contemporary design.

11. Submit practical work and drawings and sketches of an exceptionally high design, construction and finish.

12. Submit a statement that the work is entirely that of the participant.

Basketry (Canework)

Introduction
This activity should include as much practical work as possible, preferably undertaken with others through a group or club. Practical application in learning the basic skills, right choice of materials etc. is of primary importance in this programme. It is hoped that young people will be encouraged to be creative in making their own designs, especially at the more advanced stages.

The social and cultural significance and historical aspects of Basketry are to be studied.

For assessment, each individual is to produce evidence of regular application to the activity over the required period, which may be in the form of a certificate of attendance at instruction classes finished articles, notebook or log.

General
1. Throughout young people should show a knowledge of:

a) History of Canework.
b) Sources of cane, recognition of different types, gauges, grades and qualities.
c) Method of manipulation, storage and preparation for use.
d) The tools of the craft.
e) Borders—Foot, Trac, Scalloped, Plaited (3 and 5 stroke), Plain (3 and 4 rod), and Follow on Trac and Back Trac.

2. Participants should make models incorporating the basic skills and leading to an understanding of the following terms: Stakes, Bye Stakes, Upsetting (including the step up), Randing (even and uneven number of holes), Waling, Pairing, Fitching, Methods of Joining and Slewing.

For beginners
Young people should work the following on wooden bases:

1. Plant pot holder.
2. Teapot stand.
3. Wastepater basket.
4. Oblong or oval tray with plaited border.
5. Set of mats (woven cane bases).
6. Small shopping basket (woven cane base).

For those with some knowledge
Young people should work the following on cane bases:

7. Hanging flower basket.
8. Wine bottle cradle.
9. Fruit or bread roll basket.
10. Oval shopping basket.
11. Trellis basketry—various on cane base.
12. Item of their own choice.

For the more advanced
Those taking part should work *four* of the first *five* items and item 18.

13. Linen basket.
14. Oblong picnic basket.
15. Baby's carry-cot.
16. Firescreen.
17. Drink set holder—6 sections and handle.
18. Item of their own choice.

Note: If a frame is used for more advanced work, it should be designed and made by the individual. **No** work should be done by the more advanced on wooden (non-cane) bases.

LIFE SKILLS

Entertaining/Independence/Money Matters/Consumer Affairs/
Personality and Appearance/Home Studies/Furnishing and
Decorating/Democracy and Politics/Young Enterprise

Introduction

**These programmes are designed to give an opportunity for
closer work with young people on a group basis. This does
not preclude participants from following them as individuals and the programmes lend themselves ideally to a
structured course which may be followed by individual
studies or surveys to complete the time requirement.**

**Each programme contains a variety of ideas for continued
study. At all stages, participants are expected to undertake
projects in theory or practice on aspects which are of
personal interest to them and are capable of assessment.**

**The programme can be tackled as a series of visits away
from the group environment; as a way to introduce skilled
adults into the group or to the individual; or by a
combination of both. The sessions can be spread over the
whole of the required period with time for individual or
group project work, or by starting with a structured course
and then specialising in certain aspects of the programme.**

**Many of the programmes are complementary and there is
no reason why topics from more than one should not be
combined to produce an individual programme. Independence,
Money Matters and Consumer Affairs are three programmes
which may, for example, be combined to produce an alternative programme.**

Consumer Affairs

(See also Introduction above)

General

To develop skills with which to reach sensible decisions when choosing
goods or services, the emphasis here being on thinking processes. To
offer, through guided practical experience, opportunities to apply
consumer thinking processes to particular situations and to foster
awareness of the consequences of consumer decision-making processes
for individuals themselves and for others (including "society" and "the
environment").

For beginners

1. Choosing goods or services.

2. Studying selling methods including all kinds of advertising (sponsorships, direct mail etc.) drawing attention to the strong and the weak points of individual items.

3. Understanding product marking.

4. Comparing prices (inc. "bargain" offers) best buys etc., shopping basket comparison.

5. Taking care of money (saving, investing, borrowing).

6. Studying provision of one local public service e.g. buses, sheltered housing, school meals.

For those with some knowledge

7. Comparing products (performance, safety, etc.).

8. Following instructions analysing them in plain language.

9. Studying how one part of retail service works, direct mail, neighbourhood shops, supermarkets.

10. Finding out about one public service (e.g. housing, transport).

11. Finding out where to get consumer advice and further information.

For the More Advanced

12. Work of a Trading Standards Inspector, fair and unfair contracts (e.g. hire purchase agreements, package holiday terms, insurance proposals forms) and saying in which ways they are "fair" and "unfair" to the consumer.

13. Codes of practice, British Standards.

14. Consumer protection organisations and the range of work done.

15. Faulty goods, remedies and redress.

16. Finding how much it costs to buy particular products and different types of borrowing, showing in a table the "gain" and "losses" resulting from each method.

17. Study sponsorship by advertisers of some sport and assess the pros and cons.

Note: Learning may take shape through: Preparation of written reports, arranging displays/exhibitions, interview work/questionnaires, diaries/recordings, artwork, drama/role playing, and visits.

National Consumer Council

Personality and Appearance

(See also Introduction on page 190)

For beginners

1. Care of the face: cleansing, nourishing, treating and hiding blemishes, make-up. Dental care.

2. Personal freshness, healthy diet, exercise, depilatories.

3. Clothes—choice, fabrics, care, buying, colour, foundations, shapes to suit.

4. Hair care: washing, setting, ways to maintain healthy hair and scalp.

5. Manicure and pedicure.

6. Deportment and poise. Language.

7. A look at beauty in other ethnic groups.

For those with some knowledge

8. Face masks, steam treatments and other aids to problem skins.

9. Beauty salons—services they provide and home methods. Weight and diet, body building exercises.

10. Styles of clothes for different occasions, separates, mix and match, self-made, styles for figures. Catalogue buying, costs and quality.

11. Hair styles to suit; rinses, highlights, problem hair. Beards and moustaches—growing and trimming.

12. Shoe fashions and materials used. Foot problems, avoidance and treatment. Chiropodists. Exercises and other corrective devices.

13. Conversation and being at ease with others.

14. A look at fashions in other ethnic groups.

For the more advanced

15. Composition of make-ups and other beauty treatments.

16. Specialist aids to beauty, electrolysis, dental capping, cosmetic surgery. Provisions by NHS and private treatment.

17. Stage make-up and character changes.

18. Health centres and services offered, saunas, relaxation, meditation. Nutrition deficiencies—causes, effects and remedies.

19. Fashion houses; influence of the media; mass-marketing. New clothes from old.

20. Hair cutting, perming and bleaching/colouring. Transplants and wigs.

21. Confidence at interviews; giving votes of thanks and short speeches.

22. Social customs in other ethnic groups.

23. Equality of the sexes.

Home Studies

(See also Introduction on page 190)

For beginners
1. Decorating: preparation, painting, papering, estimating.

2. Electrics: plug wiring, safety, fuses, meter checking.

3. Plumbing: washers, leaks, mains supply. Emergency procedures.

4. Construction: shelves, glues and repairs.

5. Garden planning: care of indoor plants.

6. New from old—items from junk shops and jumble sales.

7. Visits to Do-It-Yourself shops and show house.

8. Preservation of family treasures, old photos.

For those with some knowledge
9. Simple wiring (lights), extension cables, ratings.

10. House repairs; cracked ceilings, wood rot, window glazing.

11. Improvements; plastering, skirtings, cornices, doors. Built-in furniture.

12. Plumbing problems: blocked wastes, ball valves, soakaways, cisterns. Central heating flow diagrams and simple maintenance.

13. Second-hand furniture: what to look for and how to renovate.

14. In the garden: patios, play-areas and ponds. Visit show houses, exhibitions, public and private gardens.

15. Ways of preserving local environment.

For the more advanced

16. Ring mains and spurs, extra lighting, rewiring. Regulations.

17. Grants for home improvements.

18. Regulations for new work—wiring, plumbing, building, extending.

19. Wall tiling, ceiling papering and tiling.

20. Making rooms larger or smaller: stud partitioning, removing walls. Creating an illusion of space: use of mirrors, screens, colour.

21. Second-hand appliances; cookers, washing machines, etc.—repairs and safety.

22. Tools for the job.

23. Outside work: concreting, bricklaying, re-pointing, slating, constructing garden furniture, sheds.

24. Improving local amenities; creating community centres; preserving historic buildings by old craft methods. Preservation orders. International conservation projects.

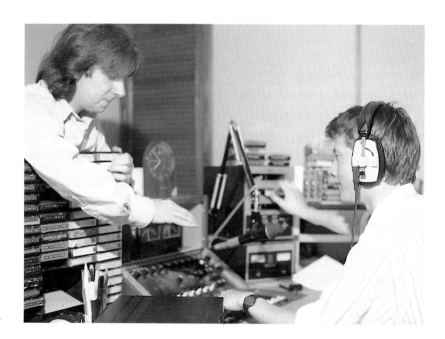

S K I L L S

MUSIC

General/Classical Guitar/Jazz/Pan Playing—(Steel Bands)/Wind Instruments/Buglers and Trumpeters/Campanology/Choirs—Church and Chapel/Choirs—Roman Catholic/Drummers/Handbell Ringing/ Military and Brass Bands/Military Flautists/Piping/Classical Music Appreciation/Folk Music Appreciation/Popular Music Appreciation

Introduction

Participants should have some understanding of the history and development and, where appropriate, of the social implications and consequences of the musical field of their choice. These might include such topics as the comparison and contrast of music from different countries or different periods, or an evaluation of the part played by music in times of crisis.

For assessment, each individual is to produce evidence of regular application to the interest over the required period.

Participants can choose from the following:

a) Play an instrument either solo or in a group or band.

b) Sing either solo or in a group choir.

c) Study a type of music, look at the life of a composer, musician or singer, or study the development of a musical instrument.

Note: Making a musical instrument or repairing them would be included in the Crafts—General group of programmes.

Playing a musical instrument

For beginners

1. Young people should choose one instrument to study. They may concentrate on one of the following sections:

Classical   Jazz   Folk   Popular   Military

or may select pieces from each of these types of music.

2. Having chosen the instrument and type of music to be studied, participants should ask a qualified teacher of the instrument to suggest an appropriate programme of study. Specific examples of possible programmes are available as listed under the heading "Music".

195

For those with some knowledge
3. At this level, participants should have some ability to read music at sight.

4. Those taking part should show competence in playing the instrument of their choice. If learning to play an instrument as part of a musical group, club band or orchestra, they should also play regularly as members.

For the more advanced
5. At this level, participants should have a good ability to read music at sight.

6. Those taking part should show further competence in playing the instrument of their choice, preferably in more than one type of music.

7. Study the development of a particular type of music, e.g. jazz, national music played on rare instruments, etc.

8. Play regularly as part of a musical group, club band or orchestra.

9. If playing a percussion instrument, show competence to follow their part from a musical notation and perform on any type of such instruments.

Singing in a group
(See also Introduction on page 195)

For beginners
1. Young people should be regular members of a singing group. They should be able to sing, hum or whistle a short musical piece at sight.

For those with some knowledge
2. At this level, participants should have some ability to read music at sight.

3. Those taking part should be regular members of a part-singing group. Specific examples of possible programmes for group singing are given in Choirs—Church and Chapel and Choirs—Roman Catholic.

4. Be able to sing three songs solo to a standard to satisfy the assessor. Each song should be chosen from a different type of music.

For the more advanced
5. At this level participants should have a good ability to read music at sight.

6. Continue as a regular member of a singing group.

7. Take part in a musical dramatic show or performance of a major work.

Solo Singing

(See also Introduction on page 195)

For beginners
1. Individuals should satisfy an assessor that they can sing three songs, each chosen from a different type of music. The types suggested are folk music, jazz, popular music, light music, or the standard repertoires.

2. Give evidence of regular and continued practice.

For those with some knowledge
3. At this level, participants should have some ability to read music at sight.

4. Young people should satisfy an assessor that they can sing a further three songs chosen from different types of music as in item **1**.

5. Give evidence of further regular and continued practice.

For the more advanced
6. At this level, participants should have a good ability to read music at sight.

7. Young people should satisfy an assessor that they can sing a further four songs chosen from different types of music as in item **1**.

8. Give evidence of further regular and continued practice.

Classical Guitar

(See also Introduction on page 195)

For beginners
Young people should:

1. Be able to prepare and tune the guitar to correct pitch and know the elementary care required for the instrument.

2. Play one piece from *The Guitarist's Hour Book 1* (Catalogue No. GA 19), either from memory or from the music. This should be a complete and rhythmic performance.

3. Play one piece from *25 Easy Sonatas* Op.80—Kuffner (Catalogue No. GA 7).

4. Play any major scale from memory to the extent of one octave, up and down, using open strings and stopped notes. Play three arpeggio patterns for the right hand on any major or minor chord.

5. Name two major keys and give their key signatures.

6. Sight-read a simple piece, not more than four bars long written in crotchets and quavers in the first position.

For those with some knowledge
Young people should be able to:

7. Play two pieces in different keys, either from memory or from the music from *24 Short Pieces* Op. 21—Carcassi (Catalogue No. GA 6). This should be a complete and rhythmic performance.

8. Play two pieces in different keys, either from memory or from the music from *A Classical Album for Guitar Solo*—John Gavall (Oxford University Press).

9. Play two major scales in different keys to the extent of two octaves, up and down, using only stopped notes. Play six arpeggio patterns for the right hand on any major or minor chord.

10. Name four major keys and give their key signatures.

11. Sight-read an easy piece not more than eight bars long.

For the more advanced
Young people taking this programme should:

12. Play two pieces in different keys from memory from *Guitar Method Part III*—Carcassi (Catalogue No. GA 1C). This must be a complete and rhythmic performance.

13. Play two pieces in different keys from memory from *Easy Pieces from Shakespeare's Time*—ed. Karl Scheit (Universal Edition).

14. Play two major and two minor scales in different keys to the extent of two octaves up and down, using only stopped notes.

15. Name two major and minor keys and give their key signatures.

16. Sight-read a moderate piece not more than eight bars long.

Note: All the music mentioned can be obtained from Schott & Co Ltd 48 Great Marlborough Street, London W.1.

Pan-Playing—(Steel Bands)

(See also Introduction on page 195)

For beginners
Those taking part should:

1. Draw a scale-chart of their pan (or set of pans) and write the names of all notes on the appropriate segments.

2. Play the chromatic scales as well as the major and minor (harmonic) scales of C, F and G, and their arpeggios.

3. Play the melody of five tunes of different rhythms and tempi, including at least one calypso, a current hit (non-calypso) and an excerpt from a classical composition.

4. Give a brief account of the history of the Steel Band movement in the Caribbean Islands.

For those with some knowledge
Those taking this programme should:

5. Play all major and minor scales and their arpeggios.

6. Read at sight or improvise on a given melody. Play a chord accompaniment for a given melody. Play a bass line for a given melody on either the cello, tenor-bass or five bass.

7. Describe the instruments in a local steel Band, and discuss their use in the steel orchestra as well as in other combinations.

For the more advanced
Young people should:

8. Prepare and rehearse for audition, an arrangement of at least four minutes for a steelband of at least six pieces, e.g. two tenors, one double 2nd or double-tenor, one guitar, one cello, one tenor-bass or five bass. Brake-hubs and other percussion instruments may be added.

9. Know the general principles of keyboard harmony, the whole-tone scales, the diminished scales and the modes.

10. Play at sight or improvise on three tunes in different keys chosen by the assessor.

11. Make a detailed study of playing and the future of the pan or pans as musical instruments.

NATURE AND PETS

Agriculture/Aquarium Keeping/Dogs—Training and Handling/
Gardening/Keeping of Pets/Ornithology/Horses—Handling and
Care/Bee-keeping/Budgerigars and Canaries/Cacti Growing/
Forestry/Orchid Growing/Pigeons/Pigs/Plant Study/Poultry/Sheep

Introduction

These activities should include as much practical work as
possible, preferably undertaken with others through a group
or club. The social aspects of the chosen programme should
be covered in group discussion and, where appropriate, the
social implications of food production and of aesthetics should
be included. Participants should also show some understanding of the historical development of the chosen activity and
its relevance to other groups in a worldwide society.

For assessment, each individual is to produce evidence of
regular application to the activity over the required period.
This may take the form of some kind of record, such as a
diary, log book or sketch book.

Studies of plants, birds, fish, animals or insects might well
be included in the Collections, Studies and Surveys group of
programmes. See pages 152 to 153 for further information.

Keeping animals larger than small pets but without specific
programmes is possible; however approval should be obtained
before commencing the activity as outlined on page 147.

Note: Participants should be aware of health hazards from
pesticides and animal diseases as appropriate to the programme being followed.

Gardening

(See also Introduction above)

General

Wherever possible, young people should follow this activity in a
group. At all stages they should understand the progression from
raising food as a necessity to gardening as a leisure pursuit, e.g.
keeping window boxes in urban areas.

For beginners

1. Maintain a plot for at least six consecutive months, and cultivate at least one indoor plant.

2. Raise several garden plants and/or flowers from any *three* of the following groups:

a) Bulbs in bowls.   **b**) Shrubs   **c**) Vegetables.
d) Bedding plants.   **e**) Herbaceous plants.
f) Fruit bushes or trees (tomatoes are included).

3. Carry out necessary plant propagation methods for the groups selected by any of the following methods:

a) Obtaining seeds or bulbs.   **b**) Preparing cuttings.
c) Division.   **d**) Budding.

4. Thin out seedlings, transplant into pots or boxes with a suitable compost, or in the open ground depending upon the groups selected.

5. Carry out any subsequent cultural requirements, such as staking, stopping, watering, manuring and pest disease control.

6. Keep a diary of all gardening activities.

7. Have a knowledge of the conditions necessary for normal healthy plant growth, such as plant nutrients, light, temperature and water. Young people should acquire such knowledge when carrying out the practical work and should note any findings in the record log.

For those with some knowledge

8. Cultivate a piece of ground over six months so that it gives vegetables or flowers for nine months of the year, and so that the crops mature and are removed in an orderly way, thus making preparation of the ground for the next crops as easy as possible.

9. Either

a) Select several types of plant, and raise a number of them to be used for a gardening feature such as an ornamental flower bed, window box, tub, or hanging basket.

or

b) Raise several vegetables and exhibit them at a local flower and vegetable show.

10. Raise a number of house plants from cuttings, and plant together in a suitable container.

11. Visit a nursery or propagation department of a local park. Note the various methods of plant propagation employed either in the open or under glass.

12. Prepare display panels, using imaginative methods of illustration, about **one** of the following:

a) Unusual propagation methods.   **b**) Climbing plants.
c) The greenhouse and its uses.   **d**) Seeds and potting composts.
e) Garden tools and their uses.   **f**) Gardening skills.
g) Indoor plants.

13. Keep records of practical work undertaken and visits made.

14. Study Health in the Garden—Importance of thorough cultivation and weeding, helpful and harmful pests; garden troubles and their recognition.

15. Study flower groups—Annuals, Biennials and Perennials.

For the more advanced
16. Undertake any **three** of the following assignments:

a) Pruning top and soft fruit.

b) Pruning ornamental trees and shrubs.

c) Propagation of new plants from old in three different ways.

d) At least one original plant experiment.

e) The raising of one specific flower or vegetable crop, e.g. sweet peas, chrysanthemums or dahlias, runner beans, celery, etc.

f) Demonstration of three gardening skills, e.g. potting, pricking out, air-layering.

17. Make a compost heap.

18. Visit a botanical garden or horticultural experimental station and discover the main spheres of work.

19. Carry out **one** of the following:

a) Design a small town garden and make a model (excluding vegetables).

b) Design a garden, including vegetables and fruit.

c) Study the principles of rock, water or roof gardens, and draw suitable designs.

d) Construct a small rock garden or miniature indoor garden.

e) An individual plant study, e.g. roses, the history of the apple, etc.

f) Design and propagate and plant a small herb garden or border.

g) Raise several recommended lawn grass mixtures from seed in boxes and note any differences, e.g. rate of germination, etc. The resulting turves should be labelled appropriately.

20. Try to visit at least one flower show or botanical garden.

21. Keep records of practical work and visits.

22. Understand the properties and uses of nitrogen, phosphates, potash fertilisers, organic manures and compost. Know the uses of potting and seed composts.

23. Compile a list of gardening terms.

Keeping of Pets—(Small mammals)

(See also Introduction on page 200)

General

Young people must recognise that in keeping an animal they undertake responsibility for its well-being, both mental and physical. It is essential, too, that before acquiring an animal they gain sufficient knowledge to look after it properly and to ensure that it does not suffer in any way. Whenever possible, young people should undertake this activity in a group.

For beginners

Young people should:

1. Be able to show that they have read about the proposed breed of pet **before** obtaining it.

2. Have some knowledge as to how to select sound works of reference relating to pet-keeping in general.

3. Show that proper care has been taken in respect of buying the pet; know how to tell whether a breeder, dealer, or pet store maintains hygienic premises and cages, and where reliable information on these points can be obtained locally; know what special points are considered important in choosing the animal or animals in question.

4. Understand the reasons for strict cleanliness in cages, and explain the ways in which they are constructed to suit certain species.

5. Look after the pet (or pets) for the time the activity is followed.

6. Know the correct diet and rules for feeding throughout the year.

7. Understand how a suitable cage should look and be constructed.

8. Know the correct way to handle the pet and have some knowledge of why any particular method is necessary.

9. Keep a written record of the habits, welfare and progress of the pet during the required time.

For those with some knowledge

Young people taking this programme should:

10. Have some knowledge of the varieties or breeds of the pet in question and their advantages and disadvantages as pets.

11. Know the correct way to sex the animals; how to plan and, if necessary, organise the mating; the gestation period; precautions to be taken at birth; duration of suckling and when to take the young away from the parents.

12. Have bred from a pair successfully.

13. Know how to groom or otherwise prepare the animals for exhibitions.

14. Where possible join a club or society specialising in the pet owned. Where this is not possible, young people should endeavour to exhibit the pet and prove that they are familiar with the appropriate "show points" and normal exhibition procedure.

15. Have some knowledge of hygiene; likely ailments and how to guard against them; also of simple First Aid treatments.

16. Be well informed about local veterinary surgeons, animal clinics and boarding establishments.

17. Keep written records during the stipulated period.

For the more advanced

18. Keep a written record of any practical work undertaken.

19. Have some knowledge of the senses on which various kinds of mammal pets rely, and know how they are used in their daily life.

20. Study the reasons why certain "exotic" species are **unsuitable** for keeping as pets. They should also have some knowledge of which species of native mammals can, at times, reasonably be kept as pets, and should cultivate judgment and discrimination in this respect.

21. Have some knowledge of the basic principles involved in the conservation of wildlife, e.g. the importance of habitats, food and food chains, predators and prey. They should, if possible, visit a Nature Reserve.

22. Make several visits to a zoo (or zoos), and having read widely on the subject, make a study, which may be illustrated, of the problems of keeping animals privately compared with those running a modern menagerie.

23. Try to obtain from their local public libraries works on zoos, and on animals in captivity by such authors as Dr. H. Hediger, Philip Street, and Gerald Iles.

24. Understand the historical background to the keeping of animals for domestic use and the transition to domestic companions.

Ornithology

(See also Introduction on page 200)

Note: **Egg collecting is illegal.**

General

At all stages, those taking part should be aware of the patterns of study by group organisations.

For beginners

1. Recognition—Be able to recognise and describe the essential field characters of 20 common species, and know something about their habitats, habits, food and nests. Suggested supplementary activities are: a feather collection, a scrap-book of press cuttings and photographs, etc. of birds (with comments on any features of special interest), or the construction of a bird-table and nestboxes.

2. Fieldwork

a) Keep a diary or field note-book.

b) Make at least one visit to some place of special ornithological interest, recording the results in a diary.

c) Make more detailed observations on the bird life of a particular area (e.g. garden, park, school grounds, wood).

For those with some knowledge

3. Structure—Have a good knowledge of the external features of a bird, including the main feather tracts.

4. Recognition—Be able to identify at least 50 species, and know something of their habitats, habits, food, nests and distribution in Britain.

5. Systematics—Candidates should extend their knowledge of the structure of the more important families of British birds (especially wing, tail, tarsus, bill), so as to be able to relate their form to adaptations for different ways of life, and to compare the major groups with one another.

6. Fieldwork—Keep a diary and field note-book, and embark on a more intensive study of a single species, making notes on, e.g. its song-period, feeding behaviour, movements, habitat-preferences.

7. Migration—One not too advanced book on the subject should be studied. Fieldwork should include the recording of arrival and departure dates of migrants, and of any "visible migration" and hard-weather movements that can be observed. A local reservoir or sewage farm might be especially suitable for this purpose.

8. Protection—Have a basic knowledge of the Protection of Birds Acts.

For the more advanced
9. Structure—Have a detailed knowledge of the external features of birds, and a basic knowledge of moult; and understanding of how the bird's wing functions; an elementary knowledge of the bird's internal anatomy (especially blood systems, digestive system, air sacs, gonads).

10. Recognition—Be thoroughly familiar with all the usual habits of the home area, including their songs and calls.

11. Systematics—In addition to the requirements for those with some knowledge, have a more detailed knowledge of the systematics of one species or genus, which should be based at least partly on a study of museum specimens.

12. Fieldwork
Either

a) If possible, take part in some national enquiry, e.g. census of a single species, nest record scheme, ringing;
or
b) Undertake a census by the mapping method of an area which might produce results of interest to conservation, e.g. gravel-pit, closed railway-line, industrial waste ground;
or
c) Keep up a study of a single species of own choosing, taking it further than is necessary for those with some knowledge. Produce a written "paper" describing some aspects of the fieldwork carried out for this stage.

13. Migration—There should be some understanding of the sociological implications of migration.

14. History—There should be some understanding of bird training as a cultural pursuit.

If possible, take an active part in a school or local society, or attend a Young Ornithologists' Club field course.

The Royal Society for the Protection of Birds, The British Trust for Ornithology.

NEEDLECRAFTS

Dressmaking/Embroidery/Knitting/Soft Toy Making/Canvas Work
(Tapestry)/Crocheting/Dressing Dolls in National Costume/
Filography/Glove Making/Leatherwork/Macramé/Patchwork/
Pillow Lace Making/Quilting/Rug Making/Soft Furnishing/Tatting/
Weaving and Spinning.

Introduction

**These activities should include as much practical work as
possible, preferably undertaken with others through a group
or club. The essence of these programmes is the practical
application in learning the basic skills, stitches and right
choice of materials. It is also hoped that young people will
be encouraged to be creative in making their own designs,
patterns and colour schemes, especially at the more advanced
stages.**

**These activities also lend themselves to some study of their
social and cultural significance and historical background.**

**For assessment, each individual is to produce evidence of
regular application to the activity over the required period
with examples of finished work.**

General Programme

The following guidelines should be used to draw up a programme
for a needlecraft that does not have a particular programme listed,
but which a participant wishes to follow. Before embarking on this
programme it should be approved by the participant's Operating
Authority.

Any needlecraft programme should include:

a) A knowledge of processes and stitches.

b) A knowledge of the type/variations of materials.

c) The making of items or samples.

d) A record of items made and processes learnt.

e) An opportunity to display samples, items should be found during
the period of participation.

f) Some knowledge of the history of the craft and its development
should be shown.

Dressmaking

(See also Introduction on page 208)

General

At all stages young people should be encouraged to make and adapt their own patterns; those with artistic flair might design the garments they make, and learn some of the processes of dress-design.

For beginners

1. During the stipulated period participants should make at least two garments. The emphasis should be on suitability of style and material and on the good finish of the garment. They should show a variety of processes and include at least *six* of the following:

a) Darts or gathers.   **b**) Pleats.   **c**) Set-in sleeves.

d) Collar.   **e**) Button and buttonhole.   **f**) Zip fastening.

g) Opening with snap fasteners or hooks and eyes.

h) Belt with fastening.   **i**) Waistband.

j) Crossway binding or facing.

There should be both hand and machine sewing included. The garments should be well neatened to give durability.

2. Where practicable the garments should be worn at assessment to show suitability and fit.

3. A folder should be made to give the following information:

a) Participants own measurements required for dressmaking.

b) Figure type with a short explanation of good or bad points.

c) Colouring.

d) A collection of pictures of garments which would look attractive on the owner or which are suitable for all occasions.

For those with some knowledge

4. Young people should be able to use correctly the more "difficult" materials, e.g. wool, nylon, rayon, knitted fabrics such as Courtelle.

5. During the stipulated period it should be possible to make at least two well-finished garments which should be different from each other, e.g. a woollen dress and a nylon nightdress.

6. Participants should, wherever possible, bring the pattern with the garments made and be prepared to discuss the method used and any special points of interest or difficulty during the making.

7. A folder should be made to contain the following information:

a) Picture of a complete outfit for participant for winter and summer, giving prices, possibly showing differences in cost between garments made by the participant and those ready-made.

b) A collection of samples of materials used giving prices, widths and suggestions for suitable garments.

For the more advanced
8. Those with experience and knowledge of dressmaking already will probably wish to specialise in one type of dressmaking. Emphasis should be on good style, fit and finish. At least two garments should be made, one of which should be shown worn by the person for whom it was made. Garments should be from two of the following groups:

a) Beachwear, including attractive accessories, e.g. beach bag.

b) Children's wear including hand or machine embroidery.

c) Lingerie including hand or machine embroidery.

d) Soft tailoring, e.g. jumper suits, slacks, jackets.

e) Costumes for drama productions (style, fit and quality of work are the important points).

9. A folder should be produced giving all details and costing of the garments made. It should include details of new work attempted (using sewing machine attachments, using belt or button making aids, etc.) describing how these are done and showing samples as suitable.

Knitting

(See also Introduction on page 208)

For beginners

1. It should be possible to produce at least two knitted garments during the period of the interest. These should show wise choice of pattern and materials which are both suitable and attractive, and which will show good knitting. One garment should be made in two-, three- or four-ply wool, e.g. jumper, baby clothes, socks, etc. The other garment should be made of thicker wool, e.g. double knitting, poodle or mohair wool. In each case the pattern should be suitable and the garment finished to wear well, and the assessor will look for good knitting which should include increasing and decreasing, buttonholes, picked up stitches, ribbing and a fancy pattern.

2. Young people should be prepared to discuss the making of the garments with the assessor and to demonstrate any of the following:

a) Checking tension.

b) Casting on by two different methods.

c) Increasing and decreasing by two different methods.

3. They might also produce a loose-leaf notebook showing samples of stiches and methods.

For those with some knowledge

4. Young people should show how they have developed the interest over the stipulated period. They should have done some experimenting with different types of wools and be prepared to discuss with the assessor the new ideas they have had.

5. At least two garments should be shown. One should be chosen from the following:

a) Fairisle knitting.

b) Four-needle knitting.

c) Tailored garment including pockets.

d) Two-ply knitting.

A good standard of finish is expected.

For the more advanced

6. The emphasis should be on interesting and experimental work and on good style, workmanship and finish. Two garments should be made from the following:

a) A complicated or traditional pattern, for example baby's shawl in two-ply.

b) Tailored knitted dress, suit or waistcoat.

c) A garment made with a knitting machine (if possible including a pattern).

d) A piece of community knitting organised by participant who should make up the completed article, e.g. a knitted blanket.

Similar alternatives may be added but these should be discussed with the assessor before starting the work.

Soft Toy Making

(See also Introduction on page 208)

At all stages safety should be considered i.e. no glass eyes, wire or other possibly dangerous materials should be used.

For beginners
Those starting this programme should:

1. Make a simple felt toy or a felt ball.

2. Turn two or more felt balls into a child's toy or make a knitted toy.

3. Make another toy of their own choice, or a glove toy.

4. Construct a toy by covering tins, boxes, lollipop sticks, cotton reels, etc. with felt.

For those with some knowledge
During the stipulated period young people should:

5. Make a washable toy suitable for a baby.

6. Make not less than three toys to represent a family of people or animals, or characters in a fable or nursery story, or to present a scene. Dress need not be removable, and embroidery may be used on the toys if desired.

For the more advanced
Participants should show a very high level of skill and finish and should:

7. Make a jointed toy.

8. Make a standing toy.

9. Make a rag doll with removable clothes.

RECREATIVE SKILLS

Chess/Fishing/Marksmanship/Table & Indoor Games/Air Pistol Shooting/Air Rifle Shooting/Athletics Officiating/Billiards and Snooker/Bridge/Clay Pigeon Shooting/Fly Fishing/ Fly Tying/Rifle Shooting (Cadets)/Umpiring and Refereeing/Fantasy Games/ Ceremonial Drill/Darts.

Introduction

Wherever possible, those choosing these activities should join a club which is properly constituted and affiliated, directly or indirectly to the national body governing the activity. Where appropriate, the participant should be knowledgeable about the equipment used and its care and maintenance, about the rules and scoring for the games concerned, about the historical and social aspects of the activity and about the organisation and work of the governing body at national and local levels.

For assessment, each individual is to produce evidence of regular application to the activity over the required period, which may take the form of club membership, attendance record, results achieved, diary or log, but should not be solely on the standards of skill attained.

Billiards, Snooker and Pool

Introduction

This activity should be undertaken in clubs affiliated to the Billiards and Snooker Control Council or in equivalent conditions in the participant's youth organisation or club. For the latter, affiliation to the Council is strongly advised.

Participants can only pursue this activity at the discretion of their Operating Authorities who should satisfy themselves that the environment in which the young person will pursue this activity is suitable.

Where appropriate, the participant should be knowledgeable about the equipment used and its care and maintenance, about the rules and scoring for the games concerned, about the historical and social aspects of the activity and about the organisation and the work of the appropriate governing body at national and local levels.

For assessment, each individual is to produce evidence of regular application to the activity over the required period, which may take the form of club membership, attendance record, results achieved, diary or log, but should not be solely on the standards of skill attained.

For beginners
Those starting this activity should:

1. Join and attend regularly over the required period an approved billiards, snooker or pool club, or play in equivalent conditions in their youth organisation or club.

2. Be conversant with the rules, and the spotting of the balls before and during play.

3. Be able to use a correct cue action, bridge and stance.

4. Know the methods of scoring, and appreciate the methods of break building in all three games.

5. Know the value of any shot; together with knowing foul strokes and the respective penalties.

6. Know the use of equipment other than their personal cue.

7. Be able to act as marker for any game, or frame.

8. Practice as much as possible and learn by **watching** more skilful players.

For those with some knowledge
Young people should:

9. Know the value of cushion angles for making cannons; making or defeating snookers.

10. Know the value of "side", "bottom", or "top" for the execution of different strokes.

11. Know the effect of playing with, or against the nap of the cloth.

12. Be learning cue-ball control, and the chief principles of break building.

13. Know how to care for their cue, and cue-tip; and know how to re-tip.

14. Know how to brush and iron a billiard or pool table correctly.

15. Study the duties of a referee.

16. Continue practice, and join in competitive individual and team games.

For the more advanced
Those taking part should:

17. Be a member of their Club team, or an entrant in individual competitive games.

18. Be able to referee any game, or frame, with confidence in their knowledge of the Rules.

19. Be, if not a player, an active member of the committee organising games and competitions.

20. Be able to give instructions to younger members.

21. Keep up to date with matters relevant to all three games.

Books for reference
Official Handbook and Rules

The Rules of Snooker booklet
The Rules of Billiards booklet

Know the Game Series—E.P. Publications
Billiards and Snooker
Pool

Understanding Billiards and Snooker
Jack Karneham—Pelham

Fishing

(See also Introduction on page 213)

Care should be taken at all times when using lead weights

For beginners
Those taking part should have a knowledge of:

1. Fishing to be found locally (Game, Course, Sea).

2. Methods of fishing these local waters, e.g. fly fishing, spinning, long trotting, worming, etc. Practical experience in these methods.

3. Elementary knowledge of any one of the different types found in these islands, e.g.

a) Game—Trout—Sea Trout—Salmon.

b) Coarse—Perch—Roach—Tench—Pike—Bream.

c) Sea—Bass—Mackerel—Shark.

4. Selection of tackle, e.g. what type of rod to use with which reel and line.

5. Basic ideas of rod-building: glass fibre and carbon fibre, cane; if possible the assembly of a rod kit.

6. Close seasons.

7. Practical work. As much fishing as possible.

8. Elementary knots.

9. Keep a diary and general notebook.

For those with some knowledge
10. Types of fishing to be found in the British Isles, Where to look for each type. What species a certain type of water is likely to yield.

11. Game, Coarse, or Sea Fishing.

12. Methods of fishing, e.g. fly fishing, spinning, long trotting, etc. Practical experience in these methods.

13. Baits. Which bait to use. When, where and how. Legal and illegal baits. Weather conditions.

14. Tackle. What type of tackle to use for different fish and conditions. Selection of rod, reels and lines.

15. Close seasons for the different fish in various parts of the British Isles.

16. Different methods of rod construction used today, e.g. glass and carbon fibre, cane, etc. Materials used in rod making and why. Differences between rods for fly fishing and spinning.

17. Fish breeding, hatchery work, maintenance of stock, etc.

18. Those taking part should gain as much practical experience as possible, both in actual fishing and tackle maintenance and making.

For the more advanced
19. Have a knowledge of game fishing of the world. Distribution; species; methods of catching.

20. Have a more detailed knowledge of British fish and fishing than required for those with some knowledge.

21. Do more practical work in spinning, fly fishing, coarse fishing. How to improve their style and technique. (Specialisation in one or two of the above). Using tournament techniques in practical fishing, e.g. double-haul in long fly-casting. Correct choice of balanced outfit.

22. Do more work in the following fields:

a) Game Fishing.   **b**) Sea Fishing.   **c**) Coarse Fishing.

23. Have a knowledge of more difficult ideas concerning rod building. Preferably build either a glass fibre or carbon fibre rod, but a rod of more advanced type than that made for those with some knowledge. Some idea of what goes into the design of a rod—type, weight, action, material, etc. Care of rods.

24. Have a knowledge of fish culture. Pollution—prevention of.

25. Have a knowledge of reel and line design. Choice of reel, use of centre pin, fixed spool or multiplier. Lines, care and choice for different types of fishing. Type of line to use and why.

National Anglers' Council.

Table/Indoor Games

(other than those listed in the Physical Recreation Section)

General Guidelines

Specific programmes have been produced for some of these topics but where there is no programme, or another related skill is being offered the group programme given below or a programme for a similar skill should be used as a guideline:

a) Whenever possible these activities should be undertaken through a properly organised society, youth club or some other recognised grouping.

b) Where appropriate the participant should be knowledgeable on the use and care of equipment.

c) A thorough knowledge of the rules and ability to score properly.

d) A knowledge of the background of the game, i.e. its origin and development.

e) Knowledge of tactics and conventions.

f) Keep a record of games played and scores appropriate.

g) Assessment should be made on the basis of regular participation, a thorough knowledge of the rules and an improved standard of play.

Because of the wide range of activities included in this group of programmes it is impossible to provide further general programme guidelines. Participants and instructors should read the introduction on page 213 carefully before drawing up any suggested programme.

TRANSPORTATION

Aircraft Recognition/Aeronautics/Boatwork/Motor Cars — Driving/ Motor Cycles and Mopeds—Riding/Railway Affairs/Astronautics/ Coastal Navigation/Gliding/Karting/Motor Sport (Competitions, Racing, Scrambling and Trials)/Power Boating/Ship Recognition/ Flying.

Introduction

These programmes contain certain safety requirements, indicated in bold type, which must be followed.

Those following water activities must either hold an A.S.A. Personal Survival qualification or be able to swim 50 metres in clothing appropriate to the activity. They should be familiar with RoSPA leaflet *On the Water, In the Water*. They must be able to fit a lifejacket of BSI specification which must always be worn when on the water.

Age

A person under 16 years of age cannot by law be in possession of a driving licence of any kind. Participants should therefore not start driving or riding programmes unless they will reach the age at which they are legally permitted to hold a provisional driving licence to ride a motor cycle or moped or to drive a car at least one month before the completion of the course of instruction, even when practice can be obtained by riding/driving on private ground. It is strongly recommended that they should have supervised training.

The law states that persons under 16 years may not fly solo. People under this age may join clubs and fly gliders dual.

Insurance

Those responsible for young people pursuing such activities should ensure that adequate insurance cover is provided whilst carrying out Award Scheme activities.

Assessment

For assessment, each individual is to produce evidence of regular application to the skill over the required period. This may take the form of a certificate of attendance at instruction classes, a notebook, diary or log or other similar means.

General

Participants should give thought to the social and environmental implications of motorised transport and of transport as a leisure pursuit. The evolution of transport as an economic necessity from its earliest to its present form is included as an aspect in each programme.

Its importance to other nations at different stages of development may also form useful areas of study.

Aircraft Recognition

(See also Introduction on page 218)

For beginners

Young people should:

1. Keep records of aircraft visiting local airports, including Civil, RAF and Foreign types.

2. Visit at least one air display and two other airfields.

3. Be able to recognise fifty aircraft of civil and/or military type, with at least 40/50 correct identifications Viewing time—ten seconds each.

4. Have some knowledge of the early history of flight and the pioneers of aviation. If possible, visit a museum of aviation.

For those with some knowledge

Those taking part should:

5. Keep records of aircraft visiting local airports, including Civil, RAF and foreign types.

6. Keep records of air displays and airfields visited during the stipulated period. At least two air displays and three airfields should be visited.

7. Take and log photographs of various aircraft in connection with the above visits and air displays.

8. Be able to take a similar recognition test as for beginners, with viewing time reduced to five seconds.

9. Have some understanding of the effect of aviation on economic and human life up to the present day, e.g. foreign travel for all; and of the effects of two world wars on development.

10. Appreciate environmental implications, e.g. pollution control, sound levels, airport planning and size.

For the more advanced
Young people should:

11. Keep records of Civil, RAF and Foreign types of aircraft visiting local airports.

12. Visit at least two air displays and four airfields.

13. Take and log photographs in connection with various aircraft observed at above air displays and on visits to airfields.

14. Through an Amateur Aircraft Society or Aircraft Club, fly in a club aircraft for at least ten hours and keep a log of these flying hours.

15. Have some understanding of:

a) Aesthetics of aircraft design.

b) The arms race; sale to underdeveloped countries.

c) International aviation projects.

Boatwork

(See also Introduction on page 218)

General
Those taking part must have access to, and use of, suitable craft.

For beginners
1. **Form part of a boat's crew.**

2. **Be able to tie the following knots quickly:** Reef knot; sheet bend; bowline; clove hitch; fisherman's bend; rolling hitch; round turn and two half hitches; figure-of-eights.

3. **Be able to make boat fast to moorings.**

4. Know construction and parts of various types of boats.

5. Know routine boat maintenance and assist with practical maintenance.

6. Know how to carry out simple emergency repairs to a boat's hull.

7. Have some knowledge of the early history of seafaring. If possible, visit a maritime museum.

For those with some knowledge
8. **Know basic rule of the road including sound and distress signals, courtesy, customs of the sea, and navigation lights.**

9. Be able to take charge and handle boats under oars and power on inland waters.

10. Be able to make a short and eye splice in rope.

11. Know emergency drills for man overboard, grounding, lost rudder, towing, anchoring with kedge, and fog procedure.

12. Carry out practical boat maintenance and simple repairs.

13. Know basic engine equipment.

14. Have some knowledge of the emergence of maritime nations, the role of sea power and environmental effects, e.g. oil tankers.

For the more advanced
15. Full knowledge of the rule of the road.

16. Understand elementary chartwork, buoyage and lights.

17. Be able to take charge and handle boats under oars and power on tidal waters.

18. Be able to make a rack seizing.

19. Be able to make sailmakers and common whippings.

20. Carry out repairs to boat and gear.

21. Know basic principles, operation and maintenance of simple inboard and outboard engines.

22. Give regular help at a recognised boatwork centre.

23. Have some understanding of:

a) Marine and maritime archaeology.

b) Recent theories, e.g. Thor Heyerdahl.

c) Spread of civilisations and cultures.

d) Seafaring as a leisure activity.

e) Philosophies and experiences of single-handed yachtsmen.

f) Social responsibility to other water users.

Motor Cars—Driving

(See also Introduction on page 218)

For beginners
Young people should:

1. Take regular instruction over the stipulated period, aimed at passing the official Driving Test.

2. Have a thorough knowledge of the Highway Code.

3. Study the leaflet DL 68 *How to pass the Driving Test* and the Department of Transport manual *Driving*.

4. Have a sound knowledge of the law relating to cars in regard to driving licences, certificates of insurance, excise licences, the Construction and Use Regulations as they affect the driver and compulsory vehicle test certificates.

5. Know the principles of braking and acceleration.

6. Know the principles of the working of four stroke engines.

7. Know the main causes of accidents involving car drivers.

8. Have some knowledge of the early history of motoring. If possible, visit a museum of motoring.

For those with some knowledge
9. Those taking this activity must hold a valid driving licence, and if they have not already done so, should pass the official Driving Test.

10. Journey Planning—Young people should:

a) Learn to read road maps—grid system, topography, symbols, etc.

b) Study route planning—average speeds, secondary roads, places of interest, "bottle necks", etc.

c) Have a detailed knowledge of the district within a radius of 25 miles of their home.

d) Carry out a scheduled journey of which half should be driving in daylight on "B" class and unclassified roads, and half in darkness on "A" class roads. Suggested total distance about 100 miles.

11. Knowledge of Vehicle—Those taking part should have a knowledge of routine maintenance as follows:

a) Daily check of oil, water, petrol and battery. They should know correct grades of fuel and oil best suited to the engine.

b) Regular check and adjustment of tyre pressures, and removal of stones and foreign bodies from the tread. Participants should understand the need for regular wheel changes, and if there are signs of uneven wear, understand the importance of discovering the cause.

c) Keeping windows clean, and checking that windscreen wipers and washers are working effectively. Know how to change wiper blades.

d) Keeping lamp-glasses clean, and periodically checking the lights.

e) Be able to change a wheel, and know the necessary precautions to be taken before and after this operation.

f) Understand the lubricating system, and be able to carry out minor lubrication operations, e.g. gear box, rear axle, and check brake fluid levels periodically.

g) Know how to adjust the carburettor.

h) Be able to recognise inefficiency in braking, and play in the steering mechanism.

i) Know how to adjust the fan-belt.

j) Know when a cylinder is not firing and how to check which one it is. Know how to change a sparking plug.

k) Know how to identify and clean fuel filters.

l) Be able to answer simple questions on the basic principles of the operation of a four-stroke engine, and the functioning of the carburettor and ignition systems.

12. Have some understanding of:

a) The effect of the internal combustion engine on economic and human life up to the present day.

b) Environmental implications of roads; effect on town planning; pollution.

For the more advanced
13. All those taking part must hold a valid driving licence, and have passed the official Driving Test.

14. Young people should have a thorough knowledge of all the points outlined for those with some knowledge.

15. Participants should:

a) Study to improve their driving technique in urban traffic and on fast open roads.

b) Have a detailed knowledge of reaction times, and stopping distances.

c) Have some understanding of momentum, stability, and force of impact.

d) Know how to handle special conditions and eventualities such as ice, winds, floods, skids, and fog, both in daylight and after dark.

e) Understand the importance of health, eyesight, mental approach, the effect of fatigue, alcohol, and drugs.

f) Have a sound basic knowledge of legal and insurance requirements, including procedure when accidents occur.

g) Know how to use a telephone in an emergency, and how to report an accident.

h) Know the meaning of traffic circulation and the importance of traffic engineering in road development.

13. Knowledge of Vehicle—Young people should make a more advanced study of the vehicle, and should:

a) Study the working of the clutch and gear box.

b) Have a knowledge of the electrical system, and be able to trace electrical faults.

14. Journey Planning—Those taking part should demonstrate their ability to plan and carry out journeys of any distance, using classified and unclassified roads. They should know how to load their vehicles safely, and the maximum load capacity.

15. Have some understanding of:

a) The aesthetics of design of cars.

b) Conservation of resources; fuel economy.

c) Social responsibilities to other road users.

Royal Automobile Club.

Railway Affairs

(See also Introduction on page 218)

For beginners

Those starting this programme should:

1. Be a regular member of a loco-spotting club during the stipulated period and take part in at least one of its outings.

2. Make a collection of photographs, sketches and notes about the railway in the vicinity of their home, and present them in a notebook or folder.

3. Visit a small signal box with a Supervisor. Study, and submit a short description of the method of signalling trains.

4. Visit a locomotive running and maintenance depot, with a Supervisor, and make notes on the work of the depot.

5. Have some knowledge of the early history of railways. If possible, visit a railway museum.

For those with some knowledge
Young people should continue to follow the interest regularly over the stipulated period, including:

6. Go to see an old locomotive and make notes about it and the work it used to do.

7. Study *two* steam locomotives designed by different mechanical engineers, making notes on any similarities and differences.

8. Study the history of any one of the former Railway Companies *or* of any aspect of railway engineering.

9. Make a study of the relative advantages and disadvantages of steam, diesel and electric traction, and submit either a written or oral account of their findings.

10. Visit a junction signal box with a Supervisor, and make a diagram of the lay-out it controls and show the position of the signals.

11. Develop the collection of photographs, sketches and notes started under item **2** above, with emphasis on any specialised aspect of the railway in an area of their choice, which is of particular interest to them.

12. Have some understanding of:

a) The effect of railways on economic and human life up to the present time

b) Environmental effects of railways.

c) Competition with other forms of transport.

For the more advanced
Young people should:

13. Attempt one of the following:

a) Join a recognised Locomotive Society, attend regularly during the stipulated period, and join in at least one of their excursions.

b) Join a Railway Preservation Society, attend regularly during the stipulated period, and either join in one of their excursions, or study the history of one of the old railways in which it is interested.

c) Take a trip behind an old locomotive, or endeavour to see it in service.

14. Make a study of the work of one of the former Railway Company's Chief Mechanical Engineers with regard to the design and construction of steam locomotives, noting the developments he introduced.

15. Visit a mechanised marshalling yard, and record detailed observations of the visit illustrated by photographs if possible.

16. Either

a) Select a locomotive, and describe how it was designed for a particular duty, with details of its parts and how they function.

Or

b) Make a diagram of any locomotives selected by participants to their chosen measurements.

17. Make a study of the Service provided by the Railways for **either** passengers **or** freight, and make notes on what improvements they think should be made.

18. If possible, buy a Regional "Freedom" ticket and give an account of their travels.

19. Have some understanding of:

a) The aesthetics of design of locomotives and rolling stock.

b) Role of rail transport abroad and different forms of ownership and control.

Note: This programme deals with Railway Affairs. Railway Modelling is covered in a separate programme (see page 150 or 186), but young people should, if possible, join a Model Railway Club, or run a Model Railway.

WORKSHOP CRAFTS

Metalwork/Pottery/Woodwork/Boat Building/Canoe Building/
Enamelling/French Polishing/Jewellery/Lapidary/Marquetry/
Pewter Working/Shoemaking/Cycle Maintenance/Car Maintenance/
Motor Cycle Maintenance

Introduction

These activities should include as much practical work as possible during the stipulated time. Those participating at any level should be given adequate instruction in the safe use of tools and equipment.

Craftwork provides an alternative and equally satisfying pursuit for those who find little motivation from other recreative activities. Like these it serves to balance more academic efforts yet, if reinforced with reading in its historical background, it can assist an understanding of the social structure and cultural development of our society.

Socially and in terms of speed and efficiency it is better to learn craftwork as part of a group. Once reasonable proficiency has been achieved, it is possible to accelerate social development through participation in group projects.

Instruction in the safe use of tools, awareness of possible hazardous materials, especially glues, and in the importance of good ventilation should be given. Due regard should always be given to safe working practices.

For assessment, each individual is to produce evidence of regular application to the interest over the required period. This should normally take the form of finished articles or certificates of attendance at instruction classes.

General Programme

The following guidelines should be used to draw up a programme for a workshop craft that does not have a particular programme listed, but which a participant wishes to follow. Before embarking on this programme it should be approved by the participant's Operating Authority.

Participants should develop a practical knowledge of the following:

a) Materials which can be used and an identification of their characteristics. This would include destructive testing of materials so that the limits of flexibility are known from the outset.

227

b) The range of tools available to any particular craftsman. Basic tools to be used in the first instance before progressing to higher levels of work demanding more sophisticated equipment including items driven by mechanical, electrical or other power sources.

c) Production of simple components which involve the basic techniques of material manipulation with the tools most relevant to the current level of skill of the participant. The degree of skill and concentration needed with progressive components to represent a continuing challenge to the individual.

d) Be able to understand drawings and other non-verbal methods of instruction and communication appropriate to their capability.

e) The opportunity to explore the historical development of the workshop craft chosen and for the predictions for the future of the Craft. The opportunity to meet experienced practitioners and to discuss current and new developments to be encouraged.

f) The chance to design and develop a product which is of interest to the participant. This would include rough draft sketches, finished drawings as well as the actual product.

g) **Instruction in the safe use of tools, awareness of possible hazardous materials, especially glues, and in the importance of good ventilation should be given. Due regard should always be given to safe working practices.**

Cars—Engineering and Maintenance

(See also Introduction on page 227)

For beginners

1. Strip a four-stroke, push rod, overhead valve, spark ignition engine, maximum four cylinders, and name the parts.

2. Re-assemble the engine, know the function of each part and understand the four-stroke cycle.

3. Understand how the power is transmitted from the engine to the propeller shaft.

4. Know how a single plate friction clutch operates.

5. Have some knowledge of the early history of motoring. If possible, visit a museum of motoring.

For those with some knowledge

6. Strip and re-assemble a single venturi, manual choke carburettor and understand its principles of operation.

7. Describe the principle of operation of a differential unit and explain why such a unit is necessary.

8. Understand the principles of steering geometry. Explain what is meant by caster angle, king pin inclination, camber angle and toe-in and explain why each is necessary.

9. Understand the principle of operation of a single line hydraulic braking system. Explain the different characteristics of drum brakes and disc brakes.

10. Understand a pressurised cooling system.

11. Have some understanding of:

a) The effect of the internal combustion engine on economic and human life up to the present day.

b) Environmental implications of roads; effect on town planning; pollution.

For the more advanced

12. Explain the different types of suspension system in common use and define the function of each component.

13. Strip and re-assemble an inertia type starter motor and understand its principle of operation.

14. Dismantle and re-assemble four-speed, constant mesh gearbox.

SKILLS

15. Remove cylinder head from a four-cylinder, four-stroke, push-rod, overhead valve, spark ignition engine. Grind in valves. Refit cylinder head and reset the valve clearance.

16. Understand how a charging system incorporating an alternator functions.

17. Service a popular four-cylinder car in accordance with the manufacturer's recommendations.

18. Understand the law relating to tyres, with regard to permissible tyre combinations and the condition of tyres. Explain the essential difference between cross-ply tyres and radial-ply tyres in relation to their construction and their characteristics.

19. Understand the essential requirements of the MOT test.

20. Have some understanding of:

a) The aesthetics of design of cars.

b) Conservation of resources; fuel economy.

c) Social responsibilities to other road users.

Pottery

(See also Introduction on page 227)

General
Throughout the programme young people should show that they have a progressive knowledge of the history of pottery-making through the ages, and should be able to explain to an Assessor or write an article on the historical and developmental aspects of the subject on completion of each part of the programme. At the higher stages, they should preferably take part in a group visit to a local studio and to a museum displaying pottery artifacts.

For beginners
Those taking this activity should have a practical knowledge of the following:

1. Pottery without a wheel:

a) Thumb pots.

b) Coiled vessels.

c) Slab pots.

d) Pottery made from plaster mould designed by them.

e) Modelling.

SKILLS

2. Decoration of hand-made pottery:

a) Pressed and raised decoration on clay.

b) Relief decoration using clay.

c) Slip decorations using trailed slip and graffito techniques.

d) Underglaze and on-glaze brush decoration using ceramic colours.

3. Thrown pottery:

a) Knowledge of the technique, beginning with the making of simple cylindrical shapes for conversion to mugs and tankards.

b) Knowledge of mixing slips and of clear and coloured glazes.

For those with some knowledge
Young people should have a practical knowledge of the following:

4. More advanced degree of pottery without a wheel.

5. Development of the technique of "throwing", leading to the making of vases and bowls of a variety of shapes.

6. Making of lipped and handled vessels, e.g. jugs (to bring in techniques of making lips and handles by slaps, coils and pulling). They should submit:

a) A coiled pot with imprest decoration.

b) A small bowl with "turned" foot on base.

7. Glazing and firing of pots. Mix glazes and learn how to stack and fire a biscuit and glost kiln.

For the more advanced
8. Make a further study of clays and glazes.

9. Undertake more advanced wheel throws, including pots having a definite function, and make the following:

a) A tankard and mug with a "turned" foot and "pulled" handle.

b) A jug with a "turned" foot and a "pulled" handle.

c) A bowl with a set-in lid (e.g. butter dish or powder bowl).

d) A coiled pot (minimum height 7″).

e) A moulded dish.

f) A table set, salt, pepper, mustard.

10. Make a wide application of the various types of decoration, e.g. slip, imprest, inlaid clays, graffito, coloured glazes.

British Pottery Manufacturers' Association.

Woodwork

(See also Introduction on page 227)

For beginners
Those starting this activity should:

1. Compile a scrapbook or design a notebook showing illustrations of small wooden articles that can be made at home.

2. Show evidence of:
a) Accurate measuring.

b) Use of nails and screws.

c) Use of glues and adhesives.

d) Use of simple woodwork joints.

e) Glasspapering.

f) Painting or staining or brush polishing.

g) Use of modern plastic coverings.

3. Have knowledge of some of the common timbers used in woodwork.

4. Submit one piece of work which should embody as wide a range of construction and ideas as possible and be well constructed, of pleasing design, correctly finished and well suited for its particular purpose.

For those with some knowledge
Young people should:

5. Have a free choice of the item or items to be made.

6. Incorporate more advanced variations of joints and construction in their work than included in the programme for beginners.

7. Make such articles as stools, small tables, simple carcase constructions or small articles suitable in the home, the workshop or garden, or connected with an interest or hobby.

8. Keep a scrapbook or design notebook showing drawings or illustrations from magazines or newspapers of articles which could be made at this level.

9. Make sketches and brief notes on the historical development of one piece of furniture, e.g. a chair, table or cabinet.

For the more advanced
Young people should:

10. Design and make the whole of the work submitted.

11. Submit drawings and sketches with the practical work.

12. Submit work which should be original, well designed and to a good standard of construction and finish.

13. Have some appreciation of the functional and artistic elements of the work submitted.

SKILLS

Skill followed:

Conjuring and Magic

DATE STARTED: 14·2·90 COMPLETED: 22-8-90

Assessor's report

Polly showed great enthusiasm in the whole sphere of Magic and Conjuring from the start. She has staged several shows for local old people's homes, children's clubs and groups and, each time, has managed to introduce new and challenging routines which have all been well received by the audiences.

SIGNED *[signature]* DATE 30-8-90

QUALIFICATION / EXPERIENCE EALING MAGIC CIRCLE MEMBER

19

Bronze

SKILLS

Skill followed:

WINE MAKING

DATE STARTED: 27·III·89 COMPLETED: 4·X·90

Assessor's report

Although a complete beginner, Wayne was quick to learn the techniques of wine making + was soon entering local competitions. He has taken an active role in The Wine Society & has made many friends. He has just been elected Membership Secretary for the coming year. Wayne has produced some excellent home made wines which are a credit to his efforts

SIGNED L. Houghton DATE 4·X·90

QUALIFICATION / EXPERIENCE Sec. Hanworth Wine Society

33

Silver

234

Aim

To encourage participation in Physical Recreation and improvement of performance.

General

This Section offers a wide range of programmes in the belief that:

■ Involvement in some form of enjoyable physical activity is essential for physical well-being.

■ A lasting sense of achievement and satisfaction is derived from meeting a physical challenge.

■ The activities listed are enjoyable in themselves and can lead to the establishment of a lasting active lifestyle.

The Section makes use of a points scoring system which enables the physically less gifted to qualify as well as the natural athlete or games player, and requires of both a reasonable degree of training, leading to improved performance.

Requirement

Assessed participation in organised Physical Recreation, and achievement of individual progress.

Types of Physical Recreation

The following list gives the choice of the activities available.

▲ Exercise to Music 279
● Fencing 252
Fives:
▲ Eton 280
▲ Rugby 280
△ Football 302
△ Frisbee 302
△ Goalball 302
● Golf 252
Gymnastics: 284
● BAGA 254
▲ Educational 281
● General 254
● Modern Rhythmic 254
▲ Olympic 284
● Rhythmic 254
● Sports Acrobatics 254
● Hang Gliding 254
Hockey:
△ Field 302
△ Ice 302
△ Indoor 302
△ Street/Roller 302
● Judo 254
▲ Keep Fit 290
△ Korfball 302
△ Lacrosse 302
● Lawn Tennis 254
● Martial Arts 254
▲ Medau Rhythmic Movement 291
● Modern Biathlon 254
● Modern Pentathlon 254
● Modern Triathlon 254
● Netball 254
△ Octopushing 302
● Orienteering 254
● Parachuting 254
▲ Petanque 292
● Physical Achievement 246

△ Polo 302
▲ Real Tennis 293
● Riding 256
▲ Rock Climbing 294
△ Rounders 302
● Rowing and Sculling 256
△ Rugby League Football 302
△ Rugby Union Football 302
▲ Running 297
● Sailing 256
● Sand & Land Yachting 256
Skating:
● Ice 256
● Roller 256
Skiing:
● Alpine 256
● Grass 256
▲ Nordic 299
● Freestyle 256
▲ Skipping 300
● Squash 256
△ Stoolball 302
● Surfing 256
Swimming:
▲ General 245
● Personal Survival 245
● Safe 245
● Synchronised 245
● Underwater 258
● Table Tennis 256
● Trampolining 256
△ Volleyball 302
△ Water Polo 302
● Water Skiing 258
● Weightlifting 258
● Windsurfing 256
● Wrestling 258
▲ Yoga (Hatha) 304

● The activities marked with this symbol are those that have relevant National Governing Body Awards or, in the case of Athletics, Cross Country Running, Physical Achievement and Swimming, set standards of The Duke of Edinburgh's Award.

▲ The activities marked with this symbol are those that have participation programmes listed.

△ The activities marked with this symbol are those which are covered by the general **Team Games** participation programme.

Note: **This list is not exhaustive, but any proposed additions must first be submitted to the National Award Office for approval via the appropriate Territorial or Regional Office.**

Conditions

1. Select one activity from the list above and **participate** in it for a minimum period of six weeks.

2. To qualify:

a) Show **improvement** in the chosen activity, assessed on the basis of effort, progress and performance during the period for which it is being followed, having regard to the criteria listed in paragraph 7.

b) **Obtain** the stipulated number of **points**, which may be built up by:

Participation alone for activities marked with ▲ or △

Participation and achieving standards for activities marked with ●

3. The minimum number of points required to qualify for each Award are as follows:

BRONZE – 24 points
SILVER – 30 points
GOLD – 36 points

4. Points are awarded as follows:

For participation – For all activities – on the basis of two points for each hourly (one for each half-hourly) session outside curriculum timetable or works time. Not more than two points to count per week or four points per **alternate** weekend.

For standards – In activities marked with ● – on the basis of the tables given on pages 250–259.

5. For each Award at least 12 points **must** be gained by participation. The balance required may be made up either by:

a) attainment of the appropriate Award where National Governing Body proficiency tests are listed.

b) attainment of the standards listed for Athletics, Cross Country Running, Swimming or Physical Achievement.

c) continued participation or by a combination of **a)** and **c)** or **b)** and **c)**.

Improvement

6. Improvement of overall performance is essential to qualification in this Section.

7. Such improvement must be assessed as a continuing process throughout the period of participation. In making what must necessarily be a subjective judgement, those assessing achievement should have regard to the following considerations:

a) All candidates should have shown **effort** during the period of participation and made **progress** based upon their initial knowledge and ability.

b) They should also have shown **improvement** in the following areas, in so far as they are applicable to the activity concerned, related to their initial standard, physical ability, and period of participation.

Application: Attendance and willingness to involve themselves during each practical session, appropriately attired and equipped.
Technique: Understanding of the techniques applicable to the activity.
Skill: Development of individual and/or cooperative skills appropriate to the activity.
Tactics: Appreciation of individual and/or cooperative tactics necessary to the activity at their level of participation.
Fitness: Improvement of physical fitness specific to the activity.
Rules: Knowledge of rules appropriate to the level of activity at which the participation is involved.
Safety: Knowledge of safety regulations and appreciation of dangers inherent in the activity.

Instruction

8. Participation sessions are to be coached or supervised by persons knowledgeable and experienced in the activity and who are acceptable to the Operating Authority. The form of participation should be approved in advance by the Assessor.

Assessment

9. At all levels points for participation are to be awarded and entered in *Record Books* by those coaching or supervising. At Silver level the Assessor should normally be independent of those coaching or supervising. At Gold level there **must** be an independent assessment at both the initial and final stage to confirm that there has been improvement.

10. Points for achievement of National Governing Body Awards or set standards of The Duke of Edinburgh's Award are to be awarded and entered in *Record Books*, were applicable, by a National Governing Body Assessor, or by suitably qualified Award Leaders, P.E. teachers, Club officials or Instructors. At Silver level, such persons should preferably be independent of those who have trained the participant. At Gold level there must be independent assessment.

Activities with Governing Body or set standards of The Duke of Edinburgh's Award ●

11. Participants can only score by achieving standards after the required 12 participation points have been achieved. If the activity has a National Governing Body or The Duke of Edinburgh's Award standard the points gained for participation and the achievement of these standards, must be in the same activity. Operating Authorities, however, have the discretion to waive this rule if for exceptional reasons, such as moving away from the area, the participant no longer has access to the required facilities. However, points gained for standards in one activity cannot be added to those gained for standards in another in order to reach the required total.

12. Only points scored for **one** standard achieved in the activity may qualify.

13. In some cases there are separate tables for young men and young women. For all other activities one table gives standards for both sexes.

14. For some activities the points awarded are related to proficiency tests laid down by the National Governing Body of the sport concerned, as indicated in the tables on page 250–259.

15. Proficiency tests passed before starting work for an Award may not be counted retrospectively. Participants should either gain the next higher proficiency award (not instructors' certificate) or take up a new activity.

16. Guide lines for participation in each activity consist of the syllabi of the National Governing Body proficiency tests, as listed in the tables, or the programmes listed at the end of this Section.

17. Standards **should** be attempted but where these are not achievable, young people may qualify by participation and personal improvement alone. In such cases they **must** use the relevant Governing Body syllabus for measurable or certified standards as a guideline.

Notes:
1. The standards used are those from the British Governing Bodies. Where these do not exist the standards of English Governing Bodies have been published. In these cases the appropriate standards of the Governing Bodies of Scotland, Wales and Northern Ireland may be used instead, where these exist.

2. Outside the UK, the standards specified by equivalent national bodies may be adopted in lieu.

Activities with Participation Programmes ▲

18. Guidelines for participation in activities without current Governing Body standards are given on pages 262–305 in the form of suggested programmes. **Safety requirements in bold type must, in all cases, be observed.**

19. Where availability of local facilities seriously limits usage, e.g. in rural or deprived areas, the qualifying points may, at the discretion of Operating Authorities, be built up by undertaking a second activity, but a minimum of 12 points for participation **must** be gained in each activity.

Participation by those with Special Needs

20. Whenever possible, participants with Special Needs are encouraged to choose an activity which will enable them to take part in the Section without recourse to variations. Many sports have versions specifically adapted for those with Special Needs e.g. Wheelchair Basketball and wheelchair dancing. Many Governing Bodies can provide information on such variations and some of these activities, especially those included within the Paraolympics, have National Governing Bodies of Sport in their own right. The list of activities is, therefore, intended to be inclusive rather than exclusive and participants with Special Needs should choose activities that interest them on a similar basis to able bodied participants. Where appropriate, further information on standards and possible variations is given in the Award publication *A Challenge to the Individual*.

Athletics

The Standard rules of the Amateur Athletic Association and the Women's Amateur Athletic Association are to apply for each event as regards safety measures, timing, judging and measurement. Weights of throwing implements are to be as laid down for the various age groups by the AAA and WAAA.

Either:

Undertake one run, one jump and one throw from the events listed and score at least 1 point in each event chosen. Maximum score in any event is 10 points.

The three events are to be performed during one session allowing reasonable rest between each event.

or:

Obtain an equivalent AAA/WAAA Five Star Award and score points as follows:

2 star-6 points; 3 star-12 points; 4 star-18 points; 5 star-24 points

Scoring—Boys and Young Men

Event	Points	1	2	3	4	5	6	7	8	9	10
100 Metres	Seconds	15.8	15	14.3	13.7	13.2	12.8	12.5	12.3	12.1	12.0
200 Metres	Seconds	35	33.3	31.6	29.8	28.3	27.1	26.2	25.7	25.3	25.1
400 Metres	Seconds	77	73	69.5	66.5	64.0	62.0	60.5	59.5	58.5	58.0
800 Metres	Mins. & secs.	3.18	3.02	2.48	2.36	2.28	2.24	2.21	2.19	2.17	2.16
1500 Metres	Mins. & secs.	6.34	6.09	5.48	5.30	5.15	5.03	4.54	4.48	4.42	4.40
High Jump	Metres	1.06	1.14	1.22	1.34	1.44	1.52	1.58	1.61	1.64	1.66
Long Jump	Metres	2.97	3.30	3.65	3.95	4.20	4.40	4.55	4.65	4.75	4.80
Triple Jump	Metres	6.7	7.20	7.90	8.50	9.00	9.40	9.70	9.90	10.10	10.20
Pole Vault	Metres	1.6	1.76	1.90	2.02	2.14	2.30	2.42	2.50	2.58	2.62
Shot	Metres	4.80	5.40	6.10	6.70	7.30	7.90	8.35	8.65	8.95	9.10
Discus	Metres	14.00	16.40	18.50	20.50	23.00	25.00	26.50	27.50	28.50	29.00
Javelin	Metres	14.00	16.40	18.50	20.50	23.00	25.00	26.50	27.50	28.50	29.00
Cricket/ Rounders Ball	Metres	34.00	41.00	48.00	54.00	59.00	63.00	66.00	68.00	69.00	70.00

Scoring—Girls and Young Women

Event	Points	1	2	3	4	5	6	7	8	9	10
100 m	Seconds	17.0	16.2	15.5	14.9	14.4	14.0	13.7	13.5	13.3	13.2
200 m	Seconds	37.4	35.8	34.3	33.1	31.9	30.7	29.8	29.2	28.6	28.3
400 m	Seconds	88	80	75.5	72.5	70.0	68.0	66.5	65.5	64.5	64.0
800 m	Mins. & secs.	3.42	3.26	3.12	3.00	2.50	2.42	2.36	2.32	2.29	2.28
1500 m	Mins. & secs.	7.30	6.50	6.24	6.06	5.51	5.39	5.30	5.24	5.18	5.15
High Jump	Metres	0.94	1.02	1.09	1.15	1.20	1.28	1.34	1.38	1.42	1.44
Long Jump	Metres	2.61	2.85	3.08	3.35	3.6	3.8	3.95	4.05	4.15	4.2
Shot	Metres	4.2	4.6	4.95	5.5	6.0	6.4	6.7	6.9	7.15	7.3
Discus	Metres	9.5	12.8	14.9	16.7	18.2	19.4	20.5	21.5	22.5	23.0
Javelin	Metres	9.5	12.8	14.9	16.7	18.2	19.4	20.5	21.5	22.5	23.0
Cricket/Rounders Ball	Metres	28.5	32.0	36.0	42.0	47.0	51.0	54.0	56.0	58.0	59.0

Cross Country Running

Either:

Undertake ten weeks training, one time trial and one race and accumulate points according to AAA Five Star Award tables.

or:

Obtain an equivalent AAA/WAAA Five Star Award and score points as follows:

2 star-6 points; 3 star-12 points; 4 star-18 points; 5 star-24 points

AAA Points	90	100	110	120	130	140	150	160	170	180
D of E Points	1	2	3	4	5	6	7	8	9	10

Swimming

Non-Swimmers:
Learn to swim at least 20 yards (18.3 metres)—12 points.
For the test, jump or dive in and swim unaided without stopping.

Swimmers:
Either: Obtain one of the qualifications below.

Scoring	Minimum			Maximum
Points	**6**	**12**	**18**	**24**
Amateur Swimming Association Awards for Proficiency in Personal Survival	Level 2			
Swimming Challenge Awards		Bronze	Silver	Gold
Swimming Teachers' Association Survival Award	Bronze	Silver	Gold	Merit
Royal Life Saving Society Safe Swimmers Award	Award II	Award III	Award IV	
Amateur Swimming Association Synchronised Swimming Award	Prelim. Synchro.	Grade I	Grade II	Grade III

or: Pass Composite Speed Test

Swim 25 yards or 25 metres without turns three times each by a different stroke and
score at least 1 point for each stroke. Maximum score for any one stroke is 10 points.
All three events to be taken during a single session, but not continuously.

Scoring—All Participants

Stroke	Points	1	2	3	4	5	6	7	8	9	10
25 yds Backstroke (without a dive)	Secs.	27	26	25	24	23	22	21	20	19	18
25 yds Breaststroke	Secs.	29	28	27	26	25	24	23	22	21	20
25 yds Freestyle	Secs.	24	23	22	21	20	19	18	17	16	15
25 m Backstroke (without a dive)	Secs.	30	29	28	27	26	25	24	23	22	21
25 m Breaststroke	Secs.	32	31	30	29	28	27	26	25	24	23
25 m Freestyle	Secs.	27	26	25	24	23	22	21	20	19	18

Physical Achievement

All the events may be undertaken outdoors or indoors (e.g. gymnasium; club hall). The only equipment needed is a size 5 football or netball, a chair or similar item, gym mat or sandpit, markers and a watch.

Undertake all 7 events and select 6 to count. At least one point must be scored in each event. Maximum score in any event—5 points.

A reasonable rest is to be allowed between each event. Tests may be spread over two days.

Scoring—Boys and Young Men

Event	Points	1	2	3	4	5
Speed test	Time (secs.)	30	28	26	24	23
Sit-ups	Number	30	45	60	75	90
Burpees	Number in 30 secs.	14	16	18	21	23
Stamina run	Time (mins. & secs.)	4.20	4.00	3.40	3.20	3.10
Ball speed bounce	Number of catches in 30 secs.	30	35	40	45	50
Standing broad jump	Distance (metres)	1.4	1.8	2.2	2.4	2.5
Push-ups or	Number	10	18	26	32	38
Bailey Bridge	Number in 30 secs.	18	22	28	32	36

Scoring—Girls and Young Women

Event	Points	1	2	3	4	5
Speed test	Time (secs.)	24	23	22	21	20
Sit-ups	Number	28	36	44	52	60
Burpees	Number in 30 secs.	11	13	15	18	20
Stamina run	Time (mins. & secs.)	4.50	4.30	4.10	3.50	3.40
Ball speed bounce	Number of catches in 30 secs.	20	26	32	36	38
Standing broad jump	Distance (metres)	1.2	1.4	1.8	2.2	2.4
Push-ups or	Number	8	14	22	28	34
Bailey Bridge	Number in 30 secs.	14	18	24	28	32

Note: Score may be counted for either Push-ups or Bailey Bridge, but **not** both.

PHYSICAL RECREATION

Description of Events

Speed test Boys: cross ten times; Girls: cross eight times—between two lines marked on ground or floor 9 metres apart. Each line to be crossed or touched by one foot.

Situps Lie on the back with legs bent and feet about 50 cm. apart. Place hands to the side of the head. Ankles should be held (e.g. under wallbar or by a partner) so that the heels are kept in contact with the ground. Sit up, curling trunk and head and turn until one elbow touches the opposite knee and then return to the starting position. Repeat the exercise to the opposite side. Scoring ceases if a rest is taken.

Burpees This is a four-count movement. Start standing upright, then bend to crouch position placing both hands flat on the floor; jump both feet backwards and together to front support position (NB.—the distance between the hands and feet in this position to be at least 70 cm.). Jump feet forward to return to crouch and then stand upright. Count each time performer stands upright in 30 seconds.

Stamina run Twenty laps of a rectangular circuit 12 metres by 8 metres, each corner marked by a small object.

Ball speed bounce   Using a netball or size 5 football, stand behind a line 2 metres from wall. Hold ball with two hands against chest. Ball must be thrown with two hands so as to rebound from the wall into both hands behind the restraining line. Count each successfully caught ball in 30 seconds. (It is recommended that a brick wall or similar solid surface is used for this event to ensure a satisfactory rebound.)

Standing broad jump   Feet may be placed in any position behind the edge of the take-off line or board, but may leave the ground only once in making an attempt to jump onto the feet. The participant may rock backward and forward, lifting heels and toes alternately from the ground, but may not lift either foot clear from the ground or slide it along in any direction on the ground. Measure from front edge of line or board to nearest point on gym mat or in sandpit touched by any part of the body or limbs.

Either:

Push-ups   Lie face down on the floor, hands under shoulders, palms flat on the floor. Straighten arms to lift body, locking elbows and leaving only palms and toes on floor. Bend elbows until nose only touches the floor, then push up to straighten arms. Repeat, keeping body straight from head to ankles. The activity must be continuous: scoring ceases if a rest is taken or if the body sags. Girls and young women may find it easier to lie face down on the floor, hands under shoulders, palms flat on the floor with legs bent upwards from the knees. Straighten arms to lift body, locking elbows and leaving only knees on the floor.

or:

Bailey Bridge   Start in the front support position with shoulders near to and facing a chair/stool/box on which rests a small object (e.g. bean bag, duster, 5 cm. cube of wood). The seat of the chair should be 45 cm. from the floor. Take the object from the chair seat with one hand, place it on the floor, pick up the object with the other hand and replace it on the chair. Continue cycle, using alternate hands. Count number of times object is successfully placed **on the chair** in 30 seconds.

Note: **Participation sessions.**   These may be used to train for the actual events, but could also include related activities such as jogging, "aerobics", pop mobility, 5BX and XBX, circuit training, and work with weights, e.g. multigym.

SPORTS WITH CURRENT NATIONAL GOVERNING BODY STANDARDS ●

Undertake any one event out of the following and score as indicated; the minimum and maximum points are marked at the head of each table. **Where standards for girls and young women are different from those for boys and young men, they are shown in brackets.**

Archery—Full programmes obtainable from
The Grand National Archery Society
Target
Flight

Clout

Field

Badminton—Obtain a Badminton Association of England Carlton Award

Basketball—Obtain an English Basketball Association Star Award

Canoeing—*Either:*
Pass Star Test
or
Obtain Proficiency
or
Placid Water Tests
or
Racing Tests: Kayak (K1)
Canoe (C1)
or
Marathon Tests 13.5 miles
36 miles
or
Achieve a result in:
Racing, Slalom, Wild Water Racing or
Marathon Race (Promotion)
or
Devizes–Westminster Race/Trans-Pennine Canal Marathon.
(Junior Class—over 19s must compete in the senior event)

or
NABC 100 mile Canoe Test

Scoring	Minimum			Maximum
Points	6	12	18	24
	—	B (A)	D (C)	F (E)
	—	165 yards	180 yards	195 yards
		(130 yards)	(140 yards)	(150 yards)
	—	Score 32 at	Score 40 at	Score 70 at
		120 yards	140 yards	140 yards
		(100 yards)	(120 yards)	(120 yards)
	—		Refer to GNAS Programme	
	Bronze	Silver	Gold	Supreme
	Two Star	Three Star	Four Star	All Star
	—	1 Star	2 Star	3-5 Star
	—	Proficiency		Advanced
	Grade 1	Grade 2	Grade 3/4	
	—	1,000m	3,000m	10,000m
	—	1,000m	3,000m	10,000m
	—	Bronze	Silver	Gold
	—	Bronze	Silver	Gold
			(% of winner's time)	
	—	150%	135%	120%
	—	9-8	8-7	7-6
	for each stage completed	—	—	For full completion of the course
	for each stage completed	—	—	For full completion of the course

Cricket—Obtain a proficiency Award from the National Cricket Association to the following standard

Cycling—Undertake *Either:*
Time Trial—1000 metres Standing Start

or:
Time Trial—4000 metres Standing Start *or:* (3000 metres Standing Start).

or:
Reliability Trial— 80 kilometres (50 miles), normally ridden in a small group on a road but the conditions are not competitive amongst the members of the group and each individual is timed over the set distance. The course may be a circuit covered one or more times, especially if the start can also be the finish, but the circuit should not be too small, i.e. not covered more than two or three times.
or:
Road Time Trials—10 miles and 25 miles.

Notes:
Time Trials to be ridden under competitive conditions on a hard surfaced cycle track. The Tests are to be judged by British Cycling Federation officials of Divisional or National status or in the case of Reliability Trials, officials of the Cyclists' Touring Club. Road time trials to be assessed by the Road Time Trials Council.

Dancing—Obtain a proficiency Award of one of the following:
Imperial Society of Teachers of Dancing; International Dance Teachers' Association; The British Association of Teachers of Dancing; The British Ballet Organisation; Royal Academy of Dancing
Ballroom, Disco, Latin American, Old Time, Highland, Acrobatic.
Ballet, Stage, Tap, Gymnastic Dance, Modern Dance, National.

Diving—Obtain a proficiency Award of the Amateur Swimming Association

Fencing—Obtain a proficiency Award of the Amateur Fencing Association.

Golf—Obtain a certified handicap of:
Royal and Ancient / Ladies Golf Union
Intervals allowed for scoring intermediate points

Scoring	Minimum			Maximum
Points	**6**	**12**	**18**	**24**
	—	1st Test	2nd Test	Final Test
Mins. & Secs.	1.43 (2.00)	1.37 (1.51)	1.31 (1.42)	1.25 (1.35)
Mins. & Secs.	6.34 (5.26)	6.16 (5.14)	5.58 (5.02)	5.40 (4.50)
Hours & Mins.	3.54 (4.42)	3.36 (4.18)	3.18 (3.54)	3.00 (3.30)

Details available from Road Time Trials Council.

	—	Bronze	Silver	Gold
Ballet:	Grade IV	Grade V or Pre-elimentary	Elimentary	Intermediate
Tap:	Stage 4	Stage 6	Elimentary	Intermediate
	—	Star Award Grade 1	Star Award Grade 2	Novice Diver
	Yellow Grade 1	Green Grade 2	Blue Grade 3	Orange Grade 4
Handicap – (–)		23 (35)	17 (29)	11 (23)

Gymnastics—Obtain a proficiency Award of the
British Amateur Gymnastics Association
Either:
Rhythmic Gymnastics
or
Modern Rhythmic Gymnastics
or
Sports Acrobatics
or
Gymnastics Award for Women and Girls
or
Gymnastics Award for Men and Boys
or
BAGA Award

Hang Gliding—Obtain a Pilot Rating Certificate of the
British Hang Gliding Association

Judo—Obtain a certified grade of the British Judo Association
Those holding a junior grade
Those holding a senior grade

Lawn Tennis—Obtain the appropriate standard from the
Lawn Tennis Association

Martial Arts—Obtain a grading from the appropriate Governing Body.
Participants **must** read the note on page 260
before undertaking this activity.

Modern Biathlon, Modern Pentathlon and Modern Triathlon—
Obtain the required number of points as laid down
in the Modern Pentathlon Association Rulebook in
the required disciplines.

Netball—Obtain the appropriate Award from the
All England Netball Association

Orienteering—Obtain an Award of the British Orienteering Federation

Parachuting—Obtain a qualification of the British Parachute
Association (minimum age 16)

Scoring	Minimum			Maximum
Points	6	12	18	24
	3	2	1	—
	3	2	1	—
	3	2	1	—
	—	Single	Double	Triple
	Primary	1st Class	2nd Class	3rd Class
	5	4	3	2
	Elimentary Pilot Certificate	Club Pilot Certificate	Cross Country Pilot Certificate	Advanced Pilot Certificate
	5th Mon 8th Kyu	8th Mon 7th Kyu	10th Mon 5th Kyu	13th Mon 4th Kyu
	Level 3	Level 4	Level 5	Level 6
	Lowest awardable grade	Second lowest awardable grade	Third lowest awardable grade	Fourth lowest awardable grade
Biathlon	1500	1800	2100	–
Pentathlon	1300	1700	2300	2900
Triathlon	3500	4200	4600	5000
	—	Preliminary	Intermediate	Advanced
	Orange	Red	Green/ Bronze	Brown/Blue/ Silver/Gold
	—	'A' Certificate	'B' Certificate	'C' Certificate

Riding—Obtain an Efficiency Standard of the Riding Club

Pony Club

British Horse Society

Rowing and Sculling—Obtain a proficiency Award from the Amateur Rowing Association

Sailing and Windsurfing—Obtain a proficiency Award from the Royal Yachting Association
Cruising

Dinghy
Keelboat
Windsurfing

Sand and Land Yachting—Pass a sailing test of The British Federation of Sand and Land Yacht Clubs

Skating—Pass a test judged by officials of the National Skating Association of G.B.
Ice or Roller $\frac{1}{2}$ mile.

Ice Dance/Figures
Roller Dance

Skiing—Obtain a certified grade from the English Ski Council
Alpine
OR European Local Ski School Test
Freestyle (ballet)
Grass obtain a certified grade of the British Grass Ski Tests

Squash—Obtain an Award from the Squash Racquets Association

Surfing—Obtain an Award from the British Surfing Association

Table Tennis—Obtain a grading from the
English Table Tennis Association

Trampolining—Obtain a proficiency Award of the
British Trampoline Federation

Scoring	Minimum			Maximum
Points	**6**	**12**	**18**	**24**
	Grade 1	Grade 2	Grade 3	Grade 4
	D Standard	C Standard	B Standard	A Standard
	Progressive	Progressive	Progressive	—
	Test 5	Test 10	Test 12	
	Water-manship or 50km	Sculling or Coxing	250km	500km
		Competent Crew	Day Skipper	Coastal Skipper
		Practical	Practical	Practical
	Level 1	Level 2	Level 3 or 4	Level 5
	Level 1	Level 2	Level 3 or 4	—
	Level 1	Level 2	Level 3 or Comp 1	Level 4 or Comp 2
	—	—	Sailing Pilot	—
Mins. & secs.	2.21 (2.28)	2.09 (2.16)	1.57 (2.04)	1.45 (1.52)
		Grades D7–D9	Pre-Dance	Bronze Dance
		Grades D7–D9	Pre-Roller Dance	Bronze Roller Dance
	1 Star	2 Star	3 Star	4 Star
	—	Bronze	Silver	Gold
	Apply to English Ski Council for programme			
	—	Bronze	Silver	Gold
	Red Star Award	Bronze Star Award	Silver Star Award	Gold Star Award
	—	Single Fin	Twin Fin	Three Fin
	Grade 1	Grade 2	Grade 3	Matchplayer
	Preliminary Award	Elementary Bronze	Elementary Silver	Elementary Gold

Underwater Swimming—Obtain an Award of
the National Snorkellers' Club or the British
Sub Aqua Club or the Sub-Aqua Association
or via PADI

Water Skiing—Obtain a National Grade of the British Water
Ski Federation

Weightlifting—Obtain a certified grade of the British Amateur
Weight Lifters Association
1) Based on two competition lifts
2) Based on all round weightlifting lifts

Wrestling—Obtain an Award of the Schools' Olympic Wrestling
Association Merit Award Scheme.

Scoring	Minimum			Maximum
Points	6	12	18	24
	—	NSC Snorkellers' Award *or* Elementary Diver *or* Basic Scuba Diver *or* Novice Diver	NSC Adv. Snorkeller *or* Club Diver *or* Open Water Diver *or* Sports Diver	Dive Leader *or* Advanced Open Water Diver
	Bronze	Silver	Gold	—
	—	Yellow 1 Star grade	Orange 2 Star grade	Green 3 Star grade
	Preliminary	Bronze	Silver	Gold

Martial Arts

Note: Participants **must** have read this information **before** attempting the standards given on page 254.

1. Due to the nature of Martial Arts as traditional combat systems it is essential that Operating Authorities closely monitor the involvement of The Duke of Edinburgh's Award participants. Those young people wishing to include Martial Arts in their individual programmes must seek approval from their Operating Authority prior to commencing the activity.

2. The Martial Arts Commission (MAC) is an advisory umbrella organisation composed of the individual Governing Bodies for each of the Martial Arts. It is federal in structure and the following member bodies control individual Martial Arts acceptable for inclusion within participants' individual programmes:

English Karate Board
English Karate Council
Scottish Karate Board of Control
Welsh Karate Federation
Northern Ireland Karate Board
British Council for Chinese Martial Arts
British Jiu-Jutsi Association
British Aikido Board
British Kendo Association
British Shorinji Kempo Association
United Kingdom Tang Soo Do Federation
United Kingdom Sulkido Federation
Nippon Dai Budo Kai
British Taekwondo Council
The Northern Ireland Martial Arts Commission
British Students Karate-Do Federation

3. Operating Authorities must ensure that in all cases participants are being trained by Instructors recognized by the MAC. The following criteria must be met and proof of such presented for examination by the Operating Authority:

a) Individual participants must hold an MAC licence. Such a licence is available via all MAC affiliated clubs and associations.
b) The Instructor must hold a Coaching Licence awarded under the MAC Coaching Award Scheme.
c) The Instructor must hold Professional Indemnity Insurance.

Participants may not be permitted to commence Martial Arts training prior to the Operating Authority satisfying itself that criteria have been met in full.

ACTIVITIES FOR PARTICIPATION ONLY ▲

Participants, Instructors and Assessors should take note of the conditions as given at the beginning of the Physical Recreation Section. These programmes are for guidance and are not to be taken as rigid syllabuses. **Any safety requirements are, however, set in bold type and must be observed.** Participants should start the programme at their own level of aptitude and experience and should cover as much of it as they can in the time it takes to qualify in this Section for each Award.

Instruction:

Participation sessions are to be coached or supervised by persons knowledgeable and experienced in the activity. The form of participation should be approved in advance by the Assessor.

To Qualify:

a) Show improvement in the activity, assessed on the basis of effort, progress and performance, during the period for which it is being followed. This is to be certified in *Record Books* by the Assessor. Participation alone does not qualify.

b) Obtain the stipulated number of points for each Award given in paragraph 3 of this section. These are to be entered in *Record Books* by those coaching or supervising.

Where practicable, young people should join a club or team which is properly constituted and affiliated directly or indirectly to the national body governing the game or sport.

Where appropriate, the participant should be knowledgeable about the equipment used and its care and maintenance.

Bowls

1. Know the basic rules as published in the *English Bowls Association Handbook*. Obtain the EBA *Guide for New Bowlers*.

2. Know the requirements regarding correct dress, i.e. whites or greys, correct footwear, waterproofs, etc.

3. Know the types and sizes of bowls and how to choose the correct size and weight to suit the player.

4. Learn how to place the mat correctly and demonstrate how to deliver the jack to a required length including the correct way to deliver a bowl for forehand and backhand.

5. Play in friendly single games.

6. Know the rules regarding singles, pairs, triples and rinks games, including ends required to be played for each game.

7. To know and be able to demonstrate according to the level of skill attained shots which can be played in a game: the draw, resting out a bowl, trailing the jack, follow through shots, fire or drive, block or stopper, touching bowl on the green, touching bowl in the ditch, resting a bowl, resting a bowl adjacent to the jack.

8. Play in Club events.

9. Learn the correct method of measuring and be able to use different types of measuring equipment: spring measure, string measure, callipers, feeler gauges and wedges.

10. Understand how to complete score sheets, how club match results are calculated and how to mark single matches.

11. Know the duties of each player in pairs, triples and fours.

12. Play in the different types of game.

13. Learn the tactics of play by taking part in club rinks games.

14. Play in individual competitions.

Carpet Bowling

1. Know the Basic Rules as published in the *Scottish Carpet Bowling Association Handbook*.

2. Know the requirements for correct equipment including knowledge of woods and how to choose them.

3. Deliver bowl competently.

4. Take part in friendly singles matches.

5. Be able to place the woods consistently.

6. Compete in a team singles match.

7. Demonstrate drawing, guarding, chap and lie and striking.

8. Compete in friendly doubles matches.

9. Play in a major competition, showing skill in all basic plays.

10. Understand the completion of score sheets and tournament draws of varied kinds.

Crown Green Bowls

1. Know the Laws of the Game as published in the *British Crown Green Handbook*.

2. Have an awareness of what the BCGBA and its County Associations stand for and what they are trying to achieve.

3. Have an awareness of what a handicap system in Crown Green Bowls means.

4. Have a working knowledge of score cards and tournament sheets.

5. Be able to deliver a bowl both finger and thumb bias competently.

6. Obtain a standard of play sufficient to compete for a position in a Club team.

7. Play in an Open Competition.

Ten Pin Bowling

Instruction and assessment should be carried out by any BTBA qualified Instructor, or School Teacher in possession of a BTBA Teachers Certificate.

For details of local instructors, please contact British Tenpin Bowling Association, 114 Balfour Road, Ilford, Essex IG1 4JD (SAE for reply please)

1. Obtain a certificate from the instructor to the effect that you have received regular instruction throughout the stipulated period, and have a full knowledge of scoring and pin positioning by numbers.

2. Know how to choose a bowling ball to fit the hand.

3. Be able to demonstrate the four step approach to right and left hand bowlers.

4. Have a knowledge of correct stance, follow-through, and the importance of hand, wrist and thumb positioning.

5. Know about the various types of bowling shoes.

6. Keep a certified personal score card throughout the stipulated period.

7. Be able to demonstrate the straight ball, hook ball, and the reasons for the use of spot and arrow markings on the lane.

8. Have a record for good manners and courtesy to other bowlers, and sportsmanship within the Bowling Centre.

9. Keep a certified personal score card throughout the period of, participation, keeping a note of any problems which resulted in low scoring. Aim to achieve a consistent scoring average.

10. Have a knowledge of lane dimensions and materials and of pin and ball composition with their respective weights.

11. Bowl regularly throughout the period of participation with a recognised League affiliated to the BTBA and consistently improve your scoring average.

Caving and Potholing

General

1. The emphasis must be on safe caving, keenness, hardiness and ingenuity. Such folly as solo caving or the use of a clothes line for safety must not be allowed.

2. All caving and potholing expeditions for beginners and inexperienced participants must be led and accompanied by an experienced adult caver who has completed the Local Cave Leader Assessment Scheme or who holds the Cave Instructor Certificate. Advice on leadership is obtainable from the National Caving Association Training Committee, 3 Valletort Road, Stoke, Plymouth, Devon PL1 5PH.

3. Experienced participants undertaking these expeditions may do so unaccompanied by an adult leader, provided that, prior to each expedition, it is discussed with and approved by an experienced adult qualified as in 2 above, and familiar with the cave in question. The adult consulted should be fully satisfied that the party has a responsible leader, is properly equipped, and of sufficient skill and strength to carry out the expedition safely.

4. Participants must realise that caves are a unique environment and any damage done will have a lasting effect. **Conservation must be learned at the outset**.

5. Participants must have knowledge of local cave rescue call-out procedures.

Programme

1. Emphasis should be on participation in practical caving expeditions through progressively more difficult cave systems.

2. Pass the casualty code in the Expeditions Section, *Award Handbook*.

3. Discuss knowledgeably the clothing and personal equipment necessary for safe caving: boots, helmet, lighting, food, whistle, First Aid, spares.

4. Know the general safety precautions to be observed: Be familiar with the advice and information contained in the leaflets *So you Want to go Caving* and *Protect our Caves*. (Obtainable from the NCA Information Officer, 3 Valletort Road, Stoke, Plymouth, Devon PL1 5PH.

5. Know the rules of good behaviour whilst caving.

6. Discuss the care and maintenance of equipment and tackle.

7. Continue to show a high standard of competence, endurance and a sense of responsibility on expeditions.

8. Organise and lead at least one expedition of reasonable difficulty.

9. Participants are required to demonstrate improving skills and commitment to caving during their participation by either descending caves of a gradually increasing difficulty (as graded in the local guide book) or by spending longer exploring caves of similar technical difficulty and gradually assuming more responsibility for leadership.

10. Organise and lead at least one expedition of appropriate difficulty.

Croquet

General

Association Croquet is a game where skill in making individual shots and a knowledge of tactics are equally important. Variations of the game are played in many back gardens up and down the country, but the official game is played to the rules of the Croquet Association, the game's governing body.

At club level, the game is played on a lawn 35 yards long by 28 yards wide, and many croquet clubs provide coaching for beginners throughout the season. Addresses of individual croquet clubs, publications to help the beginner and advanced player, and copies of the official Rules can be obtained from the Croquet Association.

Programme

1. Know the Basic Laws of the game, as published by the Croquet Association in its booklet, *Basic Laws*.

2. Join a Croquet Club, if possible, and obtain some coaching.

3. Understand the basic stroke sequence (Roquet, Croquet, Continuation shot).

4. Practise single ball shots:
Taking position   Hoop running   Roquet   Rush.

5. Practise two ball shots:
Take-off   Stop shot   Drive   Roll   Split shot.

6. Practise hoop approaches:
Rush   Croquet shot   Run hoop   Roquet.

7. Practise playing 4-ball breaks.

8. Understand common faults:
Crush   Double hit   Push.

9. Obtain a Croquet Association Handicap. Play Handicap games with other players.

10. Theory and tactics:

a) Know the theory of 4-ball break.

b) Know the theory of 3-ball break.

c) Understand the standard opening.

d) Know how to use bisques to set up a break.

11. Play games at a croquet club with experienced players.

12. Enter a Croquet Association Tournament either as an individual or a member of a team.

Practice targets:
Roquets
(6 feet): 7 out of 10
(12 feet): 4 out of 10

Hoop running and taking position: place a ball on the yard line in front of hoop 1; using 20 shots, take it through the first 6 hoops in order and then hit the peg.

4-ball break: make a 4-ball break through 6 hoops using 3 bisques.

There are Merit Awards awarded by The Croquet Association but as they are not training awards they can be used as a good indication of performance.

English Folk Dancing—Morris & Sword

General

Morris and Sword Dancing calls for a particular style of movement. The individual, while remaining natural and unselfconscious, becomes "tuned up" in pose and alertness. The dance action is performed with the whole body and not just the legs, especially when the "stepping" is at all complex. More important is the sharpening of the sense of give and take, of the neighbourliness on which good teamwork is based. Above all, the dancing promotes the sense of rhythm which can be so cultivated as to make for economy and an effortless flow of movement.

Programme

1. Be a member of a team of eight to perform the "Flamborough" Sword Dance. Each young person should be able to dance in any position in the set and to sing or play on mouth organ or other instrument a suitable tune in reel time, as accompaniment to the dance.

2. Be a member of a team of five to perform with "stepping" the "New-biggin" Sword Dance. Each participant should be able to dance in any position in the set and to sing or play a suitable "jig" tune as an accompaniment to the dance.

3. Be a member of a team to perform Morris Dance, either:

a) A stick dance (6).

b) A hand-clapping dance (6) taken from the "Morris Men of England", or a handkerchief dance.

c) One representative dance of their own locality (8 or more).

Each participant should be able to dance in any position in the set and to sing or play the music appropriate to the dance.

Irish Country Dancing

General

Care should be taken of posture, formations and the participant should be able to dance any position in a set. The use of hands in figure dances is important.

Programme

1. Be able to perform:

a) Promenade step (double jig and reel rhythm)

b) Side step (seven and two threes)

c) Jig step (rise and grind)

2. Be able to perform:

a) The advance and retire

b) The right and left wheel

c) The figure eight

3. Be able to perform:

a) The Siege of Carric   c) The Siege of Ennis
b) Rinnce mar   d) The Bridge of Athlone

4. Know, in addition to the above basic steps, the following:

a) Jig side step   b) Promenade step in single jig rhythm

5. Be able to perform:

a) The full chain   c) The square
b) Slip sides (four sevens)

6. Be able to perform:

a) Lannigan's ball   c) The Walls of Limerick
b) The Harvestime Jig   d) The Four Hand Reel

7. Be able to perform all basic steps with a high degree of proficiency, and in addition:

a) The double quarter chain   c) Telescope or down the centre
b) The variations on side step and movements as in the Three Tunes

8. Be able to perform:

a) The Glencar Reel or Fairy Reel   c) The Three Tunes
b) The Eight Hand Jig   d) The Sixteen Hand Reel

Irish Folk dancing

General

Young people should show good posture, style, movement and technique and have a good knowledge of the music required for each dance.

Programme

Steps.

1. Promenade step, showing difference in rhythm 6/8 and 4/4 time.

2. Side step.

3. The light double jig.

4. Solo reel.

Team Dances.

5. Soldier's Joy.

6. Siege of Carric.

Steps

7. Jig step and Jig side step.

Solo Dances.

8. Double Reel.

9. Single Jig.

10. Treble Jig or Hornpipe.

Team Dances.

11. Fairy Reel or Walls of Limerick.

12. Harvestime Jig or the Bridge of Athlone.

13. Explain difference in all rhythms—6/8 Light Double Jig; 6/8 Single Jig; 6/8 Treble Jig; 2/4 and 4/4 Reel; 9/8 Slip Jig; 4/4 Hornpipe.

Modern Educational Dance

General

The aim is to understand movement as a medium of expression and communication. Participants should, therefore, show that they are able:

a) To use the body with increasing proficiency.

b) To initiate each phrase of the sequence with one particular part of the body.

c) To invent a movement motif and develop it into a dance phrase.

d) To particpate sensitively and imaginatively in a group dance and dance drama.

Programme

1. Consider the body in rest exploring its four typical situations of standing, kneeling, sitting and lying. Create a sequence in free rhythm interchanging at least three of these:

a) With the whole body taking part.

b) Initiate each phrase of the sequence with one particular part of the body.

c) Show that when the body is in rest (i.e. in one of the chosen situations) there is awareness of the relationship between different parts of the body.

2. Create a sequence in metrical rhythm contrasting muscular tension and relaxation:

a) In the whole body.

b) In isolated parts of the body and produce a simple vocal accompaniment.

3. Understand that there are two different kinds of balance:

a) That which is unstable and naturally initiates forms of locomotion such as walking, running, leaping, hopping, turning or spinning.

b) That which is stable and so locomotion has to be initiated by voluntary bodily actions.

Create a short dance combining a) and b) using running, turning, hopping and find a piece of music as an accompaniment.

4. Invent a dramatic dance that is one vivid expressive action and contains an unexpected event. This may be danced with a partner or with two or more people.

5. Show increased proficiency of bodily movement:

a) By producing fluent transitions in a movement sequence containing tension and relaxation on curved pathways.

b) In a sequence containing flying and falling in oblique directions.

c) By suddenly halting the flux of movement in
i) a symmetrical, **ii)** an asymmetrical position after:
spinning, leaping, rolling.

6. Create a rhythmical dance which contains both sustained calm actions and vibratory excited actions preferably with one or two partners. The use of percussion accompaniment is optional.

7. a) Explore the differences in expression of arm and leg gestures leading **i)** away from the centre of the body, **ii)** towards it, **iii)** around it.

b) Create a dance phrase using these three possibilities together with the various degrees of extension between near and far.

c) Show a clear development of the design in space, using different levels and leading from a closed-in starting position to an open ending position or vice versa.

8. a) Observe people at work and recognise that different stresses in movement are needed to produce different practical effects such as smoothing, stirring, piercing, threshing, screwing, whisking, squeezing or tapping an object. Such actions if performed with small areas of the body such as the face, hands, shoulders, feet, etc, or also with the whole body without relation to an object, form a basis to expressive movement.

b) Produce with a partner a movement play approaching, meeting, separating, which ends on a note of dramatic tension. Clarify the expressive value of your movement actions. Use no accompaniment.

9. Invent a solo dance which should not be more than two minutes long. Take whichever season of the year in which you are working for your Award as a starting idea around which you build your dance. Musical accompaniment is optional.

10. Demonstrate a technique of bodily performance so that you can show:

a) A wavelike development of a movement from a very small to very large extension in space and back to a small one. This movement phrase of growing and shrinking must be executed smoothly and contain a climax in the largest extension.

Care should be taken that the whole body is involved in the movement so that arms and legs are able to unfold into all areas around the body, e.g. an arm backward-downward, or a leg upwards, etc., while the rest of the body helps to maintain balance.

b) A rhythmical phrase of sharp, angular movements emphasising the use of different joints of the body in a counterplay. Start this phrase in a very quick tempo and decrease its speed during the course of five repetitions to a very slow one without losing the sharpness.

c) Leg gestures combined with steps, leaps, hops, turns, leading to an advancing and receding flow of movement.

11. a) Be familar with all "the 8 effort actions", as they are called, by exploring their expressive value through large movements with the whole body, as well as through very small movements of small areas of the body.

Every physical action is the result of an effort spent. This may be a stressed one, powerfully bursting out, or an easy one, gently oozing through the body. Between these two opposite kinds of effort which produce a thrusting-punching action and a gently stirring-floating one respectively are others which result in different types of actions.

These are: dab-peck; press-squeeze; slash-lash; wring-wrest; flick-flutter; glide-smooth.

b) Perform the following scene using clear effort actions throughout: Enter a room secretly. You are anxious to read a letter which lies on a table by an open window, but afraid that somebody might discover you doing this. At last you find courage to pick the letter up but as you reach for it a wind whirls it away. In trying to catch the paper, you overturn a precious vase. Terrified and conscience stricken you leave the room.

12. Compose a movement dialogue for two or more people arguing about the different shapes and patterns in the air and on the floor.

Every movement creates a pathway through space. When stationary this occurs within your personal movement sphere, the space into which you can reach without moving away from the spot on which you are standing, kneeling, sitting or lying. You then create "air patterns". When striding, jumping, rolling, etc., you also move in the general space of the room and the pathway creates "floor patterns". All these shapes and patterns may show sharp, angular zig-zag movement forms or smoothly rounded ones such as circle, spiral, double curve, etc.

13. Choose a piece of music and create a solo dance which expresses change of mood. The composition should show interesting texture, clear rhythm and shape movement.

Scottish Country Dancing

General
In Scottish Country Dancing a knowledge of the basic steps and formation is more valuable than the memorisation of isolated dances. *Note:* Alternative dances are suggested to allow for individual preferences.

Programme
1. Perform the following steps rhythmically in reel and jig time:

a) Skip change of step
b) Slip step
c) Pas de Basque
d) The "stepping-up" step

2. The following formations:

a) Four hands across
b) Down the middle and up
c) Cast off
d) Four hands round
e) Right and left
f) Allemande
g) Poussette

3. The following dances, one from each pair to be selected:

a) The Highland Fair—Graded Book
or Cumberland Reel—Book 1

b) The White Cockade—24 Favourite Country Dances
or The Isle of Skye—Book 10

c) Lady Catherine Bruce's Reel—Graded Book
or The Bob of Fettercairn—Book 6

d) Cornriggs—24 Favourites
or The River Cree—16 Popular Country Dances.

4. Know the following:

a) Strathspey travelling step

b) Strathspey setting step

5. Formations:

a) Reel of three

b) Six hands round

c) Set and turn corners

d) Set and turn corners, followed by reel of three

e) Adaptation of all known formations except Poussette to Strathspey rhythm

6. Dances (one from each pair):

a) Dunbarton Drums—24 Favourites
or The Duke of Roxburgh's Reel—101 SC Dances

b) Jenny's Bawbee—24 Favourites
or Moneymusk—16 Popular Dances

c) Speed the Plough—24 Favourites
or The Fairy Dance—Book 3

d) Mrs Macleod—24 Favourites
or I'll Mak'ye Fain to Follow Me—Book 6.

7. **a**) One reel time setting step, e.g. Pas de Basque and coupe.

b) One Strathspey setting step, e.g. Glasgow Highlander's step.

8. Formations:

a) Set to corners, followed by reel of three
b) Turn corner and partner.
c) Double triangles
d) Set to corner, turn right to face partner, etc.

9. Dances (one from each pair):

a) Madge Wildfire's Strathspey—16 Popular Dances
or The Earl of Home—Book 12

b) Duke of Perth—24 Favourites
or Dalkeith's Strathspey—Book 9

c) Lord Rosslyn's Fancy—16 Popular Dances
or My Mither's Comin' in—Book 15

d) Lady Susan Stewart's Reel—24 Favourites
or General Stuart's Reel—Book 10

e) The Eightsome Reel—24 Favourites
or The Buchan Eightsome—Book 21

Note: This Programme has been compiled so as to make it possible to work through it using only the following books:

Sixteen Popular Country Dances
24 Favourite Country Dances
The Book of Graded Scottish Country Dances
The alternative dances, however, are chosen from other books.

Scottish Highland Dancing

General

Information on this activity and advice concerning assessment, which will be conducted by an assessor approved by the Board, can be obtained from the Scottish Official Board of Highland Dancing, 13 Atholl Crescent, Edinburgh. Only steps approved by the Board may be used.

Programme

1. Be able to dance a Highland Fling—six steps.

2. Sword Dance—three slow and one quick step.

3. Strathspey and Reel of Tulloch—two Strathspeys. Two Reels.

4. Highland Fling—eight steps.

5. Sword dance—four slow and one quick step.

6. Shean Trubhais—four slow and two quick steps.

7. Strathspey and Reel of Tulloch—Two Strathspey and four reel steps.

Welsh Folk Dancing

General

Leaders must refer all matters regarding assessors and assessment to: Mr Huw Penallt, Secretary, Welsh Folk Dance Society, 47 Hamilton Street, Pontcanna, Cardiff. The Society will either approve as assessors people whose names are submitted to them, or provide the name and address of the nearest qualified assessor.

Programme

1. Be able to perform any three dances in List A and be able to play, whistle or sing two of the tunes.

2. Be able to perform satisfactorily:

a) Any 6 dances in List A   **b)** Y Gasog Eira
and be able to whistle, play or sing four of the tunes.

3. Be able to perform satisfactorily:

a) Any 9 dances in List A   **c)** Solo Clog Dance—to include
b) Y Gasog Eira   "The Toby" (Boys)
                               d) Dance Morfa Rhuddlan (Girls).
and be able to play, whistle or sing any six of the tunes chosen in **a)** and Y Gasog Eira.

List of Dances

a) Oswestry Wake.   Evans' Jigg.
     Of Noble Race was Shenkin.
     Aly Grogan.   Ap Shenkin.
     Evans' Delight.   Dawns Gwyl Iran.
     Llanover Reel.   Meillionen.
     Three Sheepskins.   Welsh Whim.
     Dawns Blodau.   St. David's Day.
     Welsh Morris.

b) Y Gasog Eira. Leaflet available from the
     Welsh Folk Dance Society.

c) Solo Clog Dance, to include "The Toby".
     Ffair Caerffili.
     Dawns Y Pelau.

Exercise to Music

Follow the Royal Society of Art's 'Exercise to Music' programme at classes run by an RSA qualified teacher.

Details of qualified teachers can be obtained from:

The National Association of Health and Exercise Teachers, 112a Great Russell Street, London, WC1B 3NQ.

Eton Fives

The Participant should know something about the origins of Eton Fives and the method of play.

1. Mastering service throw.

2. Mastering returns of service (the Cut).

3. Returning the Cut.

4. Use of both hands.

5. Volleying.

6. Shots off the Pepper Pot.

7. Straight drives.

8. Angled shots.

9. Positional play.

10. Tactics.

11. Advanced techniques.

12. Scoring.

13. Rules of the game.

14. Equipment.

15. Participation in competitive matches.

Rugby Fives

The Participant should know something about the origins of Rugby Fives and the method of play.

1. Mastering service throw and service.

2. Receiving serve.

3. Straight drives with right and left hands.

4. Receiving shots off the wall.

5. Strokes off back wall.

6. Angled shots.

7. Volleying.

8. Lobbing.

9. Variations of serve.

10. Variations of return of service.

11. Positional play.

12. Tactics.

13. More advanced tactics.

14. Lets.

15. Scoring of singles and rules.

16. Scoring of doubles and rules.

Gymnastics—Educational

General
1. The aim is to increase the participants understanding of movement (as applied to gymnastics) and ability to make use of this knowledge. The participant should, therefore, be able to:

a) Show technical competence. This demands precision in the use of whichever bodily, dynamic or spatial factors are chiefly involved.

b) Answer with inventiveness and accuracy, tasks which can be interpreted in a wide variety of ways.

2. Partner work—While they work, participants should prove that they can observe accurately and show adaptability and sensitivity to one another's actions.

3. Sequences—A sequence should consist of three or more main actions neatly linked with one another either directly or by definite actions.

Programme
1. Floor Work—Create a sequence:

a) Containing contrasts of quick and slow movements.

b) Using bending and stretching movements.

c) Using twisting and turns with travelling.

281

d) Using rolling and balancing the weight on the hands.

2. Simple Apparatus:

a) On window ladders or wall bars, either:

i Make a rhythmic pattern of movement including climbing, hanging leg gestures and balance, or
ii Make as continuous a sequence of twisting movement as possible and include some upside-down positions.

b) Arrange a combination of apparatus (box and bars, horse and forms, etc.) and show the following on it:

i A sequence which shows contrasts of speed.
ii A sequence showing a variety of ways of vaulting on, off and over the apparatus.
iii A sequence based on a movement idea of your own choice.

3. Floor Work:

a) i Create a sequence using bending and stretching with movement on the spot, travelling and jumping and showing clear use of high and low levels.

ii Make a sequence with twisting movements (including fixing various parts of the body while moving the rest).

b) i Working with a partner, show a sequence in exact unison involving large, far reaching, slower movements contrasting with smaller more compact, quicker movements.
ii Work with a partner to show a sequence involving the bearing of one another's weight in a variety of ways and showing economy and continuity.

4. Simple apparatus. As for item **2**, but co-operating with a partner.

5. Main apparatus.

a) Design own symmetrical apparatus arrangements for working in unison with a partner on any of the **2b)** tasks.

b) On suitable apparatus, make a sequence to show the different uses of the arms in moving on, off or over apparatus, e.g. different grips with the hands, bearing the weight on both arms or one arm, etc.

Note: Action should reveal a high level of technical skill as well as the features of the second level sequences.

Criteria:

a) Skilful and accurate rather than spectacular movement.

b) Accuracy of repetition in both practised and improvised sequences.

c) A balance of work, so that no part of the body and no one type of movement is shown to the exclusion of the rest.

6. Control of Balance:

a) Show balancing on a variety of large or small parts of the body:

i On the floor.

ii On the broad side of a form.

iii On apparatus which is waist high or higher.

b) Balancing as in **a)** showing a variety of methods of launching the body away from the point of support, catching and recovering the body's equilibrium in a new place:

i On the floor.

ii On the broadside of a form and mat.

iii On higher apparatus with mats.

c) Balancing while sliding and/or spinning:

i Down inclined forms.

ii On the floor given additional impetus by a partner.

7. Control of Rhythm.

a) Make a sequence showing clear fluctuation of speed and strength containing the following actions in the order given: run, jump into roll; balance on hands; run leap; roll; spin.

i Use your own natural rhythm.

ii Change the rhythm so that the quick and/or strong stresses come at different points in the sequence.

b) With a partner compose a sequence using the five basic jumps and bearing one another's weight.

i Without apparatus.

ii Using double bars.

8. Control of Pattern.

a) Make a floor sequence using the four basic body shapes and at least four of the basic body actions.

b) Combine with a partner to make a sequence showing patterns on apparatus, e.g. a window ladder.

c) Working in a group of three show:

i Supporting and balance.

ii Supporting flight to make patterns using the four basic body shapes first on the floor and then make another sequence on suitable apparatus.

9. Apparatus Arrangement.

Devise and demonstrate the use of an apparatus arrangement which offers full opportunity for flight with:

a) Swinging.

b) Twisting.

c) Jumping.

Gymnastics—Olympic

General
Young people showing particular promise should be encouraged to enter for the BAGA Proficiency Awards Scheme in Group 1.

Programme

1. Agility.

Be able to perform:

a) Forward Roll.

b) Backward Roll.

c) Cartwheel.

d) Push to "Crab" or "Bridge" position from back lying.

2. Vaulting.
Any three of the following vaults:

a) On and off (squat onto box or horse and spring off with continuous flight).

b) Squat or through vault.

c) Straddle vault.

d) Flank vault.

3. This item for Girls and Young Women Only.
Either:

a) Beam (height 2 ft 8 ins, length 12 ft–16 ft, width 4 ins).

Be able to:

i Mount the Beam in an original manner such as a vault or supported leg circling.

ii Walking.

iii Running.

iv Dismount with jump from feet attaining height with spring.

Or:

b) High and Low Bars.

Backward circle on low bar, from front rest on low bar with forward grasp circle one leg over bar to forward straddle position, drop back bending front leg and hang by the knee (hockhang) straighten the bent leg and bring the other through between the hands to half inverted hang, and circle backwards to ground; jump to front rest on low bar, i.e. thighs level with bar, hands close to the thighs fingers facing forward (ordinary grasp), with a forward swing of the legs from the thighs swing legs backwards and push away to stand, hang from high bar, swing forward and backwards, heave and push from bar to alight.

4. This item for Boys and Young Men Only.
Be able to carry out one of the following events:

a) Parallel bars. Cross stand at end of bars facing inwards.

i From a short run, jump forward to support and swing forward and backward.

ii Swing forward and backward again and then forward to sit in upright astride position.

iii Grasp bars in front of thighs and with bent body roll forward over shoulder support to sit again in upright astride position.

iv Grasp bars behind and swing legs up and backwards between, swing forward and backward and $\frac{1}{2}$ turn of body to astride sitting.

v Grasp bars in front and swing forward and backward between to a high front vault to stand outside bars.

b) Low Horizontal Bar (approximately shoulder height).

i With hands in overgrasp, circle upward and backward to front support.

ii Swing L leg forward over bar to the left and to between the hands in support.

iii Drop backwards, hanging on L knee and hands and with the R leg acting, make $\frac{1}{2}$ knee circle forward to regain position with L leg forward between hands in support.

iv Change L hand to undergrasp and with $\frac{1}{2}$ L circle of R leg over bar make $\frac{1}{2}$ L turn of body, supported on L arm to front support.

v Drop backward and short underswing forward to dismount to stand.

c) Rings

i From straight arm hang, develop a swing forward, swing backward and on second forward swing lift body to inverted hand and hold for three seconds.

ii Lay out forward and swing backward, swing forward.

iii Swing backward to dislocate forward (inlocate).

iv Circle forward through bent body inverted hang to lay out forward and swing backward.

v Swing forward and straddle backward to ground.

d) Pommelled Horse. Sidestand grasping both pommels.

i Assume front support position.

ii Swing R leg as high as possible to R and pass if forward under the R hand = ($\frac{1}{2}$ L circle R leg).

iii Regrasp R pommel with R hand and swing both legs in astride position to the L.

iv Swing both legs back to the R and pass the R leg backward under the R hand and regrasp the R pommel with the R hand = ($\frac{1}{2}$ R circle R leg).

v Swing L leg as high as possible to L and pass it forward under the L hand = ($\frac{1}{2}$ R circle R leg).

vi Regrasp L pommel with L hand and swing both legs astride position to the R.

vii Swing both legs back to the L and pass the L leg backward under the L hand, and regrasp the L pommel with the L hand = ($\frac{1}{2}$ L circle L leg).

viii Swing legs to the R and Flank Vault to R dismount.

e) Floor exercises.

i From C facing A, raise L leg forward and arms sideways, with a short run, handspring to stand and fall forward with R leg raised backward to front support.

ii Lower R leg and squat L leg forward to between hands, raise R leg and made two L circles R leg with $\frac{1}{4}$ turn to front support facing away from B.

iii Rear vault forward to long sitting and immediate tucked backward roll to back lying with arms upward.

iv $\frac{1}{2}$ turn to prone lying with hands on floor at shoulder level, push to prone kneeling then kick to handstand, forward roll and high jump to stand.

v Step forward to front horizontal $\frac{1}{2}$ stand with arms sideways (front horizontal lever) and R leg (2 secs).

vi Swing L leg forward, making $\frac{1}{4}$ R turn and swinging arms above head, place L foot on floor sideways to the L bending and stretching that leg whilst making a full R circle of both arms to stand facing D. (This section must be executed rhythmically and without pause).

vii 2 or 3 running paces into round off (Arab spring) high jump with $\frac{1}{2}$ turn and headspring to stand.

5. Agility.

a) Dive forward roll.

b) Backward roll to straddle stand.

c) Handstand to "Bridge" position.

d) Handstand to forward roll.

6. Vaulting. (Any three of the following vaults.)

a) Straight leg squat.

b) Thief vault.

c) Front or face vault.

d) Neck spring.

7. This item for Girls and Young Women Only.

Either:

a) Beam (Height 3 ft 4 ins.).

i Squat vault onto Beam.

ii Dance steps along length.

iii Horizontal balance.

iv Cartwheel dismount from end of Beam.

or:

b) High and Low Bars.

Hang from high bar facing low bar, swing forward, backwards and forward to place feet on low bar, push on feet and press on hands to rise above the high bar to hip rest, forward circle round high bar and come to back rest on low bar. Bend one leg and place foot on low bar extend the straight leg upwards and immediately follow with the bent leg, by thrusting first from the low bar to circle around high bar to hip rest. Take the hips away from the high bar with straight arms and a backward swing, swing forwards and backwards under high bar and with a pull on the hands prior to release, alight to ground.

8. This item for Boys and Young Men Only.

Be able to carry out two of the events as listed in Item 4.

9. Agility.

a) Backward roll through handstand.

b) Walkover.

c) Arab spring or round-off.

d) Handspring.

10. Vaulting (any three of the following vaults).

a) Short arm overthrow.

288 **b)** Straddle with $\frac{1}{2}$ turn.

c) Rear vault.

d) Long arm overthrow.

11. For Girls and Young Women Only.

a) Beam (Height 3 ft 11 ins.).

i Straddle vault across beam.

ii Dance steps in sequence including a split leap.

iii Backward roll along beam.

iv Handstand along beam and return to beam.

v Handstand dismount.

b) High and Low Bars.

Facing low bar jump to grasp and place one foot between hands, swing under low bar and release foot to pass over low bar on return swing, press down with hands and rise above low bar to forward straddle sit. Mill circle forward, circle back leg forward to come to back rest, take hands to the top bar, lift legs upwards and with a pull on the hands extend the body upwards to swing outwards, release hands and alight to ground.

12. For Boys and Young Men Only.

Be able to carry out four of the events as listed in Item 4. (When an event is repeated at this stage the participant should aim at a higher degree of performance.)

Keep Fit

General

1. The aims of this programme are:

a) To keep the body in a fit and trim condition.

b) To encourage participation in Keep Fit as a recreative activity.

c) To encourage an understanding of the fundamentals of healthy living.

2. Young people requiring any help in training and assessment should apply to the Keep Fit Association, 70 Brompton Road, London SW3 1HE.

Programme

1. Wear suitable clothing and show an understanding of personal hygiene.

2. Have an understanding of the preparation of the body for exercise, i.e. have a knowledge of preliminary warming up and conditioning of every part of the body.

3. Be able (under guidance of a qualified Keep Fit Leader) to:

a) Move in a well co-ordinated way in simple movement phrases involving travelling, turning, opening and closing and jumping and combinations of these.

b) Perform simple movement sequences involving:

i The whole body.

ii Different parts of the body initiating and/or stressing the movement.

iii Variety in phrasing and rhythm stressing the weight, time, space, flow elements of movement.

c) Move with confidence in all areas of space surrounding them and be able to manage themselves with sensitivity to others when moving freely in general space.

d) Work easily with and have consideration for other members of the class, whether moving with one partner or as a member of a larger group. In this context, they should be able to discipline themselves to a class rhythm.

4. Present a simple movement sequence and explain its content.

5. Prepare and explain a simple group movement showing variety of speed and/or strength.

Medau Rhythmic Movement

General

1. Assessment should be carried out in consultation with a qualified Medau trainer.

2. The aim of the programme is:

a) To correct faults in movement and to achieve economy of effort, suppleness and the harmony of all parts of the body.

b) To encourage participation in Medau Rhythmic Movement as a recreative activity.

Programme

1. Wear suitable clothing and understand personal hygiene.

2. Show an understanding of the basic principles of Medau Rhythmic Movement and be able to demonstrate:

a) Movements of walking, running, jumping, feathering and swinging.

b) Work with balls, hoops, clubs and tambours as an aid to movement training.

c) Work on the floor exercises.

3. Develop a sense of rhythm and aural perception.

4. Have some understanding of the application of the small apparatus to movement training.

5. Understand movement in relation to health, posture and personal hygiene.

6. Have developed sensibility and adaptability to working with partners and in groups.

7. Show progress in feeling for rhythm and phrasing.

8. Show improvement in rhythmical sense and a deeper understanding of the functions of rhythm and music in Medau Movement.

9. Have some knowledge of Medau Rhythmic breathing movement.

Pétanque

Instruction and assessment should be carried out by a qualified British Pétanque Association coach. In the UK the name and address of a local coach may be obtained from the BPA, PO Box 87, Leatherhead, Surrey KT22 8LA. (Tel: 0372 386860).

1. Know something about the origins of the game of Pétanque.
2. Have an understanding of the rules associated with the game.
3. Have an understanding of how a game is organised.
4. Understand and demonstrate the different tactics required by both the pointer and the shooter in a game of Pétanque.
5. Demonstrate a good understanding of the scoring system required in the game of Pétanque.
6. Understand what is meant by the terms:

a) Cochonnet
b) Pointeur
c) Tireur
d) la revanche
e) la belle
f) la donnée
g) un Biberon
h) le Couloir
i) un Gratton
j) une Mêlée

7. Demonstrate the correct method of throwing a boule, showing an ability to apply backspin, left sidespin and right sidespin.
8. Demonstrate the correct method of shooting in Pétanque.
9. Understand and demonstrate the following:

a) un carreau
b) une raspaillette
c) la portée (or la plombée)
d) la demi-portée
e) la roulette
f) la roulette dirigee
g) Bonne Maman
h) la Devant-de-Boule
i) une Casquette

10. Understand the rules associated with throwing out the jack.
11. Compete in at least ten Pétanque games, keeping a record of their score and showing improvement.

Real Tennis

Develop the following basic skills and strokes.

1. Forehand cut length stroke.

2. Backhand cut length stroke.

3. Consistent return.

4. Service. Sidewall service—Underhand twist. American railroad.

5. Forehand volleys.

6. Backhand volleys.

7. Knowledge of basic rules, etiquette and scoring.

8. Understanding of positional play in singles and doubles.

9. Cross court and straight forehand and backhand rallies.

10. Alternate backhand and forehand volleys.

11. Sequence of service, ground stroke and volley rallies.

12. Sequence of service, and volley rallies.

13. Participation in singles and doubles competitive games.

14. Lob.

15. Basic tactics for singles and doubles play.

16. Detailed knowledge of the rules and some knowledge of the international game.

17. Advanced strokes—half volley, stop volley.

18. Participation in club or inter-club competitive games.

Rock Climbing

General

1. All participants must have completed the equivalent of a Bronze Expedition before undertaking this activity.

2. Young people must be accompanied at all times by an adult instructor who is an experienced and competent rock-climber, thoroughly versed in the particular problems of taking out beginners.

3. Emphasis should be on participation in practical rock-climbing expeditions in progressively more difficult areas.

Programme

1. Show a competence in all the requirements of the Bronze Expedition.

2. Demonstrate familiarity with the Traditional System of Rope Handling, i.e. know the bowline knot, figure of eight, the recognised spike and thread belay knots, the correct waist belay and correct method of interchanging a belay.

3. Know the different circumferences and strength of Nylon ropes, and be able to state the advantage of Nylon over other ropes.

4. Know the circumference of slings to be used for belaying and also the correct karabiners.

5. Know the five Climbing Calls used in all Climbing Systems.

6. Know why Nylon should never be allowed to run over Nylon.

7. Be able to rope down, or abseil, using both the traditional and modern methods.

8. Be able to coil a rope neatly and quickly.

9. Satisfy the instructor of ability to move safely, in particular showing care with rotten rock.

Note: At this stage young people should not be expected to lead climbs of any standard. If the instructor sees fit, participants could second any standard of climb within their own capabilities.

10. Be familiar with different types of harness, the waist belay, the correct spike and thread belays and the following knots: figure of eight, bowline, double fisherman's overhand.

11. Have had practice in choosing a good belay point, and adopting the correct stance for both rope systems.

12. Understand the grading system for climbs, and how these are affected by different weather conditions.

13. Know how to apply and demonstrate the system of running belays.

14. Have practised climbing down.

15. Understand the uses and limitations of the various types of rock climbing foot-wear, and of the value of rock climbing helmets.

16. Have second climbs of "Difficult"standard in all conditions; be familiar with and be able to demonstrate problems such as "mantel-shelf", "chimneying", "slab work", "hand and foot-jamming".

17. Demonstrate awareness of movement on rock, i.e three-point contact, rhythmical movement, standing in balance and thinking before moving.

Note: At this stage, if the instructor sees fit, young people could lead climbs no harder than "difficult" standard. The instructor would do well to give practice in holding a simple fall.

18. Be conversant with such knots as the prusik, the tape knot, the bowline-on-the-bight, the triple bowline, sheetbend, clove hitch.

19. Be conversant with British Guide Books, and be able to pick out the lines of the more obvious climbs from the descriptions.

20. Have had practice in techniques such as the lay-back, friction holds and bridging.

21. Have had experience of reasonable degrees of exposure to height, and experiences of different types of rock.

22. See the need for carrying slings of different circumference, plus tapes and for carrying snap karabiners as well as screw-gates.

23. Have held a falling second, either during an accidental slip, or practising with an instructor.

24. Have prior knowledge of the position of Local Rescue Posts and know the main points to be mentioned in a rescue message.

25. Know how to construct a rope stretcher, e.g. a Pigott stretcher.

26. Know how to "rope-up" a mountain stretcher for lowering.

27. State how morphia is administered, and know when it is advisable to refrain from its use.

28. Have seconded a climb of at least "mild severe" standard.

Note: At this stage, if the instructor sees fit, participants could lead climbs no harder than "Easy Very Difficult" standard.

Running

This programme is intended for those who wish to run for aerobic fitness rather than for the achievement of set standards in specific events in athletics. It is appreciated that as fitness improves some participants may wish to progress to social or club competitions.

Participants should keep a diary of the running undertaken including such details as distance run, time taken, terrain, prevailing weather conditions and how they felt both during and after the activity.

All participants should ensure that they wear clothing which will maintain an appropriate body temperature. In winter conditions a woollen hat is advisable. If running on roads light coloured or reflective clothing is recommended, especially at night and in poor visibility.

Programme

For those who are unfit, overweight, or who have been involved in little physical activity for a considerable period, the programme should start with gentle activity and progress gradually. It may start with walking or a mixture of walking and running. An assessment of the fitness of the participant should be made before the programme commences by the assessor, who should make suggestions about the content and frequency of the running programme.

Participants should aim to progress towards three or four half-hourly sessions of running each week, although only two of these can count towards the total points requirement of the Award Scheme. It is not essential to join a running club but participants are advised that training with a friend is both pleasurable and a motivating influence.

1. Be aware of the personal equipment required by participants i.e. training shoes designed for running, shorts, vest, tee shirt, track suit or other warm clothing for use in colder weather.

2. Understand the benefits of running and recognise the feeling of well-being generated by the activity.

3. Recognise the adverse effects of smoking and alcohol on levels of performance.

4. Appreciate the necessity of an initial period of gradual activity before vigorous exercise.

5. Understand the value and practice of gradual reduction of the intensity of exercise after each session of vigorous activity.

6. Increasing the distance a performer is able to run over a period of time (e.g. week 1 = 2 miles, week 12 = 6 miles).

7. Decreasing the time for a set distance.

8. Increasing the distance for a set time.

9. The ability to increase the number of running sessions per week (e.g. week 1 = 2 sessions, week 12 = 5 sessions).

10. A reduction in heart rate.

11. Easier breathing.

12. Improved muscle definition.

13. Improvement in recovery rate after exercise.

Participants should demonstrate knowledge of:

14. The prevention and basic treatment of injuries which might occur (e.g. blisters, sprained ankles, pulled muscles, shin soreness).

15. The nutritional and fluid intake requirements for longer distance running.

16. The use of different training procedures and terrain to maintain interest and improve performance.

17. The availability of appropriate magazines to keep in touch with trends and developments in running.

18. The value of relaxation both during and immediately after hard training.

19. The need to fit training periods into the lifestyle and commitments of the participant.

Assessors

Coaches and senior middle distance runners in athletic and jogging clubs are most suitable but they must understand that participation in this activity is not for competitive purposes.

Skiing – Nordic (Cross-Country)

General

1. The emphasis must be on safe skiing, keenness, hardiness and fitness.

2. All skiing ventures for beginners and inexperienced participants must be led and accompanied by an adult (preferably over 23) with Cross-Country skiing experience.

3. Experienced participants undertaking these ventures may do so unaccompanied by an adult leader, provided that, prior to each venture, it is discussed with and approved by an experienced adult familiar with the terrain in question and with due regard to the weather conditions. The adult consulted should be fully satisfied that the party has a responsible leader, is properly equipped, and of sufficient skill and strength to carry out the expedition safely.

Programme

1. The emphasis should be on participation in Cross-Country skiing ventures using progressively more difficult terrain, i.e. machine cut "tramline" trails; following an experienced leader cutting the tracks; making new tracks across undisturbed snow.

2. Pass the safety precautions, casualty code, map reading and use of compass sections in the Expedition Section of the Awards Handbook as applicable to sub-zero conditions and travelling on snow.

3. Have an understanding of the possible hazards of open country and adverse weather conditions. Know the precautions and equipment required for safe Cross-Country skiing.

4. Be able to:

a) Do a simple kick (step) turn to the left and to the right.

b) Climb a slope on Skis using a direct ascent and then the herring-bone.

c) Traverse downhill across a slope long enough to show complete control.

d) Travel downhill and do a snowplough turn to the left and to the right.

e) Run easily and smoothly along a flat stretch on skis.

5. Undertake suitable training. This should have some bearing on the requirements of cross-country skiing, for example, hill running, dry cross-country skiing or circuit training, running and walking.

6. Be able to make a cross-country tour on skis across undulating ground. Suggested distance of eight kilometers (five miles).

7. Be able to:

a) Perform a kick (step) turn to both the right and the left on the side of a steep slope.
b) Perform a christie or swing stop turn to either the right or the left.

8.

a) Explain how bumps can be used to help when running on the flat or climbing and be able to demonstrate this technique.
b) Travel downhill over an uneven surface.
c) Perform a skating turn on the flat.
d) Demonstrate the method of resting the arms when running on the flat or when climbing.

9. Be able to:

a) Traverse up a slope incorporating kick (step) turns without breaking the rhythm of the climb.
b) Travel downhill over varying degrees of slope with the minimum severity being as near 35 degrees maximum as possible.
c) Perform skating turns through wooded country.
d) Explain and execute the "Swedish Step".

10. Continue to make Cross-Country tours on skis across undulating ground, gradually increasing distances, e.g. from eight to fifteen kilometres.

Skipping

General
The aims of this programme are:

a) To contribute to keeping the body in a fit and trim condition.
b) To encourage participation and develop skill in skipping as a physical recreation.
c) To encourage an understanding of the fundamentals of healthy living.

Programme

1. Wear suitable clothing and show an understanding of personal hygiene.

2. Have an understanding of the preparation of the body for exercise, i.e. have a knowledge of preliminary warming up and conditioning of every part of the body.

3. Demonstrate the following steps with a backward turning rope and/or a forward turning rope:

a) Slow spring steps with a rebound (plain skips).
b) Running step (on the spot and travelling).
c) Rope swinging (on both sides of the body).
d) Step, hop (with knee raising).
e) Rope checking to change direction of swing whilst skipping.
f) Pas de Basque steps.

4. Perform a short sequence of at least 32 bars of music to include at least 4 of the above steps, and complete it with an easy finish.

5. Have some knowledge of the length, quality and weight of ropes suitable for skipping and of suitable music.

6. Demonstrate:
a) Coupe step.
b) Polkas.
c) Three travelling steps.
d) At least two other dance-like steps.
e) Methods of turning to face another direction whilst skipping.

7. Perform at least 2 sequences each of at least 32 bars; each one in a different time (e.g. 4/4 and 3/4). At least two of these sequences should include travelling. The sequences to be selected by the assessor/instructor from a list of six submitted by the participant.

8. Demonstrate steps as for item 6, and in addition show one step which can be performed in 3/4 waltz time **and** in 4/4 and arrange a demonstration sequence suitable for a group.

9. Perform four new sequences, as in item 7, one to be concerned with rope swinging and circling.

Team Sports △

Activities for this programme include (not in alphabetical order)

Football, Volleyball, Rounders, Canoe Polo, Ice Hockey, Polo, Goalball, Baseball, Rugby League Football, Street Hockey, Boccia, Lacrosse, Water Polo, Indoor Cricket, Octopushing, Frisbee, Rugby Union Football, Korfball, Curling, Hockey, Stoolball.

General

1. It is not practicable to produce detailed programmes separately for each team game, but the following programme can be adapted to meet the particular requirements of most team games.

2. Young people who are still undergoing full-time education may not count participation in school teams, if the matches and training sessions are during curriculum time. It is acceptable where it can clearly be seen that a young person is putting genuine voluntary effort into the team that is undertaking matches outside of normal school hours and that they are also undertaking training sessions in the same way.

3. Those taking part in any team games should join a club or team which is properly constituted and affiliated directly or indirectly to the national body governing the game.

Programme

1. Have a sound knowledge of the laws of the game.

2. Attain a reasonable proficiency in the basic skills of the game so as to enable them to participate in and complete a serious game.

3. Show a knowledge of care of equipment.

4. Compete in appropriate club competitions.

5. Show skills and an improvement in standard of play.

6. Appreciation of tactics and positioning play.

7. Be selected and play in a team which has proper fixtures.

Yoga (Hatha)

General

Yoga is the uniting or joining of a healthy body and disciplined mind. In the postures of asanas the quality of body use is as important as degree of accomplishment. Asanas are not intended to be gymnastic exercises, they are positions for the body in which one remains steady, calm, quiet and comfortable—physically and mentally—a balanced and harmonious state.

Programme

1. Know and understand the rules and advice of practice—precautions, clothing, hygiene, limbering, etc.

2. Develop movement and co-ordination in basic asanas, i.e. All movements of the spine. Forward, backward and side bending postures. Rotation or twisting postures. Plus inverted and balancing poses.

3. Acquire a knowledge of basic breathing techniques.

4. Learn to relax during and after postures.

5. Develop and improve ability and quality of the postures—Classical asanas.

6. Expand further the breathing control—to synchronise breathing and movement.

7. Develop the knowledge and practice of several techniques of relaxation and concentration.

8. Continue as in items 1–7 with greater quality of movement and greater depth of understanding and meaning in the asanas.

9. Develop through the practice a deeper awareness of oneself and others.

10. Study and practice of Pranayama (control of breath).

ACTIVITIES WITH RECOGNISED STANDARDS ●

ACTIVITY *Swimming*

DATES STARTED: **18/4/90**   COMPLETED: **12/7/90**

NUMBER OF HOURLY SESSIONS ATTENDED:	SESSIONS		POINTS	
NUMBER OF HOURLY SESSIONS ATTENDED:	4	AT 2 POINTS EACH	8	
OR NUMBER OF HALF HOURLY SESSIONS:	8	AT 1 POINT EACH	8	
		SUB TOTAL (A) :	16	

STANDARDS ATTAINED (check Award Handbook for points)

ACTIVITY	EVENT(S)	STANDARD(S)	
Composite	25m Freestyle	23.6	4
Speed	25m Backstroke	27.5	3
Tests	25m Breaststroke	29.9	3
	SUB TOTAL FOR STANDARDS (B)		10
	PLUS SUB TOTAL (A)		16
	TOTAL POINTS (A+B)		26

IMPROVEMENT: It is certified that this participant has shown improvement in application, technique, skill, tactics, fitness, knowledge of rules, appreciation of hazards and knowledge of safety precautions, as appropriate to the activity chosen.

SIGNED *Gill Mate*

A.S.A. Teacher Cert. 12/7/90

22

Bronze

ACTIVITIES WITH RECOGNISED STANDARDS ●
POINTS REQUIRED: 30

ACTIVITY *Physical Achievement*

DATES STARTED: **1.4.90**   COMPLETED: **15.5.90**

NUMBER OF HOURLY SESSIONS ATTENDED:	SESSIONS		POINTS	
NUMBER OF HOURLY SESSIONS ATTENDED:	9	AT 2 POINTS EACH	18	
OR NUMBER OF HALF-HOURLY SESSIONS:	4	AT 1 POINT EACH	4	
		SUB TOTAL (A) :	22	

STANDARDS ATTAINED (check Award Handbook for points)

ACTIVITY	EVENT(S)	STANDARD(S)	
Speed test		26 secs.	3
Sit-ups		45	2
Burpees		19	1
Stamina run		4mins 20secs	1
Ball speed bounce		40	3
Standing Broad Jump		1.8 mtrs	2
	SUB TOTAL FOR STANDARDS (B)		12
	PLUS SUB TOTAL (A)		22
	TOTAL POINTS (A+B)		34

IMPROVEMENT: It is certified that this participant has shown improvement in application, technique, skill, tactics, fitness, knowledge of rules, appreciation of hazards and knowledge of safety precautions, as appropriate to the activity chosen.

SIGNED *Pamela M Henderson*

P.E. Teacher   25.5.90

36

Silver

PHYSICAL RECREATION

ACTIVITIES WITH PARTICIPATION PROGRAMMES ▲
POINTS REQUIRED: 36

ACTIVITY **WHEELCHAIR BASKETBALL**

DATES STARTED: **19/9/89**   COMPLETED: **7/3/90**

NUMBER OF	SESSIONS		POINTS
HOURLY SESSIONS ATTENDED:	**18**	AT 2 POINTS EACH	**36**
OR NUMBER OF HALF-HOURLY SESSIONS:	—	AT 1 POINT EACH	—
		TOTAL:	**36**

SIGNATURE OF COACH OR INSTRUCTOR   **I. Gibb.   (COACH).**

Assessor's report:

Alan turned up regularly for the 2 x 2 hour team training evenings each week. He has played for the Phoenix Junior team and has shown great improvement.

IMPROVEMENT: It is certified that this participant has shown improvement in application, technique, skill, tactics, fitness, knowledge of rules, appreciation of hazards and knowledge of safety precautions, as appropriate to the activity chosen.

SIGNED **L.E. Ferguson.**

QUALIFICATION **EBBA Coach**   DATE **20/3/90.**

23

Gold

PHYSICAL RECREATION

ACTIVITIES WITH PARTICIPATION PROGRAMMES ▲
POINTS REQUIRED: 36

ACTIVITY **Hockey**

DATES STARTED: **5/2/90**   COMPLETED: **13/12/90**

NUMBER OF	SESSIONS		POINTS
HOURLY SESSIONS ATTENDED:	**22**	AT 2 POINTS EACH	**44**
OR NUMBER OF HALF-HOURLY SESSIONS:	**10**	AT 1 POINT EACH	**10**
		TOTAL:	**54**

SIGNATURE OF COACH OR INSTRUCTOR

Assessor's report:

Louise has trained very hard to improve her all round ability. She became a key member of the hockey team playing in every league fixture

IMPROVEMENT: It is certified that this participant has shown improvement in application, technique, skill, tactics, fitness, knowledge of rules, appreciation of hazards and knowledge of safety precautions, as appropriate to the activity chosen.

SIGNED **Bm Wally**

QUALIFICATION **Club coach g the**   DATE **17/12/90**
All England Womens hockey Assoc.

23

Residential Project
(an additional requirement for the Gold Award)

Aim

To broaden experience through involvement with others in a residential setting.

General

■ The intention is to introduce young people to some form of purposeful enterprise in the company of others who are not their normal everyday companions, with whom they live and work for a stipulated period.

■ The project should provide opportunities to develop maturity and to accept responsibility.

Requirement

■ To undertake some shared activity, either through voluntary service or training, away from home. The residential setting may be in a centre, Youth Hostel, standing camp etc. but 'home stays' or living with a family are not acceptable.

Conditions

1. Involvement is normally to extend over a total period of not less than five consecutive days (four nights away). Young people having only limited holidays may, at the discretion of Operating Authorities, spread this over a series of weekends, provided they spend at least four nights away; the weekends fall within a 12-month period; the same activity is followed and progressive training is provided.

2. Others taking part in the Residential Project should not include more than a minority of the young person's usual companions in school, work or youth groups.

3. The activities undertaken are to provide opportunities for broadening the interests and experience of participants. They may be related to those being followed in other Sections of the Scheme and may form part of the appropriate programme of training—with the sole exception of the qualifying venture in the Expeditions Section.

4. The type of residential experience is to be the young person's own choice.

5. Courses undertaken as part of educational or vocational training may be counted provided that they fulfil all requirements and attendance makes demands on genuine leisure time.

Suitable Opportunities

6. Opportunities enabling young people to fulfil the conditions can be provided by residential courses, camps and placements falling into the following categories:

- Church sponsored courses for young people.

- Coaching and activity courses.

- General training and adventure courses sponsored by local education authorities, national voluntary organisations and other associations.

- Outward Bound and similar courses.

- Special courses arranged by Operating Authorities.

- Specific community tasks such as provision of playgrounds, village halls, etc.

- Voluntary help at Homes, centres or camps for disadvantaged children, the elderly, the handicapped or with recognised relief organisations.

- Voluntary work with bodies concerned with the preservation of amenities, conservation of the environment, archaeological projects, etc.

- Youth leadership training courses.

Assessment

8. In all cases it must be possible to arrange for assessment by a suitable person approved by Operating Authorities who should be present during the period of residence.

9. Young people are to be assessed on their personal standards, relationships with others, responsibility, initiative and general progress during the residential period having regard, in the case of service rendered, to the comments of the organisation concerned. Space is available for this in *Record Books*. In the event of a young person not satisfying the Assessor, he or she should be informed of the reason and no entry should be made in the *Record Book*.

The Scheme Worldwide

The Award Scheme is operated in the following countries:

The Duke of Edinburgh's Award
United Kingdom
Antigua
Ascension Island
Australia
Bahamas
Barbados
Bermuda
Brunei
Canada
Cayman Islands
Dominica
Fiji
Gibraltar
Grenada
Hong Kong
India
Jamaica
New Zealand
Pakistan
Papua New Guinea
St. Helena
St. Lucia
St. Vincent
Solomon Islands
Tristan da Cunha
Tuvalu
The President's Award
The Gambia
Kenya
Malawi
Malta

Republic of Ireland
Sierra Leone
Trinidad and Tobago
Vanuatu
Zimbabwe
The Congressional Award
United States of America
The Crown Prince Award
Jordan
The Head Of State Award
Ghana
The Israel Youth Award
Israel
The National Youth Award
Mauritius
Sri Lanka
The Nigerian National Youth Award
Nigeria
Premio Infante D'Henrique
Portugal
The Prince Makhosini Award
Swaziland
The Prince Mohato Award
Lesotho
Prix Senegalais Pour La Promotion De La Jeunesse
Senegal
The Source Of The Nile Award
Uganda

Further information and addresses concerning: Regional Councils and Regional Officers; National and Area Award Authorities; Individual Licensed Operators is available from the International Secretariat.

5 Prince of Wales Terrace, London W8 5PG. Telephone: 071-938 4545. Telex: 919885 DEAINY G.

The Bronze & Silver Award Entrance Pack (dark blue) and the Gold Award
Entrance Pack folder (black) shown above, are required for entry into the Scheme.
Details are available from Operating Authorities or from the appropriate Territorial
or Regional Office listed opposite.

The Duke of Edinburgh's Award

Headquarters
Gulliver House, Madeira Walk,
Windsor, Berkshire SL4 1EU
Tel: 0753 810753

Territorial and Regional Offices

Scotland:
69 Dublin Street, Edinburgh EH3 6NS
Tel: 031 556 9097

Wales:
Oak House, 12 The Bulwark, Brecon, Powys LD3 7AD
Tel: 0874 623086

Northern Ireland:
Northern Bank House,
109 Royal Avenue, Belfast BT1 1EW
Tel: 0232 232253

England
North East:
(Cleveland, Durham, Humberside, North, South and West Yorkshire, Northumberland, Tyne & Wear).

The Duke of Edinburgh's Award
PO Box 2, Border House, Hadrian Road,
Wallsend, Tyne & Wear, NE28 6QL
Tel: 091 262 5306

North West:
(Cheshire, Cumbria, Greater Manchester, Isle of Man, Lancashire, Merseyside)

4 Bolton Street, Ramsbottom,
Bury, Lancashire BL0 9HX
Tel: 0706 824821

Midlands:
(Derbyshire, Herefordshire and Worcestershire, Leicestershire, Lincolnshire, Nottinghamshire, Shropshire, Staffordshire, Warwickshire, W. Midlands)

89/91 Hatchett Street,
Newtown, Birmingham B19 3NY
Tel: 021-359 5900

East:
(Bedfordshire, Buckinghamshire, Cambridgeshire, Essex, Hertfordshire, Norfolk, Northamptonshire, Oxfordshire, Suffolk)

21 St John's Road,
Epping, Essex CM16 5DN
Tel: 0992 377105

South East:
(Berkshire, Channel Islands, East and West Sussex, Hampshire, Isle of Wight, Kent, Surrey)

35 Elm Road, New Malden,
Surrey KT3 3HB
Tel: 081-949 2777

South West:
(Avon, Cornwall, Devon, Dorset Gloucestershire, Somerset, Wiltshire, Isles of Scilly)

Court Gatehouse, Corsham Court
Corsham, Wiltshire SN13 0BZ
Tel: 0249 701000

London:
(Inner and Outer London Boroughs)

150 Brick Lane London E1 6RU
Tel: 071-377 2449

Information concerning Award Authorities outside the U.K. is available from the International Secretariat, 19 St James's Square, London SW1Y 4JG (Tel: 071-839 7888).